I Am a Process with No Subject

University of Florida Monographs
Humanities Number 61

I Am a Process with No Subject

Philip Beitchman

University of Florida Press
Gainesville

Orders for books published by all member presses should be sent to
University Presses of Florida, 15 NW 15 St., Gainesville, FL 32603.

Library of Congress Cataloging in Publication Data

Beitchman, Philip, 1939–
   I am a process with no subject.

   (University of Florida monographs. Humanities;   no. 61)
   Bibliography : p.
   Includes index.
   1. French literature—20th century—History and criticism. 2.
Joyce, James, 1882–1941. Finnegans wake. 3. Literature,
Experimental—History and criticism. 4. Deconstruction. I. Title.
II. Series.
PQ306.B36   1988   809'.91   88-1344
ISBN 0-8130-0888-3 (alk. paper)

I dedicate this book to the
> *homeless*
> > within and without
> > a text

Contents

Acknowledgments

The author acknowledges with thanks the permission granted by the publishers and translators of the following editions to quote copyrighted material from their listed publications.

Samuel Beckett. *Three Novels: Molloy, Malone Dies, and the Unnamable.* New York: Grove Press, 1955.

Maurice Blanchot. *Madness of the Day.* Translated by Lydia Davis. Barrytown, New York: Station Hill Press, 1981.

Gilles Deleuze. *Logique du sens.* Paris: Éditions de Minuit, 1969.

Jacques Derrida. *Positions.* Translated by Alan Bass. Chicago: University of Chicago Press, 1981.

Louis-René Des Forêts. *Le Bavard.* Paris: Gallimard, 1946. English translation of *Le Bavard* in *The Children's Room,* translated by Jean Stewart. London: John Calder Ltd., 1963. (John Calder Ltd. has given me permission to quote Des Forêts in French and translate his prose into English, but readers are respectfully reminded that the Stewart translation is the only authorized one.)

James Joyce. *Finnegans Wake.* New York: Viking-Penguin, 1939, 1958.

James Joyce. *A First Draft Version of Finnegans Wake.* Edited and annotated with draft catalogue by David Hayman. Austin: University of Texas Press, 1963.

Michel Leiris. *La Règle du jeu, II, III, IV.* Paris: Gallimard, 1955, 1966, 1976.

Emmanuel Lévinas. *Otherwise than Being or Beyond Essence.* Translated by Alphonso Lingis. The Hague: Martinus Nijhoff, 1981.

Philippe Sollers. *Drame.* Paris: Éditions de Seuil, 1965. (*Drame* has been translated by Bruce Benderson and Ursule Molinaro as *Event* [New York: Red Dust Press, 1987]. I'm grateful to Bruce Benderson for allowing me to use his translation.

Tristan Tzara. *Œuvres complètes.* 5 vols. Edited by Henri Béhar. Paris: Flammarion, 1975–82.

Triatan Tzara. *Approximate Man and Other Writings.* Translated by Mary Ann Caws. Detroit: Wayne State University Press, 1973.

Max Weber. *From Max Weber.* Translated by C. Wright Mills and H. H. Gerth. Oxford University Press, 1958.

I would like also to express my appreciation to

Hannah Charney, who saw me through to the end of this;

Mary Ann Caws, who understood I was saying something;

Fred Nichols, who knew how to read me;

Henri Peyre, cher maître who would rather call *you* maître;

Marsha Beitchman, *sine qua non* (just about the only thing I know for sure);

Patricia Zaccardo for typing;

and the staff of University Presses of Florida for attentive editing.

1

Introduction —
Author, Audience, and Work
in the Literature of Deconstruction:
Exploratory Readings of Some
Modern Texts

Author, Audience, and Work

It will be my purpose in this work to explore literary theory and practice in seven twentieth-century writers whose texts are characterized by a high degree of thematic and stylistic experimentation and are heavily inflected by the need to reflect upon and justify their own existence. I plan to examine, author by author, certain specific texts that demonstrate these tendencies; but although I will be looking at the authors individually and most often at their "texts themselves," I will also be stressing the links, both implicit and explicit, between them and a certain common mood of apocalyptic desperation, disillusion, and readiness for change and risk that they share.

I am by no means suggesting that these are the only moderns who manifest these qualities or who are significant for their prominently iconoclastic attitude toward our Western culture and heritage. I have chosen these writers because I think their works are particularly eloquent, blatant, and obvious examples of a decomposition of our society and a dissatisfaction with its norms, traditions, and goals that are present everywhere, not only, or even mainly, in literary practice.

1

In the Literature of Deconstruction

Any theory of literature seeks out or invents the texts in which it can find corroboration, inspiration, support, and stimulation. As Jacques Derrida remarks a little dryly in the well-known essay "Force and Signification,"[1] Jean Rousset's structuralist aesthetic is well suited for Proust and Claudel (since these writers can even be seen as its progenitors) but might be dubiously relevant elsewhere. Although one of the leitmotifs of deconstruction has been a hostility to literary canons and canonization, it has generally had to find its own canon (in fact if not in theory)—or works and writers that are suitable to its outlook and in sympathy with its overall goals.

We are by no means describing here a "mountain" of literature into which theory tunnels to come out with its precious ore; for in this age of rapid communications and even more rapid judgments, sudden reversals, and illuminations, in this time when we depend so much on others for therapy, guidance, and outlet and are so permeated by others that they are who we are, theory is often enough in advance of, or at least parallel to, the practice of literature. Works seem frequently written to order (in another, more controlling sense than Valéry meant when he noted the circumstantial nature of his own productions), either by a writer in accordance with his own recent theoretical progress or with points made and arguments won by or over others at the colloquia, symposia, and other stimulating but compelling stations where our intellectual trajectories intersect. A good example of this might be the "collaboration" between Jean Ricardou and Claude Simon so comprehensively recounted in David Carroll's *The Subject in Question*.[2] Another obvious instance might be the Derrida-Foucault-Barthes connections and interconnections with the "made-to-order" creations of Philippe Sollers, Jean Thibaudeau, Jean-Louis Baudry,[3] and others of the now defunct *Tel Quel* tribe, passed on to the paradise of *L'Infini.*

The day is past, and perhaps happily, when we were sure of the difference between theory and practice of literature: it seems obvious now that criticism and creation come together and are more necessarily and inextricably intertwined than ever. For another of the corollaries of deconstruction has been the blurring, sometimes the elision, of the border between the two functions, traditionally distinct, of writer and critic.[4] Deconstruction in literature marks that phase of poststructuralism, at least in some hands, where criticism, finished with merely theorizing about the disappearance of genre and limit and the close collaboration between philosophy, vested interests, and literature, has "taken the step," come over, miraculously, to the other side of that which has no other side.

This deconstruction, then, is a structuralism that has "gone wild," taken itself seriously, and in so doing comprised a library of works that are sympathetic to its project. Thus the romantics, deemphasized if not condemned by the New Critics and traditionally regarded with a suspicion traceable back through Irving Babbitt at least as far as Matthew Arnold for imbalances in education, rigor, and judgment, become important again, for they too were no great respecters of borders and limits. Likewise, a certain modern literature, often of indeterminate genre, form, and even purpose—of which there will be much question here—is important, even fundamental, for deconstruction.[5]

If another favored idea of deconstruction has been the "end of literature" in the sense of the end of any special status accorded to it,[6] then a library of deconstruction is likely to comprise works whose essential purport is to put literature in question. A central place in this library of deconstruction (to employ heuristically a concept of centrality that deconstruction discredits for what must be a library of marginality) would be taken by the works of Maurice Blanchot—a writer whose major preoccupation has been a many-leveled examination, critical and creative, of the premises, promises, illusions, ambiguities, and hopes for the practice of literature.[7] Aside from the important and well-acknowledged role Blanchot has played in the intellectual lives of several figures who are among the most frequently cited in connection with deconstruction in America, Jacques Derrida, certainly the inventor of this "new science" (for it is he who first uses, or at least privileges, the term),[8]* considers himself to be very greatly in Blanchot's debt—a debt that he has humbly acknowledged publicly and eloquently discharged in print.[9] Blanchot's past and continuing relevance to deconstruction is amply documented in an essay by Donald G. Marshall in a volume devoted to the Yale critics.[10]

Blanchot turns out to be a kind of rite de passage for those who were to become some of the principal figures of deconstruction. Geoffrey Hartman's interest in Blanchot dates back at least to 1956, when he wrote about him for *Yale French Studies*; in a 1961 essay he introduces Blanchot to the wider audience of the *Chicago Review*.[11] Paul de Man also wrote on Blanchot, and his praise for him was positively hyperbolic, especially from a critic who is known more for cool judgment than for enthusiasm:

> The influence of the critical work has been far-reaching. More philosophical and abstract than Charles du Bos and less conducive to practical application than Bachelard's theories of material imagery, Blanchot's criticism has remained aloof from recent methodological debates and polemics. Yet his already considerable impact is bound to increase; rather than directly affecting existing critical methods, his work puts into question the very conditions prior to the elaboration of all critical discourse and in that way reaches a level of awareness no other contemporary critic has reached.[12]

---

* Derrida mentions, in *L'Oreille de l'autre* (117–18) some amazement at the way the term has taken off, the *privileging* of which is the work of others as much as his own, if not more so. At one point he didn't think it was much more important than other terms like *trace* or *différance*; deconstruction then resulted from his own attempts to redefine it in answer to challenges of meaning that had already begun to grow around it; as in the claim or disclaimer he has made in answer to the charge of nihilism that deconstruction is, contrarily, *an affirmation*.

J. Hillis Miller is no stranger to Blanchot either; in a recent speech in defense of the deconstructive mood, the basis for which was a rereading of Kant's third *Critique* as well as reinterpretations of Goethe, Wordsworth, and Coleridge, Miller used a brilliant early piece of Blanchot's about "emptiness" as introduction and conclusion to his discourse.[13]

The turn toward Blanchot was significantly a turning away from Sartre; just as Derrida in philosophy has represented a correction of what seemed to him to be the "monstrosity" of Sartre's moralistic and humanistic misreading[14] (an error that Derrida, more charitably than Heidegger, grants was necessary for Sartre's *situation*) of Dasein as Existence, so Blanchot in literature represents an alternative to the Sartrean insistence that literature be explicitly and usefully social and that it make communication with others, and *engagement* in their problems, its fundamental modus operandi. Blanchot and his friend Georges Bataille opposed what they saw as a reduction and distortion of the literary function; and both were held accountable by Sartre in *Situations*[15] for what he viewed as their asocial posture and mystifying potential; and, indeed, Sartre's review, belying its name, *Les Temps modernes,* stubbornly opposed much that was modern in literature.[16]

Deconstruction, then, by recourse to Blanchot for inspiration and example, is searching for a more open and permissive philosophy than Sartrean "commitment" can provide. Isolation, eccentricity, and social inutility, all anathema for Sartre and reasons for his condemnation of modernism, are all positive points for Blanchot.

Blanchot's innovative and original attitude toward the practice of his own criticism, as well as the sublime indifference to genre and category he manifests therein, will also provide an impetus and precedent for deconstruction to be more open and experimental in its critical methods and styles. Not only the beauty and seductive power of his writings, their "saveur" Barthes might say, but also their wide-ranging references, topicality, and allusiveness contribute to the inspiration his work affords. Blanchot violates habitually, and with impunity, the new critical strictures that, for instance, exclude biography and history from a study of the work (as in his influential series of essays on Kafka); and in defense of a vision of literature that confronts the paradoxes of modernity, he is equally willing to operate on many different terrains—philosophical, anthropological, historical, and even political. The "text itself" is as important to Blanchot as it was for the New Criticism, but for him the text doesn't stop on the border of the page where it merely appears but implies certain important changes alike for the hand that composes as well as for a world that reads or refuses to read.

Where deconstruction turns by turning toward Blanchot is toward a literature that was more open to innovation and more tolerant of discontinuity. Blanchot meant an escape from the reductiveness of Sartrean moral aesthetics as well as from New Critical and other academic strictures on the limitations and functions of critical and creative discourse. To look toward Blanchot was to look toward experimentation, risk, discovery—toward the accepting of responsibility for one's freedom that constitutes, perhaps, a deeper fidelity to Sartre than Sartre was often able to recognize.[17]

To turn to Blanchot is to turn to much more than Blanchot alone, for when we talk of Blanchot we are no longer on that relatively stable terrain where we think we know who or what exactly we are talking about (as when we talk about Hemingway, Proust, or Henry James). When we talk of Blanchot, an appropriate ambience might be that suggested by the term *network*, introduced by Michel Foucault[18] to describe the aesthetics of the New Novel in contradistinction to the linear style of more traditional fiction. For Blanchot is a catalytic writer. In a variety of eloquent ways, he lets us know of the effect that other writers have had on him and *who* is, in very large measure, his *effect* on other writers. Derrida's "nonphenomenal" Text, related to Heidegger's equally immaterial Being,[19] is made to order for a Blanchot who is very much a disappearing writer behind a disappearing text.[20] In the network, then, that comprises Blanchot, the individual writer counts for little and what he says, in the sense that it can be captured, learned, and identified, for even less; an important source for deconstruction turns out to be, suitably for a doctrine that has turned against origins (and doctrines), no source at all but an example of a certain style of thinking and writing that infinitely and indefinitely proliferates, explores, refers, and circles "in the air," as it were, but never *lands*.

If deconstruction also leans toward a conception of art as *bricolage*,[21] or spontaneous ingenuity, which comes to it through Lévi-Strauss's anthropological insights and their literary application by Gérard Genette, then it seems appropriate also that the almost exclusive concern of Blanchot has been with writers of what he has termed "the fragmentary." These are writers who proceed, or seem to, by fits and starts, who profess no allegiance to any external or prior restraints for unity, completeness, and finality, but whose thoughts and whose lives are their writing, which they put together like the *bricoleur* on the basis of methods that are more often intuitive and haphazard than organized according to preexisting plans. Tristan Tzara's and dada's and surrealism's general emphasis on primitive and Eastern "nondirected thought"[22] as opposed to the calculating Western "engineer's" mentality has much in common with Blanchot's aesthetics of fragmentation, spontaneity, and intuition with which deconstruction also is deeply imbued; and Nietzsche, whose antagonism to systems and plans is almost legendary, is perhaps the perfect example of "nondirected thought" in action and therefore the fragmentary writer *par excellence*, inasmuch as he is still very important for deconstruction.[23] Hölderlin, Mallarmé, Musil, and especially Kafka are also frequent themes for Blanchot, for they are all inveterate writers of fragments, whose tentative, problematic, and functionally interminable art is largely what they write about. Very prominent in Blanchot's library are also his contemporaries Michel Leiris and Louis-René Des Forêts. Michel Leiris' approach to autobiography eschews all linearity and orderly progression, emphasizing instead the evanescent, momentary, and contingent nature of a life that resists intrinsically all totalization and rationalization; and what Des Forêts suggests in his writings is perhaps that the things that matter most to us are incapable of reliable explanation, articulation, or admission—as man's plans and projects, and the image of himself and others he forms to go along with them, are incessantly "surprised," derailed, and reduced by unconscious, social, and natural contingencies over which he has little control.

This network that we see reaching through Derrida and the Yale critics to Blanchot and the "writers of the fragmentary" we may also envision as connected laterally to Philippe Sollers and *Tel Quel.* There is a sense in which Sollers and *Tel Quel* take Blanchot literally in a way that perhaps he was never meant to be taken: they make institution and ideology out of writers that resist such articulation.[24]

Sollers is a peripheral if still significant figure for deconstruction and other poststructuralist movements, impossible to ignore if only for his importance at a certain conjuncture in the discourses of Derrida, Barthes, Kristeva, and even Lacan. It has been argued recently that Derrida has been necessarily "domesticated" for American deconstruction,[25] but Sollers would have proved more resistant to domestication, at first because he is too radical and recently because he is too conservative (politically, at least). His pertinence, in the context of this project, is that he makes an explicit ideology and practice out of the intuitions, passions, and visions of other writers whose rebellion was implicit in their art rather than contained in any concrete statement they were making or even style or technical device they were using. Sollers becomes contrarily the consummate stylist and technician, a writer who, for instance, is able to pursue with astounding, obsessive, and obstinate rigor a preconceived plan to dislocate the reader systematically. A paradox that may vitiate this effect is the very premeditation of the spontaneity and surprise, as in those "time to be creative and original" periods in school that can become dull routines in their own right. Compared to the less programmed and less predictable shocks that Blanchot, Bataille, and Leiris spring on us, Sollers may fall a little flat. His work, nevertheless, is still interesting and worth perusal as an accomplished and comprehensive repertory of the most experimental techniques of twentieth-century prose (for Sollers is as much an intersection and crossroads as Blanchot). With him the network that was going to extend into deconstruction attempts impossibly, paradoxically, and dramatically to become system, method, reliability. Subversion and revolution in art become institutionalized; for us, and in the perspective of what we have been describing alternatively as Blanchot's network of the fragmentary or the literature of deconstruction, Sollers may represent a moment of temptation and impatience that it is best to recognize and leave behind—that is, the illusion of exercising real power and influence directly in any real world. A deeper power of writing and a more effective subversion may lie in insisting on, and continuing to say, *nothing*.

National identity and even language are no barriers to this network I am describing. *Finnegans Wake*, vitally important and exemplary for Sollers and *Tel Quel*, was also an illumination for Derrida;[26] and Beckett, whose connections with Joyce come close to being lineal, has his very experimental novels introduced to the French reading public by Blanchot.[27]

The qualities, attitudes, and characteristics that I focus on in this network also do not belong to any programmatic theory of deconstruction, whose existence would be questionable if not contradictory.[28] I am instead describing certain aspects and moods that I find to be shared by some of the works that deconstruction and the intellectual ambience it grew out of tend to favor. I am far from implying, for instance, that a slippage from a declarative to an interrogative function is either new to literature or any exclusive property of the network I trace; I am merely pointing out that deconstruction and the readings I perform necessarily focus on these interrogative aspects. I am equally far from suggesting by my use of the concept of subversion in these works that subversion is indeed their exclusive concern or primary purpose (except possibly for Tzara and Sollers); instead I am saying that deconstruction, committed to looking through and beyond everything, including itself, has a natural affinity for subversion. The "subversive" is an essential element in the vocabulary that enters deconstruction from Blanchot, Derrida, Foucault, and so blatantly from *Tel Quel* and from other influential sources (Guy Debord and the Situationists);[29] and so "subversion" now figures prominently in a few chapter headings of Vincent Leitch's recent *Deconstructive Criticism.*[30] Such are the avatars of a word, from iconoclasm to what Marcuse would have undoubtedly qualified as "repressive desublimation."

In the reflections that follow on the dissolution and merging of author and reader, the "withering away" of plot, the general assault on character, and the turning away from all goal and finality, including the very palpability of the text as a last recourse, I am not implying that these developments were waiting for deconstruction or the network it draws from to be noticed. Deconstruction simply is necessarily attracted to works whose authors, characters, plots, and purposes become questionable, uncertain, and labile, being all of these things itself. This is at once to alter slightly Paul de Man's wonderful title,[31] its blindness as well as the way it sees.

By the "literature of deconstruction," then, is meant the works so mordantly critical of the world that gave them birth and a fortiori of themselves that they are remarkable less for the statements they make or conclusions they come to than for the doubts they cast and the questions they pose and leave permanently open.[32] We move with these authors from a declarative mood that, whatever its reservations, accepts the world as it is to an interrogative one that incessantly questions, denies, and subverts it. I do not mean to underestimate the traditionally subversive role of writers and writing, alternately honored and vilified exiles from Plato's *Republic,* but instead to call attention to an acceleration of this iconoclastic role for literature —perhaps because of the closing off of other outlets for protest in our tightly controlled and rationalized modern societies. For, after all, the targets of Plato's opprobrium, and those of his Puritan progeny, could congratulate themselves and, who knows, even take pride in the seductive grace or power that earned their "lies" the sentence of exile. This role of writer—variously identified through the ages as outsider, divinely inspired madman, or visionary, underground man, irrational or existential hero, intellectual nomad, scapegoat—though plentifully subversive of established order, does not call itself fundamentally into question. On the contrary, this traditional role for the writer may entitle him to self-esteem for his contribution to the overall health of a social organism in which he performs the function of antibody. Even those famous exceptions, self-interrogating works that delight our modern sensibilities, from Rabelais through Sterne and Diderot to the anguished self-probings in the last century of Poe, Baudelaire, Rimbaud, and Lautréamont—these works glory more in the flexibility of a tradition that can allow such liberties than disallow its fundamental premises. With what I call the literature of deconstruction, however, the time for such celebration is past. As Roland Barthes observed, a writer, no matter how blatantly subversive his work, fulfills an essentially decorative and ornamental role in bourgeois society;[33] for here, as the situationists argued so efficaciously,[34] power no longer passes by way of the consensual word, but prefers to inundate, intimidate, condition, and control by a vast panoply of subliminal strategies that render the subject's agreement the merest formality. In such a society the only unquestionably subversive art may be a terrorism willing to imitate selectively the total violence of state power.

Along with the self-esteem that its exile (whether in the officially sanctioned and well-quarantined "culture" of the academy, the marketplace of commercial publication, or rapidly co-opted pockets of "underground" activity) no longer entitles it to, modern writing has been stripped of many of the fictions and comfortable illusions that traditionally accompanied and facilitated its practice. Among the most prominent of the illusions that this literature undermines is that of *author*, that quintessentially fictional entity who is assigned by our society or who assigns himself credit and responsibility for the world of his work. This authorial entity is now to be elided in favor of a text to which the writer merely appends his signature, as under constraint, but which is seen as a product of a collaboration between society and individual, reader and writer.

Not only author but also *character* in this literature of deconstruction becomes an unstable element. Just as reader and writer tend to become interchangeable if not totally synonymous qualifications, so the fictional creations become engaged in a process that renders them unstable, labile, and unreliable. The author himself becomes a factor of ambiguity, doubt, and uncertainty, as difficult to define as to demarcate from his narrators and characters, for a common reality or unreality suffuses both creator and creation: rather than the author creating the work, it is the work that creates and demands its author.

This unreality is further enhanced by the parallel existence of a tendency for the characters to be named casually, if at all, as if for convenience's sake, or to be flatly unnamed, reduced to a pronominal existence: these are the "I"s, "he"s, "she"s, "you"s, and "they"s that substitute, in novels by Blanchot, Sollers, and even the more conventional Des Forêts, for personages that have no other designation. In Leiris' case the autobiographical "I," of all entities seemingly the most reliable, is derealized in successive and simultaneous avatars that contradict and deny each other, as the character that is supposed to be himself takes on the qualities of fiction and myth and thereby becomes subject to endless deconstruction. Beckett's unnamed protagonist of the final novel of his trilogy, named aptly and paradoxically *The Unnamable*, is another example of this disintegration of solid identity, as is also the hero of Tzara's long iconoclastic poem, *Approximate Man*, about whom we are reminded so often that he is no definite entity but instead an amalgam of writer, reader, man-of-the-past, and "new man" in process of gestation.

Very pertinent also for a reading of *Finnegans Wake* is an awareness of the often-remarked phenomenon of the "porosity"[35] of Joyce's characters one for the other, so that they frequently speak with each other's voices. In so doing, they become interchangeable, elusive, and evanescent, keeping the reader from being able to depend on any fixed notions about them and the work they participate in by directing attention always elsewhere—to a process and an incessantly renewed activity or task that *they* merely exemplify.

Just as in the universe of this ceaseless Brownian movement the author and his narrators and characters become so many motes that merge, collide, and lose their distinct place and separable shape and contour, so do the stories they tell and the plots they invent become increasingly questionable, fragmentary, nonsensical, repetitive, and circular. In this literature of deconstruction, as in structuralism, diachrony tends to yield to synchrony. Wherever you cut into *Finnegans Wake* you will come up with, remarkably enough, the same "piece of pie," as a handful of mythologized stories are infinitely refracted and retold from an infinite variety of points of view. Beckett's work also eschews linear development, circling obsessively and permanently round a few precious threads of story and argument; Leiris' autobiography, in spite of its massive length and pyrotechnic display of avowal and vulnerability, actually says very little about the author's life in any chronological or comprehensive sense. A little like Proust's great *Recherche*, it instead circulates obstinately around a very small number of scenes, incidents, ideas, or even words that are endlessly ruminated, commented, reinterpreted, and deconstructed.

The fact is that very little of note or worth remembering happens in this literature of deconstruction. We are here in that limit world that Beckett likes to evoke where "nothing happens"—no great battles fought, lovers parted and reunited, ancestral lines extinguished, revolutions carried out or failed, talents developed and matured, sins visited upon oneself or one's progeny—all that constituted a world for Stendhal, Balzac, Dostoevsky, Tolstoy, Dickens, Zola, Poe, Hawthorne, Melville, and even Thomas Wolfe. Action in that minimal sense in which it is present, though endlessly cogitated, as in Kafka, Proust, Musil, and Woolf, is missing here; for here nothing is written with one hand that the other does not soon erase; nothing is affirmed that is not ineluctably denied, the emphasis always being more on "how can we be sure it really happened" rather than on the significance of what is only supposed to have occurred. The stories or plots in this literature tend to describe their tellers and listeners more than any objectively ascertainable referent or reality; and the environments in which they develop, the backgrounds against which they are played, tend to avoid specific definition and location—from the "anywhere cities" of Blanchot, Des Forêts, and Sollers to the vague vacant lots, roads, beds, and fronts of restaurants of Beckett, to the purely symbolic landscapes of Tzara (which the hands of a clock that tells no time are likely to dominate), to the very cerebral reality of Leiris that the memory of a provocative painting, which incarnates his sexual obsessions, and the recollections of a few hypnotic syllables, which convey the clash between child and society, are likely to punctuate.

Motivation here is all-important, as recently in Derrida's work "why am *I* telling *you* this at this *time*"[36] becomes an overriding concern, while what is actually being said becomes secondary; and so these stories, or what is left of them, inevitably break down under this insistent, obsidian gaze into the words that compose them, which are then interrogated for meanings and values that are so painfully missing from the larger units of phrase, sentence, paragraph, chapter, and finally book that they cannot help but form. For this is a literature that is obsessively *molecular* in its outlook and profoundly etymological in its mood, a style not dissimilar to the attention to glosses in the influential philosophy of Heidegger and more recently Derrida. "What have these words meant in the past?" "What do they mean now?" and "Do they really mean what we think they mean?" are recurrent lines our authors take. Beckett, Leiris, Blanchot, and Sollers pose these questions constantly and explicitly; Joyce's mistrust of the words he has inherited is so extreme that he must invent innumerable new ones; a major preoccupation of Tzara's is a revolutionary critique of the traditional meanings of heavily charged concepts like Beauty, Art, and Talent and a corresponding attempt to change or float their meanings and uses. (Thus in one of his major texts Tzara advises, at least half seriously, a compulsory change of language on a weekly basis[37] so as to combat our complacency about the words we employ and the ideas we have received with them.)

The mistrust that our other writers show in the attention they lavish on the meanings of words, Des Forêts manifests in another way in his *bavard's* or "gabber"'s sublime indifference to them; the latter advertises the attitude that words all mean the same thing—that is, *nothing*, except the overwhelming need of a speaker to capture the attention of a listener. Des Forêts' talky narrator accordingly assures the reader that he remembers not a single word of what is after all a central event of the novel, if there is one, and certainly a scene about which the narrator has gone to great lengths to make the reader curious—his exalted, drunken tirade or monologue before an enraptured then disgusted audience in a dancing bar; it no longer matters in *Le Bavard* what exactly is said or left unsaid, as all attention is focused instead on the acts or gestures of speaking and listening—and the motivations they obey or are meant to fulfill.

This, then, is a literature that has been "stripped" and reduced to what Barthes, in his famous formulation, has called its zero degree—one that is devoid of any real and enduring finality, goal, or purpose outside of the necessity and contingency of its performance and its style; for everything here has become temporary and fleeting, a Nietzschean world where the only certainty is the lack of all certainty. This is a literature of the disinherited, as Erich Heller calls it, of transition; and although it can assume the proportions of apocalypse and an eschatological grandeur, especially in its more dramatic moments, which seem to coincide with those all-too-brief interludes when History seems to be offering some hope (Republican Barcelona, France of 1936 or of May 1968), it is equally insistent on the inapplicability of all past solutions to man's actual predicament. There is nothing *conservative* about this literature, no longing for some pristine, less confusing world; and here it parts company with Drieu La Rochelle,

Céline, and with (whatever their experimental modifications) the American tradition of innovation incarnated in Gertrude Stein, Ezra Pound, and even William Faulkner, Henry Miller, and, currently, John Barth.

Tzara's diagnosis of Western culture is so severe and his prognosis so desperate that he is ready to give up on it and try to start over on different premises; and Blanchot is not so very far away from this apocalyptic mood, at least in his more extreme formulations, except that for the latter, perhaps edified by more History (Hiroshima), "starting over" is no longer an option, since all that remains for the latest Blanchot is a kind of tragic recognition of the damage man is and has caused. There stays for Beckett and Leiris a similar sort of noble dignity in the obduracy with which they endure and continue insistently to deal in their works with a futility from which most others (have to) hide. However, these writers who will never "give up" are far removed from a literature that actually had, or still thinks it has, "something to say"; and as we describe it above, Des Forêts' masterful reduction of his author-narrator to the marginal predicament of obsessed, culpable, and compulsive talker (whose situation is universal in a world where humanity has been relegated to marginality) attacks equally any claim of literature to transcendence, special status, or privilege. This denial of finality is something common, also, to Joyce and Sollers, as both work in this same direction of flattening writer into reader and both into the elemental all-too-human needs that underlie their rapports.

Joyce's ultimate recourse is to produce a new language to be compatible with twentieth-century advances in the arts and sciences; but now it seems likely that the language of the future (in itself far from guaranteed) is to be the digital, monotonous, monophonic, and tyrannical "computerese" rather than a fascinating, polyphonic, and democratizing Wakese (the language of the Wake respects no position or privilege but undermines all hierarchy in its onslaught on the stability of all perspectives). At all events, critics seem to agree that the Wake is a profoundly "decentered" and "decentering" experience and work, which by the very laws of its being can neither constitute its own finality nor refer the reader to any transcendent one beyond an inherently mutable and relative act of reading. The *Wake* can neither represent an absolute nor constitute one by its very existence, the first because it insists on meaning nothing unqualifiably, the second because that would require the kind of tautological faith or blind fetishism that for our suspicious modern temper is manifestly obsolete as well as deservedly discredited.

It is perhaps Sollers' impatience with this "writing as its own absolute" that led him to look for more substantial anchors, standards, and referents for his later work. His notorious, well-publicized, and successive flirtations, experiments, and involvements in (a kind of) Maoism and now Christianity have at most seriously reduced the perdurability and universality of his creative works (although he continues to astonish, delight, unnerve, and enrage through what are obviously very great resources of invention, stamina, and just plain nerve) and, at the very least, propelled him outside of the parameters of this literature of deconstruction that his earlier work seemed to accommodate. This evolution or devolution in his work may serve as an example of the consequences of insisting on wresting a finality from a world that is no longer capable of supplying one.

The literature of deconstruction, while incapable of being its own absolute, is equally incapable of attachment to any other transcendent goal or finality. This is a literature of the lost—those who have given up all hope of ever attaining to any further shore and who remember indistinctly, if at all, where they came from; and it is not as if there is no urgency involved in this situation. For this time, as Joyce so aptly names it in Wakese, is the "pressant," within which our present and pressing task is no longer to abide by or even pretend to understand any code or system that is beyond, above, beneath, or even within ourselves but only *to stay afloat* and to decline, politely if possible, any offer of rescue or hope of deliverance.

This is a literature that is attached to nothing, not even itself; it resists intrinsically any attempt to understand it because it refutes in advance that literature or life can be, or was meant to be, understood; and it resists categorization and classification as ineluctably as it does comprehension. What these works elicit, encourage, and provide, and what deconstruction seems so well placed to facilitate, is the opportunity of entering the worlds of these works and playing by their rules. These texts are not objects seen more or less clearly from the outside but experiences we feel or sense from within. They are houses where we know someone or something goes on living, but though we go scrupulously through every room we will never find out exactly who or what that is; and if our obstinate search should turn up a name or two on a mailbox, as it were, we can be equally sure that the labels refer to no real entity but are there as joke, convenience, or mere consolation; or, alternatively, the names and therefore dwellings are our own, for it is we who now inhabit them—and the responsible ones, or authors, we are seeking are ourselves.

This perhaps may be a deeper meaning to deconstruction's controversial assault on the separation between creative writing and criticism and to the "answerable style"[38] that one prominent figure in deconstruction has advised as suitable for critical discourse. In other words, instead of clinging to a dated myth of objectivity and the pose of analytic neutrality, criticism should participate in and extend the method, spirit, and enthusiasm of the disseminated work. Such an "answerable style" might be the entry of Hegel and Genet (and Sartre) into the confessional, philosophical, political, and typographical alembic of Derrida's *Glas*, to which Geoffrey Hartman replies in the eccentric complexity of *Saving the Text*. A deconstructive strategy depends on the notion that we no longer so much write about a text as explore its ramifications and continue its development by becoming part of a process that intrinsically knows no end or beginning.

This is the spirit in which the essays that follow were written. In each case I have tried to answer the author with a style and a thematic content that reflects and conveys a participation in the process of his work. This accounts for the variety of the approaches I use (among others, intuitive, analytical, sometimes even eschatological-apocalyptic) and for the varying distance I assume from and tones I take with the text or author in question. It accounts also for my use of the rubric and reputation of deconstruction to introduce these essays; for deconstruction releases me, as does modernity in general according to Blanchot,[39] from the necessity and obligation to unify what I know under the command of any single idea or governing system or concept. It allows me to follow the texts I explore and extend where they take me, as it releases me from the tyranny of map and plan for a journey that, like each one's life, has never been traveled before.

Exploratory Readings in Some Modern Texts

"Il n'y a pas de hors-texte"—Derrida*

1. Symbolism in the Streets: Tzara

The essay opens with an analysis of the dada of Tristan Tzara as a rewriting of the heritage of symbolism. Although in agreement with the symbolists in their critique of bourgeois society, Tzara parts company with them for their reliance on what I call "exotic remedies." He rejects specifically a symbolist aesthetic that privileges artistic possibilities as alternatives or antidotes to the necessary boredom and dreariness of life in the "civilized" world. For him the real must be transformed, not merely escaped.

---

* "Il n'y a pas de hors-texte" means, approximately, that there is nothing but text, so that prefaces, afterwords, summaries, commentaries on texts are texts too, therefore worth as much or as little. I find this phrase impossible to translate, at least literally. Rodolphe Gasché in *The Tain of the Mirror: Derrida and the Philosophy of Reflection* translates this as "there is no extra-text" (281); but this misses the gustatory suggestion. Gasché, however, is insightful in saying "Derrida could just as well have stated *there is no inside of the text*" (281). The Derridean, which Gasché calls the "general text," is nothing that can be entered or left.

Tzara's early play, *Le Mouchoir des nuages* (*Handkerchief of Clouds*), is then examined for the ways in which it absorbs and then reworks many of the elements in what Tzara saw as symbolist escapism. The poet, for instance, in this play is devoured by a society from which he can no longer even pretend to stand apart; and Tzara uses masterfully a panoply of techniques to shock and surprise his audience and to ensure that, far from being able to contemplate the dramatic event as just an evening's diversion, it is involved in and shares responsibility for what is happening.

A reading of *Approximate Man*, an epic-length poem of 1931, goes on to show Tzara accepting the challenge of attempting to transform a world it is no longer possible to escape. Fundamental to Tzara here is an anti-Platonism that refuses to recognize in man the avatar or expression of any idea but insists on the possibilities of purely physical, sensory, and sensual presence. My discussion of this poem explores and extends Tzara's attacks on a false culture of museums and concert halls and a degrading, quantifying time of clocks and machines. Tzara's iconoclasm works toward breaking out of the ghetto wherein, in order to protect itself against their dynamic and disruptive energies, society confines and quarantines its poets and thinkers.

The strange, hallucinogenic, paradoxical, and preposterous implications of the social and personal metamorphoses that Tzara demands are spelled out in grimly and fanatically (sur)realistic detail in a later extended tract of prose-poetry, *Grains et issues* (1935). This work, which I take up in conclusion, propounds an uneasy but ambitious alliance, on the basis of the dream's power to abrogate ordinary logic, between the idealism of the libertarian-radical tradition (Rousseau and early Marx), which insists on the feasibility of an end of alienation, and the more cynical realism of thinkers like Dostoevsky, Nietzsche, and Freud, who saw man as a creature incapable of happiness, who would be bored enough to wreck any utopia he might attain.

2. A Question of Culture/Culture in Question: Beckett

For Samuel Beckett's writer the restrictions and limitations against which Tzara chafes so adamantly no longer pertain. Far from being a domain of privilege, delight, and glory, art has become inseparable for Beckett from the boredom, uncertainty, and insecurity of daily life: "waiting for Godot" is what we all do all the time.

My essay on Beckett, then, is concerned with aspects of the human condition as revealed and developed by a voice that only *happens* to be that of a writer. First of all I look at the words of *Molloy*, where stoic humor and stark pessimism carry the reader into a world too senseless and paradoxical to be objectified and understood but which can only be felt, lived, and experienced. Ideas, abstractions, and prejudices are so many hopes that must be abandoned at the gate of this particular inferno.

I then go on to show how it is the cunning of *Malone Dies* to bring the reader behind the scenes of the novel-in-process so as to share in the responsibility for the illusions being created. The reader is being duped not by the author (who, like Socrates, knows how little he knows) but by himself and by his own need to believe. No credit or blame is assignable, however, for what fools him fools everyone else.

The voice of the third novel of Beckett's trilogy, *The Unnamable*, no longer belongs to any specific being, for with Malone died the principle of identifiable character, class, and function. This book, then, is pure text, words of uncertain provenance and even less sure purpose, by no one to no one, pleading for some anomalous, unwanted, and impossible favor. The voice that speaks here knows all too well that the specific violence characteristic of our culture is assassination by classification; and so anonymity, elusiveness, disappearance, disembodiment (close to Joyce's "silence, exile, and cunning")—all synonyms for contemporary "textuality" (Derrida: "a text that does not 'hide' is not a text")—are the necessary recourses, guaranteeing nothing, for the chance of living on.

3. The Rules of the Game: Leiris

The individual is for Michel Leiris a no less permeable, unstable, and questionable entity than it was for Beckett. For Leiris, however, the "subject in question" is no fictional construct, not even a transparent one, but the author and narrator himself. The uprootedness, derealization, and loss are accrued and intensified compared with writers who are willing or able to set up intermediaries between themselves and emptiness. For here Leiris strikes a telling blow at Western man where he is seemingly most assured and at home: in the very notion, guaranteed in countless journals, diaries, life stories, that there still remains, whatever else has been swept away, the remnant and consolation of a self—about which something can be known, claimed, represented, and written.

What has dissolved in Tzara is the myth that poetry is still possible in a bourgeois world that knows no *real* exception to the universality of its stifling commercial rule and logic; and we have seen how Beckett takes down the myth of the possibility for individuality and character in a culture whose basic rule is to destroy whatever can be *found*. For Leiris it is life itself that dissolves into the myth and crypt of art.

My essay proceeds to bring out this unreality and impossibility of life along the axis of a structurally irreconcilable opposition that I apply to Leiris' work between a subjective pole of pure imaginative and emotional freedom and an objective one of social constraint and conformity. That "mirror stage," as Lacan has described it, where you discover yourself as reflected for others, is never terminated for Leiris; for the self ripe for alienation and exploitation, which is all the mirror can reflect, is an entity that Leiris is as little ready and able to accept as he is to deny. That self for Leiris, hesitant, undecided, and reluctant, is forever in pursuit of a harmony that remains always out of reach. This is at once the pathos and charm of his autobiographical art, whose unique quality it is to retain a childlike innocence and wonder in an imagined space and time that for all its guarantees of factual veracity and actuality is none the less magical and mythical; and that "art of memory," which for Proust was healing and redemptive and for Rousseau justifying and explanatory, is for Leiris a mere strategy of composition, or modus operandi and vivendi. For Leiris the wounds of existence are permanent and irremediable, and education, sentimental or otherwise, a joke or misnomer, for his text separates itself from any pretension that it should be granted any special status or make any difference—that is, be more than the complaint that one man was helpless not to utter against a world that denies him the reality he was born to demand.

4. The Fragmentary Word: Blanchot

The implications of this modernity that denies any absolute or enduring finality to art or to any other activity have never been pursued more relentlessly than in the texts of Maurice Blanchot; Blanchot is especially significant for the ways in which he is able to deduce and deal with the disruptive consequences of philosophical conjecture (Hegel, Nietzsche, and Heidegger) and historical conjuncture (the bomb, genocide, May 1968), integrating them into the practice and example of his writing. Blanchot invents a text that assumes the task of responding to and taking responsibility for a world that can no longer be understood and explained, much less excused and justified. In so doing, he practices a writing that resigns pretensions to totality, control, and glory but must admit, in all respect to the countless victims of "progress," the abjectness and insufficiency of the effort it must, nevertheless, continue to make.

My own essay follows the thread of his recurrent formulations on what he has called "fragmentary writing" through their explicit statement in his critical writings to their refraction and dissemination in his fictions. The fragmentary writer, exiled from his own work, as from a society whose achievements and logic he puts into question by the very act of picking up the pen, all the same corresponds to the most advanced elements of modern consciousness. He has taken his history and philosophy

seriously and so has refused to be lulled or consoled by
popular myths like scientific meliorism or redemptive art.
The eloquence and perseverance of this attitude of refusal
is what accounts for the importance of Blanchot for
experimentation in literature. It may also account for his
catalytic role in the formation of specific iconoclastic currents in literary criticism, like *Tel Quel* and deconstruction, that are exploratory in mood and libertarian or radical in potential.

5. The Endless Question: Joyce

This "limit-experience" of ceaseless defiance and interrogation, known to readers of Bataille, and that Blanchot projects as the natural terrain for the writer, is also
where James Joyce is very much at home. In my essay on
Joyce I concentrate on three passages from the relatively
accessible book 1, chapter 6, of *Finnegans Wake*. I show
how a paternal figure, identified with authority and tradition, in the first passage looms mightily over the history of
Ireland (a microcosm for the human race) as over the
imagination of Joyce. I then go on to describe the multifarious ways in which this figure is reduced, engulfed, and
elided in the very same process whereby he has been built
up and celebrated. The deconstructive energy of this process is then carried over into a second passage where an
incestuous lover's discourse is made into a model for the
kind of communication that undercuts and subverts all
rationality, abstraction, and logic (except its own). The
third moment of the process I study is then presented as
the hilariously hypocritical harangue of a Professor Jones
—and here I try to show how the very mechanisms of his
presentation, through the noise and interference it absorbs and invites, cancels out any sense it is likely to
make.

My conclusions are that Joyce, in *Finnegans Wake*, is
engaged in a complex action whereby he takes down and
plows under any structure he erects. Subject, story, character, even the solidity and dependability of words themselves dissolve in the sea of incessant qualification and ex-

ception that constitutes the *Wake;* and the reader is thrown back inevitably from a text that refuses him any firm hold to integrative and disintegrative moments in his own experience and culture. The *Wake* undoes itself so as to leave its reader alone.

6. The Strategy of Interruption: Sollers

Equally alone is the reader of Philippe Sollers, though perhaps less surprised by his solitude. Common to these writers who participate in what I have been calling this library or literature of deconstruction is a tendency to push the reader away from hypnotic or entranced involvement with the text. As in Brecht's renowned "Verfremdungseffekt," styles of discontinuity become important in that they remind the reader of the "produced" nature of the event that is the text. Nowhere are these styles more blatantly, comprehensively, and insistently put into operation than in the works of Philippe Sollers; *Drame,* for instance, his novel of 1965, comprises an ample repertory of techniques whereby the reader is reminded of the process that resulted in the book he is reading. The process of the book's creation is indeed the subject of the book in a much more explicit way than it was for the already self-conscious fictions of Beckett, Joyce, and Blanchot, and even for Leiris, who shows himself to be so frequently and painfully aware that he is (only) writing a book. Sollers, however, takes the self-consciousness of these texts one definite step further, for *Drame* absolutely refuses to be read in any other way except as a permanent and incessant critique of itself.

This essay then focuses on what I call Sollers' strategy of interruption in *Drame,* those means whereby he obliges his reader not so much to read as to wonder what reading is all about. By excluding his audience in advance from any continuous involvement in the text through a series of cunningly prearranged disturbances, Sollers means to exile his reader from any comfortable experience of the text and, from this distance, to make him curious (as only the disturbed are) about the premises under which reading and, a fortiori, thinking and writing take place in our culture.

With *Drame* literature moves definitively, even programmatically, into a territory that had already been explored by the other experimental writers in our network—where it no longer matters exactly what words are said because what is being shown is the process that permits their saying. The words then tend toward becoming interchangeable, modifiable, and unreliable; they point to a kind of noise, cry, sub- or paratext, or to that invisible, indeterminate, but compelling world (perhaps that miracle that Artaud puts us into contact with in his Rodez notebooks) where we become aware not so much of someone's thoughts as of *thought* itself.

7. A Deconstructed Epiphany: Des Forêts

Louis-René Des Forêts' masterful novel and tour de force, *Le Bavard* (1946), makes reading and writing just as problematic and questionable in its own way as Sollers' later *Drame*. The problem of motivation is uppermost here, for the text of Des Forêts' unnamed narrator is strangely *pretext* for the expression and satisfaction of needs that turn out to be human-all-too-human rather than eclectic and literary, as the literal dimension of these words is elided in favor of an image of their speaker and listener. For just as the subject of the book is man's infinite capacity to deceive others as well as himself, the signified of these signifiers is always their speaker's need to have others believe in his version of reality, or at least to listen to it until he has accomplished his purpose.

In this essay I discuss the cultural, social, and political etiology and ramifications of the narrator's malady, *a compulsive need to talk,* and I describe the ways in which the author builds this metaphor for the human condition into a device that subverts and derails, while guiding, the reader's involvement in and reaction to the text. In the end, author and reader stand gaping at one another, as it were, across an emptiness where once there was a text. The mysterious operation of this book is more to finish with author and reader than to be finished by them.

2
Symbolism in the Streets:
Tristan Tzara

The danger of an exclusively technical civilization, which is devoid of the interconnection between theory and praxis, can be clearly grasped; it is threatened by a splitting of its consciousness, and by the splitting of human beings into two classes—the social engineers and the inmates of closed institutions.

That the strategic action of those who have decided to engage in the struggle, and that means to take risks, can be interpreted hypothetically as a retrospection which is possible only in anticipation, but at the same time not *compellingly justified* on this level with the aid of a reflexive theory, has its good reasons: the vindicating superiority of those who do the enlightening over those who are to be enlightened is theoretically unavoidable, but at the same time it is fictive and requires self-correction; in a process of enlightenment there can only be participants.

—Jürgen Habermas[1]

I

In addition to being an inventor of dada and a participant in surrealism, Tristan Tzara is one of the writers of the twentieth century who was most profoundly influenced by symbolism—in the sense that he obviously had absorbed the doctrines of this literary movement and utilized many of its methods and ideas in the pursuit of his own artistic and social ends. Symbolism in particular seems to have been distinguished by an antihistorical bias. Symbolism constitutes, at least in part, a reaction to a school of thought culminating in Hegel and the English utilitarians that believed in progress and reason and adulated the historical process. Symbolist writers were unanimous in rejecting this attitude; they saw all too clearly its ethnocentricity, its flatness, and the ways in which it reduces men and women to a purely material dimension. Their disdainful attitude toward "what really happened" perhaps culminates in Proust, whose narrator paradoxically resuscitates a "past that never was," making it a function of pure subjectivity.

Although the symbolist aesthetic rejected history as a purely factual process, it did admit some purpose for history insofar as it supplies material—metaphors, images, and *symbols*—that have a role to play in the thought-world of the writer. So it is that one of Virginia Woolf's characters muses in *The Waves:*

> Now I will go to the bathroom and take off my shoes and wash; but as I wash, as I bend my head down over the basin, I will let the Roman Empress veil flow about my shoulders. The diamonds of the Imperial crown blaze upon my forehead. I hear the roar of the hostile mob as I step out on the balcony. Now I dry my hands, vigorously, so that Miss, whose name I forget, cannot suspect that I am waving my fist at an infuriated mob. 'I am your Empress, people.' My attitude is one of defiance. I am fearless. I conquer.[2]

History becomes a vast storehouse of costumery, where the artist is free to choose the items (masks) that correlate objectively with his subjective moods and fancies. Such is the fundamentally ahistorical approach common to such diverse works as Wilde's *Salomé*, Huysmans' *À Rebours*, Flaubert's *Salammbô*, Yeats's astrological survey of world history in *A Vision*, and Oswald Spengler's appealing but dangerously unreliable account of this same history in *The Decline of the West*. We may sum up this attitude in the word "exoticism," which for us means the attempt to escape from an intolerable present into either a past that never existed or an equally unreal geographical space.

While Tzara has obviously learned with the symbolists to disdain history and geography as such, he doesn't find much consolation in their "exotic remedies"; for Tzara, as for dada and surrealism in general, the problem is deeper and more serious than a dialectic of fact and fantasy can cope with; a novel can be trusted no more than a biography, since invented facts imprison us no less surely than "real" ones; for Tzara the great fiction and the great enemy is time, symbolized by that omnipresent machine that man has set up to rule over him, the clock—which Tzara, in a utopian mood, prefers to imagine without hands.[3]

The symbolists had rejected a historical past, but they had held on dearly to the faculty of "memory" with which they consoled themselves by inventing and then believing in a past that never was. For Tzara, however, it is memory itself that is the problem, since it deludes man into thinking there was something where there was nothing. This delusion, while understandably comforting and attractive, has negative consequences for any future for humanity; Tzara therefore carries on a systematic critique not only of the faculty of personal recollection but also of the institutions that serve as a culture's memory—libraries, museums, and academies. His idea is that as long as we do things the way we think we once did them we will be unable to achieve any kind of livable society. Either we will be applying our past routines and formulas to situations for which they are inappropriate or we will be attempting to live totally in our vision of what the past was; we will never be able to be more than alternately melancholy or manic survivors who live on the flotsam and jetsam of a civilization and who take it for the real thing. Memory is the great villain in this process, since it sets limits we can never go beyond. We waste our time, then, living (or writing) in terms of a future that can only be inhibited or confused by the marks we have made, just as we, for the most part, are more harmed than helped by the insistence of our ancestors on giving us something to remember them by:[4] the Gothic cathedrals were created not by individuals who wanted to be remembered but by a people that wanted to be saved.[5]

II

The marks of memory, as Tzara describes them in his play *Le Mouchoir des nuages* (*Handkerchief of Clouds*, 1924), are like the pebbles we drop behind us in the morning on our way through a forest. When we return at night we can no longer see these markers, and we must take a different way back anyway:

COMMENTAIRE

C.—Où sont-ils, maintenant, le poète et celle qu'il découvrit comme une note claire de chanson sur le bord de la route? Ils sont en train d'égrener les histoires de leurs vies, comme un chapelet de cailloux qu'ils laissent tomber sur la route pour la retrouver a leur retour.

B.—Mais alors il fera nuit et ils ne pourront plus retrouver le chemin qu'ils avaient indiqué au moyen de cailloux sur la route, car le lendemain les cailloux ressembleront aux autres et tout rentrera de nouveau dans la confusion d'où chaque jour nous essayons de sortir.

C.—Tu a raison, on ne peut jamais retourner sur le chemin de la mémoire. A bicyclette ou en auto on retourne au point de départ, mais sur un autre trajet que celui que la mémoire a parcouru.*

---

* "C.—Where are they now, the poet and the woman that he discovered like the clear note of a song on the side of the road? They're now telling each other their life stories, like a rosary of pebbles they drop by the way in order to find their way back later.

"B.—But by that time it'll be dark and they'll no longer be able to find again the road they've marked with pebbles, for tomorrow the pebbles will blend into the surroundings and all will return to the confusion that we constantly try to avoid.

"C.—You're right, you can never find your way back memory lane. Whether by bike or car, we always return to the point we set out from, but by another way than memory"; *Œ. C.* 1: 309.

Tzara's critique of memory is even more total than the surrealists' well-known distrust of this faculty; for, although the surrealists distrusted conscious memory, they exploited and used elements coming from the recently discovered continent of the subconscious mind; they therefore found value in dreams, automatic writing, and gestalt approaches to literary creation.[6] But for Tzara, subconscious, even "racial," memory may be no less an obstacle than the conscious traces we intentionally follow or leave. We may dream, fantasize, even hallucinate according to patterns no less rigid than the ones that rule our waking lives. It is these very waking lives that, according to Freud, provide the content and focus the needs upon which our dreams are founded. Our subconscious memories, or what we are convinced are such, may then comprise an obstacle no less surely than the ones we are aware of. Memory becomes for Tzara the discredited faculty par excellence because it incarnates man's temptation to escape from the duty of creating the world anew by duping him into the illusion that the *world has already been created*. These and other subterfuges— whether through real or invented history and geography, and whose definition we may widen to include permutations and combinations of tourism, drugs, romantic love, mysticism—we characterized above by the term "exoticism."

Together with a judgment, both stated and implied, that "exotic" remedies have outlived their usefulness, Tzara's play, *Le Mouchoir des nuages*, is nothing less than a repertory and a summary of the clichés of exoticism: the bored bourgeois wife who falls in love with the poet, the banker who loses his money in order to win back the love of his wife, the poet who travels to a deserted island where he now realizes he loves the banker's wife who no longer loves him, the reproduction of a scene from *Hamlet* which serves the poet as a correlative to his own situation, and the final flashback, twenty years later, at the "follies of youth"—all of this extensively "deconstructed," we would say, by a chorus of commentators who reflect on such themes as the irrelevance of poetry to life as proved by the inanity of this particular effort:

A.—... Mettez vous à sa [the poet's] place, *il a besoin*
de prendre la poésie pour une réalité pour du mirage.
B.—Quant à moi ... je n'hésiterai pas une seconde à
proclamer que la poésie est un produit négligeable de la
folie latente, et qu'elle n'est aucunement nécessaire à la
marche ascendante de la civilisation et du progrès.*

To make sure that we can never forget that we are being "put on," the acts, fifteen of them, flash by with the
speed of light. We make a veritable tour of the world to see
nothing. We go from Venice, to Monte Carlo, to the South
Pacific, and back to l'Avenue de l'Opéra; we even make a
little side excursion to the cliffs of Hamlet's Elsinor; and
we end up in a squalid little garret twenty years later
where the poet, out of ideas, like a banker out of funds,
tritely takes his own life—after which "action" his soul
ascends to be sold at a heavenly auction to that supreme
bidder in the sky:

A.—... Ils font monter aux enchères son âme dans
le ciel. Ils l'achètent par des chiffres. ... Ils font monter
sur l'échelle des chiffres l'appréciation de son âme.†

The actors themselves can't even escape for the brief
duration of the piece from the trap of their own personalities, since they address each other, and are known to the
audience, by their off-stage names—and the commentators
double as the minor roles to make doubly sure that we're
not likely to believe anything that is happening in front of
us, even in a theatrical sense:

---

* "A.—... Put yourself in the poet's place, he *needs* to take poetry
for reality and reality for a mirage.
  "B.—Personally ... I wouldn't hesitate a moment to proclaim
that poetry is a negligible product of latent madness, and is not at all
necessary for the forward march of civilization and progress"; *Œ.C.*
1:332.
  † "A.—They place his soul on a heavenly auction block. They buy
him with cash. There is, finally, appreciation of his soul, in the sense of
an augmentation of its cash value"; *Œ. C.* 1:351.

C.—Voilà pourquoi cette pièce est mal faite. Quoique nous soyons les commentateurs, c'est-à-dire le subconscient du drame, il ne nous est pas permis de savoir pourquoi le poète n'aime pas Andrée.

E.—Elle est pourtant jolie et intelligente, je la connais bien, vous savez.

B.—Le fait que vous jouez sur le tréteau le rôle de l'amie d'Andrée ne vous donne pas le droit de croire que vous l'êtes en réalité.

A.—Mais elle pourrait bien l'être, en dehors de l'action, en dehors de la scène, dans la réalité vraie, qu'en savez-vous?

C.—Oh! c'est ennuyeux, toujours la même discussion sur la différence entre le théâtre et la réalité.*

This handkerchief made of clouds is not one you could put in your pocket. This is a world of shadow, not of substance; these actors are interchangeable to their root essence, which is nothing. They relate not as authentic personalities but as play-actors who are uncomfortably aware of the artificial nature of the roles they are playing. It is as if the two-thousand-year reign of Aristotle over Western art ends with this little play of Tzara's. Nothing is left of the great philosopher's "tragic hero but flawed" in this comedy where the protagonist dies at the end, when no one cares anyway; and to emphasize this vacuity and utter nullity the poet is not even named. The poet is ultimately no different from the banker—not named either —for each tries to maximize his profit from a minimal outlay of resources, whose only value is one of exchange. Becoming someone of

---

* "C.—That's why this is a bad play. Although we're the chorus, that is to say, the unconscious of the play, we're not allowed to know why the poet doesn't love Andrée.

"E.—Nevertheless she's young and beautiful; I'm well acquainted with her, you know.

"B.—The fact that you're playing the role of Andrée's friend on stage doesn't give you the right to suppose you're her friend in reality.

"A.—But she could well be that, outside of the action, outside the scene—in real life, what do you know about it?

"C.—Oh, how boring, always the same discussion about the difference between theatre and real life"; Œ. C. 1:320.

consequence and thereby winning love, or whatever other prize accrues to "good behavior," is a function of pure social status. One has become poet or banker simply by following certain rules; whether these pertain to the "dérèglement de tous les sens"* dear to such poets as Rimbaud, Lautréamont, Gilbert-LeComte, and our own Jim Morrison or the procrustean fit of reality to a preconceived pattern that results in the fortunes of a Rockefeller, Morgan, or Rothschild, is a matter of complete indifference. In Feuerbachian–Hegelian–early-Marxian terms, one is alienated because one has located one's identity outside of oneself. The poet is therefore interchangeable with the banker: the aesthete with the philistine. The banker has only to obey a different set of rules, in particular the hallowed revolutionary-mystic maxim "the more you have the less you are" (slogan, in our time, of Baader-Meinhof, German revolutionary group); he has only to lose his money gambling to become an entirely different character and thereby win the love of his wife, which just happens to accrue to that kind of personality.

An entire generation of Russian symbolists (Blok, Bely, Sologub, and others) woke up one morning in 1917 to realize that the Revolution meant the abolition of *all* private capital—artistic, cultural, poetic, intellectual, and philosophical no less than monetary; a generation of French-educated Cambodian intellectuals recently faced, nor did they survive, these same typical revolutionary exigencies;[7] and in this play we can see how systematically Tzara, certainly well versed in revolutionary themes by 1924, if not yet a member of the Communist party, dynamites all the claims made during the preceding symbolist period as to any privileged position for art. The poet, for Tzara of the *Mouchoir,* is simply the *banker of the absolute:*[8] he is richer and cannier than the banker, for he has made investment in securities that are more likely to weather the vicissitudes of an unreliable market. When the banker realizes the superior *return* the poet is col-

---

* "Disorganization of all our senses."

lecting on *his* investment, he is, in typically capitalistic style, ready to embrace the methods of the competition, that is, to become the poet, *overnight* as it were.

By working to destroy not only the *factual* past of the empirical philosophers and historians but also the *invented* past and present fantasies of the symbolist writers, Tzara works out a vast and comprehensive delegitimation of contemporary culture together with all the privileges and inequalities that are its sacrosanct givens. If the past is the eminence upon which the "great" of history stand, if their privileged access to the "memory of culture" is the reason for the respect and devotion accorded them, then Tzara, by reducing these eminences and obliterating that memory—cultural as well as personal—is sapping the very fortresses of power of their ability to defend themselves.[9] Tzara here in *Mouchoir* is performing the operation that he recommends so persuasively at the Eighth Dada Evening (April 9, 1919), which he was understandably prevented from delivering:

> ... Le talent QU'ON PEUT APPRENDRE fait du poète un droguiste
> ... HYPODROME DES GARANTIES IMMORTELLES
> Il n'y a aucune importance il n'y a pas de transparence ni d'apparence.
> MUSICIENS   CASSEZ   VOS   INSTRUMENTS AVEUGLES
> sur la scène ... J'écris parce que c'est naturel comme je pisse ...
> L'art a besoin d'une opération
> L'art est une PRÉTENTION ... L'hystérie née dans l'atelier ...
> nous ne cherchons RIEN

---

*   ... The talent THAT YOU CAN LEARN makes of the poet a shopkeeper
... SUPERMARKET OF GUARANTEED IMMORTALITY
Nothing is important. Our art is neither transparent nor apparent.
MUSICIANS BREAK YOUR BLIND INSTRUMENTS on stage ... I write naturally, like I take a piss

nous affirmons la VITALITÉ de chaque instant. . . .*

The ongoing relevance of Tzara to the problems of Western culture is amply demonstrated by the now banal action of rock musicians smashing their instruments on the stage; and not so long ago the best among us were singing "tear down the walls." Sooner said than done, as we now all recognize—but that need to erase the difference between artist and public, that intolerable suffocation of being reduced in humanity because one is *only* a performer, or *only* part of an audience—these demands constitute some of the fundamental questions of our time, questions that have not been solved by simply being adjourned. As a recent article linking Tzara to punk rock indicates,[10] this dissatisfaction will not evaporate simply because psychologists point out to us what we should already know by now—that we still crave inwardly the illusions of security provided by the petty hierarchies that we outwardly pretend to despise, so that we make at once leaders and scapegoats of our most "beloved" artists, those who by choice or by destiny have been frozen into the essentially inhuman role of cultural hero. One thinks of the "youthfully dead" Janis Joplin, Jimi Hendrix, or that suicidal genius sacrificed on the altars of consciousness and who claimed Rimbaud as his major inspiration, the poet Jim Morrison, angrily smashing a microphone against the stage that night in New Orleans, when, still on the young side of thirty, his strength ran out for good.

Art needs to be operated on
Art is PRETENSION . . . hysteria born in the atelier . . .
we're looking for NOTHING
we affirm the VITALITY of every moment

(Œ.C. 1:369)

(The anomalous dada typography brings out the iconoclasm much more forcefully than I can render it in quotation.—PB)

III

In his epic-length poem of 1931, *L'Homme approximatif* (*Approximate Man*), Tzara deepens and further defines his rejection of exoticism and points to the possibility of realizing an authentic destiny and purpose for mankind; as a preliminary to this evolution, man must strip himself of the excess baggage of his past and the notions, based on insufficient logic and reason, with which he has hitherto tried to control his life. Tzara is now looking forward to a future that is as utterly new as the first page of an unread book:[11]

> but let the door open at last like the first page of a book
> your room full of unconquerable loving coincidences
>   sad or gay
> I shall slice the long net of the fixed gaze
> and each word will be a spell for the eye and from page
>   to page
> my fingers will know the flora of your body and from
>   page to page
> the secret study of your night will be illumined and
>   from page to page
> the wings of your word will be fans to me and from page
>   to page
> fans to chase the night from your face and from page to
>   page
> your cargo of words at sea will be my cure and from
>   page to page
> the years will diminish toward the impalpable breath
>   that the tomb already draws in.
>   (*Approximate Man and Other Writings*, 61).

Tzara conceives of man, in this poem, as stretched on the cross of memory, sheltered from reality by words and notions that keep him from knowing effectively what he is supposed to do. The poet is special only to the extent that he is aware of things that others can't or don't want to face. As Tzara so often reminds us, "the approximate man is like you, reader, and so many others." The poet, as the ultimate intellectual, he who takes words for things, is uniquely situated to tell of the limits and pitfalls of intellect:

> we have displaced the ideas and confused their clothing
>   with their names
> blind are the words which from their birth can only find
>   their place again
> their grammatical places in universal safety
> meager is the fire we thought we saw kindling in them
>   in our lungs
> and dull the predestined gleam of what they say
>
> (103)

This is the same intellect that has converted our world into the desert, where at the conclusion of the poem the approximate man pledges himself, in repeated refrains, to wait:

> and stony in my garments of schist I have pledged my
>   waiting
> to the torment of the oxidized desert
> to the unshakable advent of fire
>
> (127, 129)

Tzara, of *Approximate Man*, has absorbed and transcended the aesthetic of symbolism, a philosophy whose attractions and limitations were so frankly summed up by Walter Pater when he said that the purpose of life was to appreciate beautiful things; Tzara finds in an aestheticism of this sort no cause for celebration, or even consolation, but rather a pretext for some savage irony:

> continue sharp fears to click above our heads
> your surgical instruments
> vague forebodings sound the shouting depth of the
>   walls

where we pile up pell-mell knowledge and poetry
but from our fists clenched and cemented with destinies
you can never take what the trial of the laughable grain
seizes from the indecision of a consoling day
take one step back leprous thoughts of death of vermin
consolation
leave to the cultivators of colors and of skies the
    succulent promise
of man carrying in his fruit the burning and propitious
    blossoming of morning

(107)

Tzara prefers to think of man, instead, and maybe Pater would have approved at least of the image, as a slow fire—a blaze that consumes and was meant to consume everything in its path—past, present and future, and working toward an unknown destiny, whose approximate nature is the only sure sign we have of its authenticity:

a slow furnace of invincible constancy—man—
a slow furnace rises from the depth of your slow
    deliberation
... a slow fire brightens in the gaping fear of your
    strength—man—
a fire grown tipsy on heights where the coastal traffic of
    clouds has earthed over the taste of abyss
a fire climbing supplicant the ladder to the stains of
    unbounded gestures. ...

(130)

This fire, whose essence is constant motion and pure change, will live as long as there is something to burn; however small the combustible, it will not be disdained, but like a fading wick the flame will jump across the rim of the candleholder in search of more beeswax; for what remains when we have left behind all those illusions by which we lived, when we are no longer moved by ideas nor motivated by abstractions—like words of praise and blame? Tzara in this poem is looking for some residue of humanity, some solid ground from which to greet the coming of the future, some excuse for hoping:

> morning morning
> morning sealed with crystal and with larvae
> morning of baked bread
> morning of shutters in madness
> morning keeper of the stable
> morning of squirrels and of window cleaners cool by the
>   river
> sweet-smelling morning
> breath clinging to the striations of the iris
>
> (111)

This repetition is not only visual and olfactory in its variations; it is incantatory and prayerful in its tenacity. A song with words that could be other words that it will take a "new man" to understand.

What will this "new man," this amnesiac creature, be like—as on that first morning of creation—this man whose lack of a past keeps him from defining a future? It would, of course, be perverse of us to assign him an essence that would be affirmed only to be denied, but one can't help feeling that this "new man" of Tzara's will be physically sensitive to a hitherto unknown extent, that the Cartesian breach between mind and matter will be healed as people begin to think with their bodies and act by intuition rather than by calculation. "No, I am not a thinker," Tzara tells us (and we *almost* can believe him)—and elsewhere the refrain imposes itself, "Do not close your eyes yet" (118), in other words, "do not make up your mind." For when you have done that you are finished, a (dead) object among objects.

Tzara emphasizes in particular the importance of *hands*. The "new man" will rely much more on these nonverbal means of communication. He will say all that need be said with a wave, a caress, a blow:

> hands that lift from the stern forehead the thick layer of
>   notched thoughts

carry to the lips the glass where worlds expand
offer alms and debase man's proper bearing
hands tense on the plank that will bear away the lowly
    body
hands that pray before that plank of air—unable to
    grasp it—
telling other hands of the unspeakable possibility . . .
cool hands musicians of serene discoveries
hands adept at saving or destroying . . .

(113)

Tzara finds not only things for these hands to do, he is also conscious of reality as worked upon by hands. The above passage (before my quotation) starts with the image of a street being kneaded, like bread, "under the coming and going of wheels." Those hands, which for Rilke were symbolic of an absolute limit for communication ("ours is to touch, nothing more") or for an infinite yearning for contact with an earthly astral being, the "angel of Beauty," these "mystic" hands have been stripped by Tzara of the gloves of their metaphysical destiny. They become as naïve and human as a voice and as innocent as the desire to help another human being. These are active hands, not only praying or resigned ones. These are hands that we humans use to satisfy or to destroy each other:

hands that catch and tame the beasts come forth in hu-
    man bodies
forged in the tension of celestial births
and also hands that kill . . .
hands cut off
but there are also hands that write
peace to some disillusioned wealth to others according
    to the chance of the wells we fall in
incendiary hands
the only ones that shine

(113–14)

The poet of *Mouchoir*, stripped of all transcendence, knocked off his pedestal, and forced to sink or swim in a sea of banal humanity, has evolved into this "approximate man" who, as is so insistently repeated, "like you reader and so many others," has only his hands to protect himself against nothingness. Tzara, as is apparent above, stresses that these hands are not, nor should they always be, so kind. Images of cruelty, blood, and destructive fire abound in this poem; and there is obviously some type of compensation attempted here for the aseptic utopias of the positivists that no one could stand to live in. In a larger sense the hypocrisy of all the utopian dreamers has been to deny the animal in man. The attempt to manufacture a man according to a prototype that has been purified of all ambiguity, whim, and spontaneity has given rise to that monstrous, unbalanced figure that alone is "adapted" to survive in modern society, a machine among machines, and that we may doubt, along with Foucault, that we can still call "man." The bomb has dropped, as Marcuse said, at least half-seriously, and *we* are the mutants. Now Tzara's man is not really man either, which is why he calls him "approximate." "My horizon is limited to the face of a watch" (113), the poet now proclaims; but then what makes him any different from any other cog in the social machine? Machines, introduced as servants, have become the masters and models, as Hegel predicted they would; and the most relevant biblical fable is not the one that so fascinated Kierkegaard, that of Abraham and Isaac, nor is it Gide's favorite lullaby, the return of the prodigal—it should be rather that of Esau, who sold his birthright for a mess of porridge. A half million years of human evolution so approximate man can wind up in a third-class railway carriage with a timetable on his knees:

> so many men have preceded me in the noble furrow of
>   exaltation
> so much soul has been squandered to build the chance
>   I gamble
> in the lonely jail where a blood prowls thick with re-
>   morse . . .

                                                    (83)

And elsewhere the clock is remembered, probably Poe's Big Ben, "which cut off heads to tell the hours" (71). The clock and all it stands for here come to resemble the savage god of the Aztecs, who demands human sacrifice as his constant diet.[12] Still, Tzara's war is not against time, in the sense of a sobering and necessary reminder of our transience that renders to life the value it has, but instead against the measurement and quantification of time that cannot help but become an obsession and compulsion;[13] the reason why clocks and all other similar devices are so seductive lies in our anguish with our uncertainty. With clocks, thermometers, calendars, speedometers, etc., we can pretend to absolute truth. They are Platonic ideas come to visit us in this instamatic age—and in the flesh. Here is a truth that we can know and be familiar with, and that can even talk, or at least beep, back at us. Yes, here it is in all its naked majesty, the great unquestioned absolute: since we no longer pretend to the big things, we can at least be certain of the small ones; so it *is*, for instance 10 P.M., and we *have* just taken two aspirins. Or maybe our senses deceive us; but we can measure that too. This we know.

These clocks that were brought out in time of dearth,[14] we have made into the gods that we are afraid to face:

man so fears the face of his god that deprived the
    horizons he trembles
man so fears his god that at his coming he stumbles he
    drowns
horizonless man. . . .

                     (*Approximate Man*, 78)

We are ashamed to face these machines we have made into idols because we can't but laugh at what they have to say; this is because, except for the clocks that aren't working, they are never right. According to clocks it is never *time* and it can never be *now*.

But the approximate man has turned away from these illusory certitudes; he is willing to admit that he cannot know or be *exactly* anything; he has dealt with the need for certainty in his own soul, which is why he is at once so attractive and so threatening to others. The approximate man is only pretending to have pledged his waiting:

to the torment of the oxidized desert
to the unshakable advent of fire

(130)

This is clearly a mask for those who still need the comfort of a disguise that words can furnish.[15] The approximate man is instead "impossible man"—impossible to locate anywhere; because you have found him do not think he's there: this is Tzara's message for all searchers of identity (and who else would read him?), as it was in a more blatant way Nietzsche's before him. This Tzara, who appears from the East, suddenly, with all the knowledge of a Gurdjieff, all the talent and strange, obdurate patience of a Brancusi, this Tristan Tzara, whose very name, adopted, means the marriage of contraries, that of heaven and earth—he is not about to take us anywhere we have ever been before. His *disguise* is that of the poet, his *persona* that of the performing artist he was while at Cabaret Voltaire in Zurich and the famous dada "happenings" of his early years in Paris, but you will never get him to say exactly what he means. This is because what he means is more or less than what can be said. Above all, he is not asking for your admiration, your esteem, or the confession you have to make of his "greatness," that is, superiority over you, which would excuse you from the responsibility of your own freedom. His goal is not to create another time-honored cultural monument for humanity to abase itself in front of. Tzara talks to his reader not across a distance, formally, like a lecturer, but familiarly, intimately, like a brother, a friend, or a lover. The human condition is his major argument, its transiency, its futility, and the fleeting nature of the sensations that constitute the best of what it has to offer:

you know you will fall apart at your life's end but you
conceal yourself and come in

flower knot of ribbons of human skin . . .
in stations—but I could never say enough of
   stations—there are born fragmented pleasures greetings too brief in shabby hotels
where even love is only part of a dusty legend

(50)

Tzara's apostrophe to "stations," though reminiscent of the *via crucis* (Way of the Cross), would of course be apostasy, since crucial to Christianity is the conception that the trip is made only once; for Tzara, as for those "noble pagans" of antiquity that St. Augustine so took to task, the journey is cyclical and interminable, as Tzara emphasizes the virtues of rootlessness and transiency in this existence "which we have only rented" (79). As if the best we can hope for in life is to enjoy the passage through it.

The *Approximate Man* comes across, in this mood, as an alternately strident and tender appeal to the reader to abandon the gods of the past, those that man worships in the form of History and Memory and that merely represent our nostalgia for a stability that is no longer to be had. Once, when we thought the sun revolved around the earth, we were confident in our own existence; now that we know better we must feel equally sure and confident about our nothingness. For only the knowledge that we have nothing left to lose can enable us to face the future with hope.

IV

Occidental civilization . . . must ultimately end in disorder and demoralization. . . . Peaceful equality can
only be built up among the ruins of annihilated Western states and the ashes of extinct Western peoples.

—Viscount Torio[16]

In a later and fascinating poem in prose, *Grains et issues* (*Seed and Bran*, 1935), Tzara is ready to describe more concretely the future he has in mind.[17] There will still be subways, for instance, but no one will use them because there will be no reason to hurry. Sexual desire will be satisfied in ways that are at once polymorphous, sudden, and spontaneous. The slightest touch will be sufficient to release orgasm or its equivalent in satisfaction. Human contacts in general will be free and unencumbered by the social hierarchies—which will have been abolished. Tzara has taken seriously Rimbaud's slogan, "il faut changer la vie" ("we must change life"), as well as Lautréamont's leitmotif of a poetry that will be made by all. In this sense the symbolist theme of the irrelevance of poetry to daily life in a mechanical age reaches its fruition in Tzara's notion of a daily life that is transformed by and infused with poetry,[18] that is poetic to its very core—a change that can only take place at the "end of History," as Hegel never imagined it to be, when Revolution and Poetry finally meet, as they must (for only one can justify the other), to translate the routines of our lives into endless possibilities.

This new culture will be based on oblivion, that is, on the abolition of memory. Tzara here, completing a critique of language commenced by dada and carried on by surrealism, operates a thoroughgoing devaluation of the word, both written and spoken. To make sure that the new attitudes don't become frozen into new compulsions, there will be a change of language every Saturday. People will hesitate to trust their thinking to words (and all the more their words to paper), so that gradually the habit of thinking in words will die out. This verbal faculty that Western man has exaggerated comes in for some serious reappraisal: words in the future will have a decorative function only—a little bit like the brief greetings and inquiries we exchange when we are in a hurry.[19]

Crime and cruelty will be key elements in any future utopia.[20] Tzara in the earlier *Approximate Man* had more than hinted at the importance of these sides of human nature—an importance that the bourgeois epoch has hypocritically chosen to ignore, while practicing real savagery more systematically than any ruling class before it:

let crime at last flower young and fresh in heavy
   garlands along the houses
fertilize with blood the new adventures the harvests of
   future generations

(*Approximate Man,* 48)

For the bourgeoisie the willful violation of order, incarnated in the concept of crime, is the enemy it pretends to fight, while it perpetuates ever greater crimes in the very name of the order it is defending.

The critique that Nietzsche and Dostoevsky have made of the *perfect worlds* as imagined by the English utilitarians (Bentham, Spencer, Mill) as well as the French social idealists (Saint-Simon, Comte) has had a telling effect on Tzara. A world of complete harmony, peace, and material well-being would be completely unlivable—and Tzara's contemporaries, Artaud and Freud, were as well aware of this as he was. A society that pretends its job is over when the needs of its citizens have been met is doomed to be destroyed by this same citizenry. Closer to psychological reality is the ancient Roman world of frank violence and mass sadism.

The major writers of the symbolist period—Baudelaire, Mallarmé, Rimbaud, and Lautréamont—all condemn this bourgeois version of paradise as if with one voice, as had Stendhal, Flaubert, and the romantics before them; and Tzara is, of course, in fundamental agreement with his predecessors on this point. But he pushes beyond the past denunciations and "refusals" in going on to visualize in positive, concrete terms a utopia that will be a pleasure, or at least interesting, to live in, in more than the merely quantitative sense meant by the bourgeois planners. If for the writers of symbolism, for instance, "boredom" remains the fundamental characteristic of bourgeois society, which, while they remain a part of it, they accept as inevitable, in Tzara's utopia boredom becomes simply a redoubtable enemy that can be eliminated with the help of a little imagination. "Sooner murder an infant in its cradle than nurse unacted desires" and "he who desires but acts not breeds pestilence" are two mottos from Blake's *Marriage of*

Heaven and Hell that could well serve Tzara in this connection.

Roger Gilbert-Lecomte, in a remarkable essay contemporaneous with the prophecies of Tzara, "L'Horrible Révélation la seule" ("Horrible Revelation the Only One"),[21] proclaims that human beings are in the process of turning into *insects.* He allows that, consistent with this mutation, men will become so busy that they will lose their ability to dream, symbolizing the reduction of man to the narrow "one-dimension" of waking consciousness wherein he follows his interest doggedly like an ant under a bread crumb. For Tzara this dreamlessness is instead a positive phenomenon; in this utopia men will no longer dream because their desires will have been satisfied by their waking lives.[22] The subtitle, then, that Tzara gives to *Grains et issues*—"Rêve Expérimental" ("Experimental Dream")—is strangely provisional in this sense. As he explains in a note, he means by this phrase a kind of "waking dream" that operates on the frontiers of consciousness and whose purpose it is to facilitate an interpenetration of the worlds of logic and the irrational. Dream here for Tzara is furthermore expressive of the lyric impulse and as such is not exclusively dependent on the will of the poet (one does not simply *decide* to dream, though one may find oneself in a situation where one is likely to) but must await the proper concatenation of social forces and personal needs. This dream-poetry is only a provisional strategy and must be abandoned when it has served its purpose—when reality will have become a revery, and poetry, from being a more or less tolerated deviation and the affair of specialists, will evolve into the principal means whereby men come to know their world. In the end, for Tzara, poetry will equal love.[23]

Tzara is working to resolve some uncomfortable antinomies here. On the one hand, he adopts enthusiastically the communist-anarchist critique of bourgeois society. On the other, he refuses to be blind and naïve about human nature, so he relates elements of his vision of utopia to the necessity of cruelty and crime as representing authentically human drives—aggression, sadism, hatred—that will need to find outlets. It is as if he is trying to marry the Marx of the *Manuscripts of 1844* with the Freud of *Civilization and Its Discontents*. Small wonder, as Micheline Tison-Braun comments in her perceptive book on Tzara,[24] that eyebrows must have been raised in Moscow and Paris over the dubious political orthodoxy of this attempt as well as over the sanity of its originator. Pickled tongue of aristocrat would have been difficult for even the angriest proletarian to digest:

> Dogs gorged on gasoline and set afire will be turned loose in packs against naked women, just the most beautiful among them, of course. Old people will be pressed and dried between the leaves of great wooden books and then stretched out in the carpets of middle-class salons. Crystal globes filled with aristocrats' tongues will be exhibited among the pots of jam and mustard in store windows.
>
> ("Seed and Bran," *Approximate Man*, 217)

This is of course no realistic scenario and was never meant to be one. Tzara is merely stating that in his version of communism life will be a complex and interesting affair, something that May 1968 well understood with its renowned slogan, "l'imagination au pouvoir" ("power to the imagination"). The fact is, as Freud came to realize with the theory of a "death-instinct" that inflects his later writings, we kill ourselves more than we kill each other (or we do one because we have been brought up not to do the other) because our progress-oriented society, whatever its actual achievements, is bound to increase the guilt each member feels. Such guilt, which is based on the inability of the individual to exchange anything with society for those "benefits" he reaps from it, augments with each of the inventions that supposedly make life easier.[25] The death wish, or Thanatos, becomes more than Eros (there is acceleration here too: hippies, nudity, promiscuity, center-folds, aphrodisiacs) can cope with. We accelerate our speed,[26] take to toxins, and engage in what the social professionals call "self-destructive behavior." When war, inevitable concomitant of the aggressions pent up in each individual, finally breaks out, the tension is lifted as socially sanctioned outlets are provided. Antismoking, antidrug, safe-driving campaigns, and the like, as well as legislation, pretend to deal with the problem; but they result, even in the rare cases where they succeed, only in a change of symptom. "Let the lost get lost," Artaud once remarked in defense of the opium users' right to stone themselves out.[27]

What makes Tzara's vision so interesting is not finally its oddness, it is the practicality of it all, for Tzara was an eager reader of Wilhelm Reich and certainly well acquainted with the latter's theories linking the development of fascism with sexual repression.[28] Our technical civilizations have lengthened life and made it easier for the masses, only to have the average man act as if he were already dead. In Tzara's utopia the individual (although the survival of such an entity is highly problematic) will owe society nothing,[29] except the dubious privilege of having been born. What Tzara is saying is that we need to pay more attention to the qualitative side of life, which we have neglected for the quantitative. We need to take more into account when we make our plans, or even our revolutions, than simply statistical well-being, literacy, nutrition. ... There is such a thing as desire.

V

In this insistence on universality, this refusal to accept compromise, Tzara carries on the symbolist rage at a reality principle that won't let the dreams of totality be realized. The symbolists, for Tzara, were right up to a certain point, but they surrendered too soon to the vagaries and escapes that we have summed up in the word "exoticism." They gave in to nostalgia, aestheticism, tourism; they rejected the crass cultural memory of the bourgeoisie (history as *facts*), but they refused to let go of the "pasts" or the "elsewheres" that, like Yeats and Proust, they invented for themselves to live in. Now it seems to have been pretty much the vocation of dada and surrealism to have cut off man definitively from all such recourses. This was done by a vast delegitimation of cultural prerogatives and privileges and an absolute insistence on the present moment as the only valid area of operation; but Tzara of *Grains et issues* and its inexplicably unpublished companion piece, *Personnage d'insomnie (Personage of Insomnia)** is not searching for simply another point of view, another philosophic retreat or school of thought to replace a past one that has become unworkable; for here he parts company as definitively with surrealism as he had previously with symbolism. What Tzara is searching for is deeper than any merely artistic movement can express or satisfy;[30] as long as it is still "art," no matter what its formal content or what kind of ideological dynamite it carries, bourgeois society can tolerate and ingest it—even use it for its own purposes.[31] The very "freedom" of the artist serves to justify and legitimize a society based on injustice and exploitation for the vast unfree majority—since the formal principle of freedom has been preserved as a theoretical possibility.[32]

By abandoning this pose of the artist, by insisting on the universal poetry of everyday life, and furthermore by proclaiming that one must take risks[33] to realize this dream, Tzara is violating the quarantine that bourgeois society imposes upon art; he is "breaking the frame," as it were, by insisting that he has something to say that can be neither postponed nor confined: look around you, he is saying, who really is enjoying, getting off on all of this?—who doesn't in his heart of hearts, who can't help but wish for the destruction of Western society (together with the "compensations," aesthetic, material, or moral, with which it deflects opposition) and its "culture," which it pretends can make up for the eventless nullity and boring "order" it has created?

The work of defending himself that man has to undertake, and the compensations that he creates for himself by way of transference, by trivializing him, by

---

* See chap. 2, n. 17.

disconnecting the lively force of his instincts, while attacking, little by little, the full enjoyment of life by the augmentation of the quantity of waste and of substitutes and by keeping him from ever getting back again any of this life he has lost, scattered as it has been by the wind around him for the greater glory of things and iron, so that even his smile tends to disappear ... (all of this) leads him inevitably to wish to destroy the established order of the present world ...

The psychic situation, socially speaking, of man, of this hypothetical but conceivable being formed of a human residue, of that which has not yet been quashed by the aggressive interventions of the material conditions of existence and of a morality promulgated for the purposes of reducing him and wresting from him whatever pieces of flesh are still alive,—the psychic situation in relation to the outside world and to the laws that this world has created, and to the laws that man creates for himself due to the decay of his vital instincts ... is characterized by an *anguish at living* in the present-day society.[34]

What else indeed did the symbolist writers, in their day and way, tell us but that somehow things have gone terribly wrong for us? The birthright has been sold for a mess of porridge. Tzara simply takes that impotent rage of symbolism into the streets, cabarets, and trains where he denounces the deal and asks for his birthright back.

3

A Question of Culture/Culture in Question: Samuel Beckett

And having heard, or more probably read somewhere, in the days when I thought I would be well advised to educate myself, (or amuse myself, or stupefy myself, or kill time), that when a man in a forest thinks he is going forward in a straight line, in reality he is going in a circle, I did my best to go in a circle, hoping in this way to go in a straight line.[1]

—*Molloy*

I

Our narrators do not feel themselves lucky to have been born; far from being even a mixed blessing, birth has been for them an utter curse. The rewards that being alive may or may not offer cannot possibly balance out the pains and sufferings of existence: "the mess,"[2] as Samuel Beckett has called it; not only is there no easy way out of this situation, there is no way out at all. Suicide looks inviting for a while yet turns out to be a disappointment, not only because the decision to end one's life, as Schopenhauer has pointed out, is one more example of an individual's inordinate attachment to the "goods of the world," and thus turns out to be a reaffirmation of the very life that suicide attempts to defy, but also, as E. M. Cioran[3] and others[4] who have elegantly reformulated the problem have shown, killing oneself does nothing to alter the fact that one was born in the first place! Gestation and birth then substitute in our narrators' cosmos for the place of original sin, previously reserved by the Christian tradition for "pride," or "overweening thirst for power and knowledge."

53

One's parents, then, are nothing less than criminals, for it was they who committed that gross imprudence that resulted in our conception and birth. If one has accounts to settle with anyone, it is most certainly with the authors of our days—especially with the mother,[5] who, by neglecting certain elementary precautions, ensured our appearance among that motley cast of characters selected for the dubious distinction of playing at being alive. One's mother, if anyone, owes one an explanation certainly—and this is one of the *logical* senses of Molloy's pilgrimage, although this "settling of accounts"[6] is going to be a doubtful procedure; as after an accident when one has been maimed for life (and birth, for Beckett, is nothing less than this accident) the damage can never really be paid for, so it is equally with the unfortunately unalterable fact of having been born.

One can, of course, and one is most likely to, take one's parents' place: Molloy has ended up in his mother's room, sleeping in his mother's bed, and giving birth unto words —which is also a form of "procreation" and therefore a kind of helpless perpetuation of the primordial crime or inevitable mistake. It is as if our narrator were caught in the web of a vast conspiracy whose purport is to point man inevitably toward the future and to ensure the survival of a (kind of) world. One was born not because it is good to be alive but because man's cosmos is a self-perpetuating mechanism that cannot change by any rebellion or disobedience: "Can it be that we are not free? It might be worth looking into" (*Molloy*, 44).

Language, as Barthes suggested in his inaugural lecture at the Collège de France, is fascist; and he meant this in the sense that as soon as we start to speak (and we are all condemned to speak, since even silence is a language) we are caught in a network of circumstances and determinations over which we have no control. Language is a tyranny; the words are all there well before we arrived on the scene and will exist long after we are gone. "Best it is never to have been born," said the Greek skeptic that Nietzsche cites (disparagingly, it is true) in *The Birth of Tragedy*, and Beckett certainly knows this ironclad argument inside and out; however, the desire to cancel one's birth can never be more than a form of nostalgia, or wishful thinking, as when the narrator of *The Unnamable* later speculates: "I'm looking for my mother to kill her, I should have thought of that a bit earlier, before being born" (544). This enunciation of regret over having been born punctuates the prose of Beckett's trilogy and constitutes a kind of seriocomic consolation to which our narrators unceasingly return; yet the rhetorical lament, which expresses the attitude of the "reluctantly alive," cannot alter the fact that the damage has been done.

II

The words are there waiting for us, and our narrators have no choice but to use them. An assumption that has seemed natural to make about words is that they evoke a referential or expressive dimension and owe their significance and importance to it. Our narrators tend to treat this assumption as myth, for here there is an undeniable movement of these words toward meaninglessness —toward what Barthes has called, in his classic study, the "zero degree of literature."

Our narrators' words, first of all, are endlessly repetitive, ceaselessly redundant, and self-duplicating. Duplication, thought of by Heidegger as man's original response to and admission of the "insufficiency of pure being," has been described recently by Jean Baudrillard[7] as the very place of oblivion: we moderns duplicate everything and at an accelerating pace because the fundamental direction of our culture and kind, our driving passion, is to *erase* everything. Baudrillard's dramatic example of the operation of this principle on its very grandest scale is the World Trade Center in New York City, where the Twin Towers endlessly duplicate and nullify each other. "As above, so below," a familiar cabalistic slogan, may then take us into the world of repetition and self-reflecting language that constitutes Molloy's modernist discourse, as self-effacing on a textual level as the infinitely proliferating "cubes" are on an architectural one. So it is that Molloy's preoccupation with repeating, ostensibly for the purpose of analysis and examination, those seemingly innocuous phrases like "yet a little while," "from time to time" (110, 117), etc., results in a derealization of language and its corresponding reduction to the status of mere noise.

The operation of Beckett's insistently sardonic and molecular curiosity on these "little phrases" is of course far from innocent. To examine is, ineluctably, to destroy; "we murder to dissect," the poet said; and Cassirer's book on Einstein[8] merely proves what we have known intuitively all along, at least since Mary Shelley's Frankenstein: that the inquisitive glance of the experimental scientist is not neutral but is bound to alter the objects of his attention. Likewise, those we have described as the "molecular"[9] writers, of the tribe of Joyce, Sollers, Leiris, and here Beckett, so interested in what our most seemingly familiar words "really mean," are hardly to leave the language exactly as they found it.

The real effect of our curious narrator's obsidian gaze on language is, then, to alter that which it contemplates. Language is reduced, stripped, cut down, thrown in the waste basket, taken out again, examined for any residual pieces of meat (meaning) adhering to these dry bones, and then tossed definitively, or at least *dramatically*—since we know we are married to words, for better or for worse! —into the "ashcan of history." The sense of Molloy's aporetic method, certainly designed to paralyze (Beckett's favorite word) even a minimal confidence in meaning, is to challenge the referentiality of language, or language as we helplessly misuse it, so that those very words that were supposed to approach us to reality can only snatch it teasingly farther away: "A and C I never saw again. But perhaps I shall see them again. But shall I be able to recognize them? And am I sure I never saw them again? And what do I mean by seeing and seeing again?" (*Molloy*, 15). What indeed; if we haven't agreed in the first place about what constitutes seeing, it seems unwarranted and premature to introduce the redundancy of "recognize." This is, of course, but one of many hilarious but slyly corrosive semantic divagations that inflect Beckett's text; and the outcome of this "investigative" passion for mysteries that are functionally incapable of solution is to establish a separation, or "écart," between the babble with which we fill our days—and from which our nights give us no surcease, filled as they must be with the dreams and words of *others*—and any real world.

Yet, comically, and we should know by now *absurdly*, language goes its merry way as if all of this wasn't so, the way, perhaps, we continue to ask each other how we *are* when we haven't the slightest idea of what would constitute *being*: "it would ill become me not to mention the awful cries of the corncrakes that run in the corn, in the meadows, all the short summer night long, dinning their rattles. And this enables me, what is more, to know when that unreal journey began, the second last but one a form fading among fading forms" (16), our irrepressible Molloy has the gall to utter, as if such transparent phonic ploys had any meaning other than the physical pleasure of repetition or the mockery they make of all pretensions to "culture."

Man is alienated, in Beckett's world, not only from the language he is forced to use, that is, from the self he is obliged to be, but also from the language that others are forced to use and selves they find themselves occupying and protecting. If knowledge of one's self, given these circumstances, is improbable and fleeting at best, communication with others and, a fortiori, community, must be downright impossible: we are all terribly *mistaken*; and that is, if any, a basis for such a concept as the "human condition"—which may account for the enduring popularity and appeal of his work over the years, at least for a certain public. But what obstructs and largely negates our efforts to relate to each other is that we have each made a different *mistake* as we supply "the words of the tribe" (Mallarmé) with our own definition and, more importantly, significance. The Tower of Babel or Leibniz' bumping monads might be apt descriptions of this kind of infernal topography, although with Beckett, quintessentially modern, our plight has no beginning, creator, end, or meaning; it is simply *funny*: "I had no papers in the sense this word had sense for him, nor any occupation, nor any domicile, that my surname escaped me for the moment" (24), ruminates Molloy about what must be going on in the policeman's mind. The duplicated and therefore devalued "sense" of the word for Molloy must be something like "toilet paper," and were our hero furnished with suitable documents he would doubtless have used them for what the officer would have thought of as unsuitable or even unpatriotic purposes: "I was bound to be stopped by the first policeman and asked what I was doing, a question to which I have never been able to find the correct reply" (77). This situation seems entirely natural in view of our narrator's previously assuring us, "For I no longer know what I am doing nor why" (57), which teases the reader into supposing he ever knew what he was doing, as does the subsequent "I knew how difficult it was not to do again what you have done before" (113). The lack of solidarity with others in this crucially important area that makes social life harrowing also makes living with oneself questionable. The repetition[10] of "to do," in its various verbal forms, has an inevitably corrosive effect on its meaning: the word tends to be emptied of its significance, becomes something that people only say, a noise they make and that one makes along with them.

This same divorce between word and referent that we have been describing may also be shown to operate on seemingly meaningful statements that Molloy is sometimes given to, such as, we have seen, "I had been bent on settling this matter between my mother and me" (*Molloy*, 84). But these words, as all others, turn out to be comically inappropriate if not irrelevant, as if one's feeling about the "crime of being born" could be handled with the same tranquil equanimity as a business matter arranged by negotiation between partners who disagree! But the wound of existence is too deep to be patched over by words, which have been "reduced" in function to a mere demonstration of their utter inappropriateness. Instead, a radical and comic discontinuity is established between words and what they eventually don't even purport to be able to represent: "Yes, it seems to me some such incident occurred about this time. But perhaps I am thinking of another stay, at an earlier time, for this will be my last but one, or two, there is never a last, by the sea" (98). This language informs of nothing; we would need a miracle (the possibility of which our narrators frequently entertain) to get water from these rocks; yet mere awareness of the irrationality of the structures that dominate and distort our social and linguistic realities is insufficient to shake us loose from them. On the contrary, the oppressive system finds itself strengthened and even legitimized by the "liberties" it has seemed to allow: the machine doesn't cease functioning and destroying because its components have been intellectually discredited; it overrides all choice with its own categorical imperative of ceaseless, even if senseless, movement: "It is forbidden to give up or even to stop an instant" (107). The passive voice here excludes the reader from the problem of responsibility that Beckett's maieutic-Socratic method[11] teases us at times into pretending exists. Thus it will do us no good to ask for a more definite subject or a change of voice from passive to active—so that the natural question "who?" could be connected to "has forbidden."

"Everything that is not forbidden is compulsory"[12] could well be the motto for such a world. For the process not only interdicts but also enjoins: "To him who has nothing it is forbidden not to relish filth" (*Molloy*, 27), or not to pretend that you like it. These are the laws of our time that have replaced the biblical injunctions, the metamorphosis of Jehovah and Jesus alike into an impersonal machine that renders nugatory any attitude, whether of agreement or rebellion, on the part of subject-become-object who is either telecommanded or programmed to obey.

Words are clearly useless, but this only makes more urgent the need to talk:

Here is the time for the Tellable, *here* is its home.
Speak and proclaim. More than ever
the things we can live with are falling away, and their
    place

being oustingly taken up by an imageless act.
Act under crusts, that will readily split as soon
as the doing within outgrows them and takes a new
    outline.
Between the hammers lives on
our heart, as between the teeth
the tongue, which, nevertheless,
remains the bestower of praise.[13]

Rilke, whom of course we quote above, still thought that words, though dubiously reliable as description, could still be used to direct us toward a nonverbal, mystical realm. The justification of the "tellable" is that it leads to the "nontellable":

Praise the world to the Angel, not the untellable: you
can't impress him with the splendour you've felt; in the
    cosmos
where he more feelingly feels you're only a tyro
... Tell him *things*.[14]

Beckett, however, like the stubborn and intransigent Tzara, has rejected in advance all mystical or aesthetic options; the situation for him is at once more critical and more desperate. There is only the tellable, since silence either doesn't exist or is not allowed;[15] and the tellable is incapable of utterance by a discredited language that can only distort or alienate the reality it pretends to transmit. It is as impossible to speak as it is to stay silent, like the child worshippers of T. S. Eliot's *Ash Wednesday* who can neither pray nor go away,[16] or the characters of Maurice Blanchot's fictions who are confronted by a system that can neither be conformed to nor rebelled against.

For Beckett, language has lost all referential function and has acquired no mystical one, in the Rilkean sense, in exchange. The writer thus approaches his task like a penance, a strange and incomprehensible duty, irrevocable like having been born, and which ultimately absolves, means, and justifies nothing. Cioran and Blanchot have eloquently articulated this attitude as the "fall into writing."[17]

Molloy has destroyed the words, but he is obliged to begin where Moran ends—as a writer. The same writer whose language has been stripped of meaning still maintains what we can call an "authorial pose," in spite of the fact that language now is more to be mistrusted than confided in or relied upon, so that in large measure the writer has been deprived of the tools of his trade—he must write without words, or as if the words meant something other than they say, or can only expose their own fatuousness. In spite of this devastation, what Blanchot was to call the *disaster* and Beckett likes to call the *catastrophe*, there remain still some physical and social concomitants to the act of writing that give it a certain minimal coherence. There is still a hand, though disembodied, such a hand as Blanchot describes Kierkegaard and Proust becoming in their isolation when they wrote their masterpieces.

There is in *Malone Dies* also an exercise book, and for Molloy some kind of social exchange has been established by means of a mysterious person who comes every week to take away the new writings and bring older ones that have been marked by unknown critics with incomprehensible feedback. "Yet I don't work for money," Molloy says, sounding like Beckett replying when asked why he wrote in French, "I don't know why I write at all."[18]

III

After we have been led to the point where we must admit that language is saying nothing and leading nowhere, we are still left with the figure of a writer and furthermore the idea of there being such a thing as literature. To attack such desultory but tenacious notions, *Malone Dies* gives us an inside look at the process of the fabrication of illusions that any artist, just like any sleight-of-hand magician, is forced to enter. Malone takes us into very close proximity, almost inside, the story he is inventing, treating us to a "behind the curtains" view of the mechanism of deception, calculation, and implausibility. This technique of the work revealing and commenting on itself we have of course seen operating in Tzara's play, *La Mouchoir des nuages*, for there, as in *Malone Dies*, the fabricated and artificial nature of the inventions is laid bare. Brecht's famous *Verfremdungseffekt* (distancing effect)[19] and corresponding mistrust of the "hypnotized" spectator is relevant here: our insight into the totality of the process and our ability to alter it gain at the expense of our ability to lose ourselves in the illusion.

Now I think it is precisely Beckett's goal in *Malone Dies* that we see more of what goes into the making of literature and believe less in it. It is easy of course to overestimate the liberating potential of such self-revealing art. Borges, for instance, is very cunning in making his reader believe what he has told him is the sheerest fabrication;[20] and there is a sense in which we fall back into involvement with Malone's "tall stories" because the human animal may be incapable of thoroughly living up to that fundamental truth that Beckett in so many avatars expresses —that it's always the "same old story." Nevertheless, Beckett's self-stripping art here in *Malone Dies* may be working to raise or enhance his reader's consciousness rather than fundamentally alter it, which would be the province of extraliterary action anyway; and in this sense I think he is in solidarity with the similarly transparent fictions of his contemporaries, Louis-René Des Forêts[21] and Maurice Blanchot,[22] as well as with the literary tradition of the self-discussing work from Rabelais through Sterne and Diderot to Lautréamont and Joyce. In contradiction to the tradition of the invisible author, as recommended by such a writer as Henry James[23] and as demanded by the kind of reader that doesn't want to see anything get in the way of the story, Beckett's narrators have a tendency to become visible and manifest, and inevitably they remind us of the creative hand (and social process) in relation to the creations or products on display or for sale.

This is, then, the sense of the "full programme" (*Malone Dies*, 248), nothing less than an informal outline of the illusion he plans to pull off, that Malone ironically announces at the beginning of his discourse. By incorporating the "present state" of the narrator-writer into this program and furthermore by interrupting his (by now) transparent fictions with blow-by-blow accounts from the realm of this intrusive reality, he both invites the reader to be aware of text as production and makes correspondingly impossible a *total* immersion in the illusions of fiction. "What tedium" becomes the habitual refrain with which he interrupts the course of his narrative. "I fell asleep," he says, as he explains another hiatus, while implying that the glory of art was not enough to keep him awake and emphasizing the artificial nature of fictions by reminding the reader of the narrator's own schedule: "There is no time for sleep in my timetable" (265). "Live and Invent," he adds shortly afterward to underline the unreal aspect of his whole project, while not letting us forget the kind of assault on language that Molloy had carried out by examining these words for their *real* meaning: "Invent. It is not a word. Neither is live."

Here our narrator attacks a certain kind of traditional author-reader relation, which was based on the latter's being a more-or-less hypnotic subject of the former, but he takes us to a place where even his experimental French contemporaries might be shy of by exploding the myth of the author who explodes his own myths.[24] Malone, the writer who is violating the gospel according to Henry James by revealing the secrets of his craft, becomes just another one of the gallery of rogues, or metaphors that are no longer necessary, by the time we get to *The Unnamable.*

Malone finally makes the ultimate authorial intrusion and exclusion by dying along with his tale. True, he has been wondering intermittently, "There is naturally another possibility ... and that is that I am dead already" (*Malone Dies,* 300), and he evokes also a Hell-on-Earth landscape, with echoes from Dante and T. S. Eliot, in a macabre description of an all-too-real cityscape where "in the corridors of the underground railway and the stench of their harassed mobs scurrying from cradle to grave to get to the right place at the right time ... till you begin to wonder if you have not died without knowing and gone to hell or

been born again into an even worse place than before"
(310). The fact is that such an outlandish, though in a way
logical, hypothesis is necessary to account for the critical
nature of this situation. What is being attacked here is not
only the power of words to render reality but the night-
marish nature of this reality itself—whatever the words
used to escape or express it we always wind up back in
"the mess."

Not only does Malone constantly seek to frustrate the
reader's belief in his creations (though this is not to deny
that they convince us momentarily through their eloquence, humor, and humanity) by his frequent interruptions, musings, and divagations, he also attacks the sub-
stantiality of his characterizations by changing the names
of his characters, denying them consistently any useful social purpose or minimal identity, and even presenting the
reader, by way of (non)conclusion with seemingly subhu-
man or teratological imitations of human life. There is not
much to do with such a cast except push it over the brink,
and this our narrator does with his last remaining
strength. He has stopped eating, or "they" have stopped
bringing nourishment; any remaining exchange with the
world is thus curtailed. This story is not to be continued,
as the narrator, who is its main (maybe only) character, is
no more. Literature has followed in the wake of language.
The writer is dead. "I am lost. Not a word" (361). Malone
has been felled by the same ax that finishes off his creation McMann. The author no longer plays at God, pretending to exemption from the contingency of his creations. "Like you and me, and so many others," as Tzara's
approximate man has it, Malone dies.

IV

Beckett has never let us forget for long the presence
of Malone not far behind his creations, however pictur-
esque; we are inevitably told, "to hell with all this fucking
scenery" (383). If there was a real story it could only have
been Malone's struggle for survival; and the world we are
left with when this struggle is over is a desolate one

indeed, deprived equally of past and future, of culture and hope "as if nothing had ever happened or would ever happen again" (385),[25] like a stage where there will be no more plays, not only because language has lost its ability to communicate or even designate but also because no audience could maintain, for long, an awareness of this.

Malone had dealt with "the crime of being born," which resulted in his being assigned the role, which he did not choose, of entertainer or storyteller, by being reborn—that is, by being, as he puts it, "given ... birth to unto death" (391). This "afterlife" image (as in the Hell-on-Earth fancy *Malone Dies* likes to entertain) is too frequent in Beckett's, and, symptomatically, in other modern fiction, to be a mere clever or comical figure of speech. At the "end of history," as Nietzsche-Hegel-Kojève would have it, why should we expect literature to live on?[26] The writer has become a *writing* that responds to the "crime of reality" (having been born, having to be) by revealing itself incessantly as that which could not, indeed, *should* not have been. By tirelessly working to reveal the artificial, social, contingent, and conditioned nature of the role of writer (just another producer), *writing* has brought literature and the cultural illusions for which it stands to the brink of nothingness.

The Unnamable must now carry on without language and without literature—that is, without words (legs) that can take us anywhere or means (hands) with which to write. Beckett's avatar is now nameless as well as a quadruple amputee. He is called upon to face nakedly the absolute terror and inexplicable mystery of existence without the defenses that man has used to protect himself from knowing too much or too little. He is deprived even of a name; and the words that he still must inevitably use are branded immediately as the property of others. His role, quadriplegic signal for a restaurant menu, is a ridiculous parody of any role at all—and in any case is as frequently disallowed as evoked—to leave us essentially with only a voice, severed irremediably from any identifiable human substance—a "someone," a "you"—a "they" that can be an "I," or an "I" that is just an "eye," as is also the

case with the *nouveau roman*. Flaubert, and all that he
stands for in terms of the artist's painful toil and all that it
is no longer capable of redeeming, is dealt more than a
glancing blow when it is said, "It's like shit, there we have
it at last, the right word" (*The Unnamable*, 507).[27]

Writing still goes on, of course, even in this apocalytic
universe; somehow something that must go on continues,
although, as Dorrit Cohn suggests,[28] we need to make almost a "leap of faith" to believe our narrator when he assures us he is a writer. Yet this writing is barely recognizable as such, stripped of all its institutional supports and
nonessentials, perhaps a throwback to the times of oral
poetry. Writing, in this sense, has been disinvested of its
identity; it has become the interchangeable murmur that
passes between an "anyone" and an "anyone," as a French
critic observes.[29] Here we certainly may experience the
eerie feeling of the "absence" of the writer from his own
work so celebrated by Blanchot as the hallmark of modern
art[30] and the "book without an author" theories put into
practice by the creators of the *nouveau roman*.

The Unnamable, in this perspective, takes on the aspect
of a foreign object newly arrived from outer space, bringing
us inklings of a kind of experience so unusual that as yet
we can have no name for it. Perhaps this is so only because what is being said is so obvious that it has been
easy to overlook: "Is it possible we're all in the same boat?"
our narrator (we'll call that him for convenience) suggests
at one point, only to retract it immediately, "No, we're in a
nice mess each one in his own particular way" (517),
which only reaffirms this hopeless sympathy with the universality of the human predicament; earlier we had been
told, this time unequivocally, in a statement ringing with
Sartrean overtones, "We have all been here forever, we
shall all be here forever, I know it" (404).

It is no longer a matter here of writer talking to reader,
within the security of a classic unilateral relationship
brought to its end by the destructive efforts of the previous
narrators. In spite of the fact, and who would argue
against it, that "all change is to be feared" (407) and in
spite of our narrator's comical denial, which might be

meant to throw us off (or onto) the track—"I have my faults but changing my tune is not one of them" (464)—there has been a significant shift in emphasis. We are no longer being addressed as writer to reader but somehow as "secret sharers" of a common fate. We have all been victims of the same crime, in the same place, "this being the place, according to them, where the inestimable gift of life had been rammed down my gullet" (441). The "instruction," so sardonically described, was our common curriculum, although some of us seem to have been selected for the dubious distinction of swallowing more of it than others; above all, we have all been branded by a name, which is nothing less than a label to facilitate our being bought and sold, in a word, exchanged.

"But the days of sticks are over": no one now is privileged in this desperate game; we are all equally naked and defenseless before the incontrovertible evidence. *The Unnamable* is particularly hostile to intellect, which deceives more than flat ignorance since it pretends to offer explanation and excuse where there is none: "They gave me courses on love, on intelligence, most precious, most precious" (411). This is the end of an evolution that our previous narrators had certainly helped along. Molloy had been prone to Faust-like summaries of his disappointment with the sundry fields of knowledge (*Molloy*, 48), and Malone casts more than a shadow of a doubt on the validity of the written word when he observes, "My notes have a curious tendency, as I realize at last, to annihilate all they purport to record" (*Malone Dies*, 357). By the time of *The Unnamable*, however, the intellectual structure, previously under scrutiny, has suffered a complete collapse, along with the particular points of view that were characteristic of it. Time itself, as an intellectually divisible and quantifiable entity, does not survive the attack: "I say years, though here there are no years. What matter how long? Years is one of Basil's ideas. A short time, a long time, it's all the same" (426). Basil (intellect) has served his purpose, which was to be the butt of ridicule, and is replaced by Worm, who cannot take notes, is "the first of his kind," and "has not yet been able to speak his mind, only murmur" (468).

The property of intellect has clearly been to separate and divide, to cut oneself off from others by means of illusory feelings of superiority that turn out to be based on "merits" that cannot survive as such under scrutiny. The post-Cartesian primordiality of intellect, which has gotten along so well with the class divisions of an unjust society,[31] cannot survive the weight of an investigation in the light of one of its own basic postulates—that is, to examine everything. We should not, however, interpret this anti-intellectuality, which comes across so boldly in *The Unnamable*, as any crusade for the "rights of the flesh" as represented in our century by Henry Miller and D. H. Lawrence and in the last by Walt Whitman; for Beckett, as for Mallarmé, "the flesh is sad, alas," as sad as the intellect.

The "discourse," then, to which our narrator refers so frequently, especially in the earlier part of the monologue (*The Unnamable*, 404, 413, 422, 424), is not meant as a unilateral communication to readers who expect to be entertained and instructed. Like Nietzsche, who tolerated such "mere readers" as little in his time as Beckett does in ours, our narrator shows nothing but disdain for such an audience: "It's the old story, they want to be entertained, while doing their dirty work, no, not entertained, soothed, no, that's not it either, solaced, no, even less, no matter, with the result they achieve nothing" (*The Unnamable*, 516). Perhaps a more relevant analogy might be to Baudelaire, whose assault on the privileged and sacrosanct nature of the author-reader relation so impressed T. S. Eliot: "Hypocrite lecteur, mon semblable, mon frère" ("Hypocritical reader, my likeness, my brother").

On a less exalted but equally important level, that is, the grammatical, the assault on the pronouns that our narrator carries out with all the methodical insistence of a terrorist completing an assignment results also in a deconstruction of the traditional barriers between writer and reader: "No sense in bickering about pronouns and other parts of blather. The subject doesn't matter, there is none" (*The Unnamable*, 500). As we will see also in the work of Blanchot and Sollers,[32] what we are left with when all our pronominal categories have been eliminated and made interchangeable is no place to hide our precious identities.

There remains only "the terror-stricken babble of those condemned to silence" (*The Unnamable*, 492), that is, of those who can no longer make meaningful statements because their language has been subject to a massive devaluation. Language is no longer the exclusive property of those whose claim to the goods of intellect is fortified by the unequivocal certainty with which their fictive "I" addresses an imagined "you." The "discourse" in *The Unnamable* takes on, instead, the quality of a common project and responsibility that we all must share.

In addition to the "onslaught" on the pronoun, the "questioning" style of the prose, or distillation of the maieutic-Socratic method, certainly prepares the way for this development. *The Unnamable's* interrogation of existence is as perpetual and inevitable as it is functionally unanswerable. The work is "open," in the sense of Umberto Eco's well-known formulation,[33] because here nothing is or can be concluded or resolved and everything invites curiosity and reader participation. The prose of *The Unnamable*, dreamlike, insinuating, endlessly iconoclastic, and interrogatory, accelerates a process that was already in evidence in the two previous narratives: here, it is as if our own minds were speaking and we were actively creating and destroying this book as we read it.

4

The Rules of Michel Leiris' Game: *La Règle du jeu, I–IV*

I

We have been concerned with a literature very much directed at a more or less explicit violation and subversion of the culture in which it occurs. Tzara's efforts have been aimed at abolishing society as we now know it in order to prepare the way for a new, more just, equitable, and livable one. We have thus called Tzara a *revolutionary poet* because of his never-flagging sense of the urgency and primordiality of a radical change in the social factor in the human equation. Beckett is, of course, less grandiose and explicit, if no less effective and determined in his iconoclasm; for what he puts into question is, first of all, the literature he practices along with the roles, assumptions, and functions it involves and distributes.

Although Leiris shares with Tzara an ardent desire for social change and, in common with Beckett, is incessantly suspicious of the "literature" he practices, there is a sense in which his writings bypass the level of theory and abstraction (which they nevertheless "play with" interminably) and work instead to engage, involve, attract, and/or repel a reader that our other writers treat more formally. Leiris' appeal is fundamentally *subliminal;* whatever its formal structure or ideological charge of the moment, his work asks us, as perhaps in a letter from a close friend or relative, to listen, to be aware of something beneath the surface of the words: a pulse, something sexual and/or affective, a communication whose significance is not what is said but in the bond that saying creates between speaker and listener.

While Tzara may be seen to be operating on our consciousness and Beckett on our sensibility and sensitivity,

Leiris works surgically and remorselessly on our human sympathy and on the mechanisms that obstruct or unleash an emotional identification with the other. Leiris' art, like the threat of the suicide of its author (which is one of his text's most involving recourses), is consummately an art of *intimidation*, one that, like a suicide, rejects any enduring accommodation with the world as it is and resists and defies, by dint of its own terrible irrevocability, all attempts at domestication, rationalization, and explanation.

II

A fundamental premise of Leiris' literary works, one as often announced as "regretted," is an inability or unwillingness to leave the terrain of personal life and experience.[1] Like Artaud his contemporary and Van Gogh before him, Leiris is perpetually in process of assembling the fragments of a portrait of the self—this self that turns out, of course, not to be *there*, except in the highly problematic "finished product" yielded more or less unwillingly to public consumption. It is surely no coincidence, then, that Leiris' literary speciality, really the only genre he practices with any consistency and ultimately to the exclusion of all other forms, is *autobiography*.[2] The irony here is dizzying, vertiginous, in view especially of the history of the genre —traditionally meant to accompany, crown, justify, or correct impressions about a life that was important for *other* reasons. This "supplementary" form becomes an end of a life, becomes its substance, meaning, direction, and content: the container becomes the contained, the frame the picture, the legal plea the act one is submitting for judgment—in a life's work that assumes, in a view of its massive length and stubborn persistence and competence, the dimension of a colossal "détournement" or subversion of the relation that society establishes between the contingencies of personal existence and the necessities of public life.

Autobiography, already problematical and a latecomer as a legitimate literary form (since whatever its pretensions to significance or relevance, it involves an essentially secu-

lar and individualistic attitude), becomes with Leiris, by
reason of the very skill and determination with which he
practices it, an absolute scandal. Justifications for indulging in this autobiographical "vice" have varied of
course with epoch and author, from St. Augustine's rationale of the positive example of the story of his conversion to Rousseau's preparation of his earthly dossier for a
heavenly tribunal; and to these we may add the rendering
of Proust's life into the work of art that inscribes and
redeems it. What has not changed, until Leiris, was an unquestioned and unquestionable assumption that we must
have some compelling reason—social utility, religious
duty, or aesthetic endeavor—that transcends while excus-
ing our narcissism in submitting our personal lives to the
dangerous and slightly bizarre joys of public scrutiny.

Justifications in another sense, of course, abound in
Leiris' books—explanations, rationales, excuses, and arguments. Leiris is acutely and constantly aware of the
pressures upon him to demonstrate the cogency, sense,
and relevance of the stunning and often compromising
revelations he makes about himself and those who were
close to him. However, the very plethora, variety, and mutability of these justifications, which are likely as not to
contradict each other, militate against their being taken
either literally or seriously except as aesthetic ploys or fascinating baroque mental games. Leiris, in fact, likes nothing better than to hold up to the most intensely critical
scrutiny the arguments with which he had excused presentation of his previous writings. Ultimately, all Leiris'
"reasons" can only cancel each other out or constitute an
extension, modification, or mask of what he has already
said.

There is no stable place, value, or standard in Leiris'
text from which to judge the worth and validity of the writing as a totality—for the same turbulence, unreliability,
and relativity that inflect the events the work narrates also
infect the critical statements it makes about itself. The
book's innumerable apologies for itself become in their
turn other "events" of doubtful reliability that call in their
turn for further commentary and excuse, in an ongoing,

functionally endless process. Here there is no immutable or even fairly stable standard, whether religious, social, or aesthetic, that can serve as aegis or roof under which Leiris can claim exemption from the taboo, all the more stringent for its being unwritten, against assuming and demanding the world's interest in one's life. If Tzara has been called, deservedly I think, "the intransigent" and if Beckett deserves the name of "the inconsolable," then we may also presume to apply to Leiris the appellation of "the inexcusable."

This is not to say, either, that a writing as personal and vulnerable, as *precarious* as Leiris', whatever its eloquence, power, and sheer ingenuity, can stand on its own, a more or less frozen and independent artifact that leads its own autonomous existence—of the nature of the works of Henry James, Flaubert, and even Proust. Just because this work cannot be excused does not mean that it does not need to be. The situation is reminiscent of Camus' *absurd*, located in the gap between human need and nature's silence; for although Leiris' work is incapable of justification, rationalization, or excuse, in the sense of anything being capable of bearing the enormous weight of its own obdurate self-scrutiny, neither can it stand alone—for it is compelled by the very nature of the traditions and taboos it has inherited and is obliged to function within to seek a confirmation and validation that must remain equally elusive and unfindable.

The *lack*[3] in Leiris' text is thus inherent and endemic, a void or vacuum, a desire that no entity can fill or fulfill: what is missing is what is there and what is there is what is missing. This functional *incompleteness*, to adapt to Leiris Derrida's description of Blanchot's text,[4] conveys at once the essence, paradox, and pathos of Leiris' project. It is at once its sublime gift and its staunch refusal: its gift, in the sense that the reader's sovereignty over this masterless text must equal at least that of its author; its refusal, in the revolutionary sense that it permanently denies to the world the possibility of filling the void that it constitutes, thereby rejecting any conceivable domestication or recuperation by any existing society.

III

This *lack*, endemic and perpetual, gives rise to an
equally inevitable and ceaseless *search*. The writer may
have forgotten, if indeed he ever really knew, what exactly
it is he is looking for, but that only makes more pressing,
urgent, and desperate the effort to find it; for that something is missing is impossible to deny:

> L'espoir de trouver ce que je cherche s'est, pour moi,
> réduit peu à peu à celui de trouver, non pas la chose que
> je cherche, mais quelle est exactement cette chose que je
> voudrais trouver. Bref, ce qu'aujourd'hui je cherche, c'est
> *ce qu'est* ce que je cherche. (A la limite, j'en viendrais
> presque à me demander si, ne cherchant même plus à
> savoir quel est l'objet de ma recherche, je ne chercherais
> pas tout bonnement à chercher, empruntant couloir
> après couloir, le coeur toujours battant, dans l'attente
> jamais détendue de la trouvaille.)*

The need becomes pure, essential, obsessing, and all-
consuming, incapable of cathexis on any object as well as,
as we see in the parenthesis concluding the above excerpt,
of acceptance of itself. What is required is everything in
general but nothing that can be named.

It is this very dissatisfaction of Leiris, unhappy even in
his unhappiness, that lends to his text its undeniable
movement and ceaseless dynamism, although the very re-
lentlessness of its uncompromising drive may deprive it of
a mass audience that seeks, even under the name of art,
perhaps more consolation and confirmation than illumination and confrontation.

"Comment nous attarder à des livres auxquels l'auteur

---

* "The hope of finding what I'm looking for has, for me, been
reduced little by little to that of finding, not what I'm looking for but
what exactly this thing is that I want to find. In short, what I'm looking
for today is *what* I'm looking for. (At the limit, I could almost ask
myself if, not even looking any further for the object of my search, I
wouldn't be seeking really only for the sake of seeking, taking corridor
after corridor, heart beating fast, in the never-fulfilled expectation of
finding something.)" *La Règle du jeu IV*, 311.

n'a pas été contraint?"* Leiris' friend Bataille once asked;
and Leiris certainly is as "driven to write" as any, and to
write on. Eschewing a naïve meliorism and rejecting in
advance that all our busy and self-complicating flurry
represents either progress for ourselves or the world, it
is as if the only real purpose Leiris has in getting to or
making any particular point—whether aesthetically, politically, or amorously—is to leave it behind; and Leiris'
persistent irony and unyielding skepticism may be seen
as the means as well as the consequences of this philosophy of perpetual movement that is content not even
with itself. It is the function of Leiris' irony to bring out
the contingent and provisional nature of even his most
apparently "committed" acts and valued memories; and
his skepticism is a caustic substance that consumes everything it touches upon, no matter how seemingly
noble, well-constructed, or secure. Leiris writes with a
kind of double or at least plural vision whose delight it
is to bring out the equal validity of mutually contradictory elements. Whether the opposition is between the
personal and the historical, the solitary and the social,
the aesthetic and the political, Leiris' intrinsically endless ratiocinations, recriminations, divagations, and in-
spirations forbid in advance all definite conclusion, for
the realm of this text, as in Derrida's deconstruction, is
that of the *undecidable.*

This mordancy is exercised not only upon the elements
that Leiris finds or creates but also, as is characteristic in
this literature of deconstruction, *primarily* upon the process itself. Leiris thus also incriminates his own irony or
his own pretense to stand apart from the life he observes,
as ineluctably his motives fail to withstand the weight of
his own scrutiny. An especially frequent pattern in the text
is for the younger Leiris to fail before the test of the older,
or the other way around, as maturity fails to live up to the
dreams of youth. The outcome of this style is that a sense
of doubt, untrustworthiness, unreliability, and deception

---

* "How do we linger over books that the author has not felt
constrained to write?"

is attached to the statements that the text makes as well as to the way in which they are made—this *uncertainty* follows the text even into its most apparently enthralling and hypnotically convincing flights of fancy and imagination. The effect of this style may be to make the reader more or less uneasily aware of the contingent nature of the work (and indirectly of all literature and the culture in which it occurs), as in versions of the Brecht-like distancing effect that we have seen operating in Tzara and Beckett. However, what in these two writers was an occasional if important recourse becomes for Leiris the very texture and nature of the work—almost as if the words themselves secrete a kind of repellent that keeps the reader (and, of course, the author) at a certain distance and from *settling* on them.

This is the self-erasing, self-interrogating, contingent, and "tormented" style that seemingly sets up objects to venerate and respect only to tear them down, in a double movement of creation and destruction that cannot even rest in itself because it moves on ceaselessly to devour its own motives, postures, and pretensions. As such this "principle of uncertainty" was doubtless one of the enduring, if ambiguous, legacies of symbolism in poetry, for in this movement the symbol is notoriously unreliable and mutable in contradistinction to its status as quasi-absolute in romantic-Platonic aesthetics. This symbolist "duality" may be illustrated by Baudelaire's poem, "À Une Madonne," which sets up an ideal of feminine beauty as an object of rapt, if blasphemously sensual, worship and devotion only to corrupt it all the more surely in the final lines of the poem:

> Enfin, pour compléter ton rôle de Marie,
> Et pour mêler l'amour avec la barbarie,
> Volupté noire! des sept Péchés capitaux,
> Bourreau plein de remords, je ferai sept Couteaux
> Bien affilés, et, comme un jongleur insensible,
> Prenant le plus profond de ton amour pour cible.
> Je les planterai tous dans ton Cœur pantelant,

Dans ton Cœur sanglotant, dans ton Cœur ruisselant.*

Yet Leiris' "deconstruction" is a good step beyond Baudelaire's already shocking one, where we may nevertheless sense, as Sartre has, a certain choice and satisfaction, if not "bad faith" and complacency, in the sacrilege and self-laceration itself. If for Baudelaire, and even more obviously for Villiers de L'Isle-Adam, Huysmans, and Barbey d'Aurevilly, a certain aesthetic-sexual "frisson" can take the place of the missing absolute or symbol as idol, consolation, or guide, no such "échappatoire" or safety-hatch is allowed for Michel Leiris—for the latter had certainly cooperated with Tzara, Breton, Artaud, and others in a rejection and demystification of symbolist "remedies" that, as we have pointed out in a previous chapter, was one of the fundamental ways in which dada-surrealism demarcates itself from its predecessor, symbolism.

Leiris will therefore subject the very process of creation-for-the-purposes-of-destruction to a consistently skeptical and critical analysis. This is a truly dizzying manner here, as is true for Leiris' autobiographical project in general, as Leiris just as commonly will analyze himself analyzing himself ad infinitum. Descartes, in a crucially important moment for Western culture, promised to doubt everything; but he did not doubt, as Leiris does, that he doubts; or, more exactly, *why* he doubts. Leiris is, for instance, especially mistrustful of the pretensions of any mere "literature" to the status of a self-justifying activity; and it is, indeed, a different literature, more involved, involving, concerned, and contingent, that emerges from this suspicious attitude. Leiris' belated preface to his first autobiography

---

*   Finally, to complete your role as Mary
And to mix love with barbarity
Black voluptuousness! From the seven capital sins,
Executioner full of remorse, I'll make seven knives
Well sharpened, and like a cold professional
Taking your deepest love as target
I'll plant them all in your panting heart,
In your sobbing, streaming heart
          Les Fleurs du Mal (*Flowers of Evil*), 96

sets forth his condemnation of this ideal of the "purely literary work" in a passage that is fairly well known:

> Je me résignais mal à n'être qu'un littérateur. Le mata-
> dor qui tire du danger couru occasion d'être plus bril-
> lant que jamais et montre toute la qualité de son style à
> l'instant qu'il est le plus menacé: voilà ce qui m'émer-
> veillait, voilà ce que je voulais être. Par le moyen d'une
> autobiographie portant sur un domaine pour lequel,
> d'ordinaire, la réserve est de rigueur —confession dont
> la publication me serait périlleuse dans la mesure où
> elle serait pour moi compremettante et susceptible de
> rendre plus difficile, en la faisant plus claire, ma vie
> privée—je visais à me débarrasser de certaines repré-
> sentations. . . . Faire un livre qui soit un acte, tel est, en
> gros, le but que m'apparut comme celui que je devais
> poursuivre, quand j'écrivis l'Age d'Homme . . . puisqu'il
> était évident . . . la façon dont je serais regardé par les
> autres ne serait plus ce qu'elle était avant publication
> de cette confession.*

In order for the game to be worth the candle there has
to be some kind of contact between the game of literature
and the game of life; in particular, the literary game has to
make a difference in the life of the author. The Hegelian
prejudice[5] is as fundamental here for Leiris as it is for
Tzara and others of his generation: only that belief is

---

* "I found it hard to resign myself to being nothing more than a
littérateur. The matador who transforms danger into an occasion to be
more brilliant than ever and reveals the whole quality of his style just
when he is most threatened: that is what enthralled me, that is what I
wanted to be. By means of an autobiography dealing with a realm in
which discretion is *de rigeur*, a confession whose publication would be
dangerous to the degree that it would be compromising and likely to
make more dificult, by making more explicit, my private life—I in-
tended to rid myself for good of certain agonizing images . . . To write a
book that is an act—such is, broadly, the goal that seemed to me to be
the one I must pursue when I wrote *Manhood* . . . since it was apparent
that . . . the way I would be regarded by others would no longer be what
it had been before the publication of this confession" (*L'Âge d'homme*,
10–13; "Afterword" to *Manhood*, 55–57).

worthy of the name whose proponents are willing to shed their blood for it. All other "texts," however clever, apt, or attractive, are relegated to the status of inanity—by the very reluctance or inability of their progenitors to stand behind them with their bodies.

This supplementarity and ostensible "inferiority" of literary endeavor to other areas of more unqualified action and risk (the "dangerous" sports, war, revolution, or just plain "dérèglement"—getting "spaced out") are other frequent recourses in Leiris' text, as they inform both his generally culpable attitude and the way he handles words and ideas, dangling them, as it were, always provisionally and teasingly before himself and his reader. In order to compensate for this "inferiority" Leiris is going to have to make a point, maybe even a spectacle, of venturing out on limbs that will possibly not be strong enough to hold him—and that he will furthermore dare and encourage his reader and critic (himself, first of all) to saw through.

In the kind of literature that Leiris practices, therefore, there is generally a deflation of the words themselves together with their "signifieds" in favor of a sense of the author's adventure and gesture in proffering them—always in the context of a personal and social conjuncture. The excitement his works afford arises not so much in the things they say (although undeniably original and fascinating) but in the nerve and intention they reveal, convey, and, most important of all, serve as an example of[6]—that moment "before the writing" where Blanchot locates and celebrates the essence of modern art.

What draws and holds our attention to Leiris' text is not the words themselves, or what they mean and why they are said (since all such meanings and justifications proliferate so extensively that they erase each other), but instead something that by its very nature, akin to the "leap" of Kierkegaard or the "fissures" of Artaud and Bataille where *Tel Quel* found its stormy home, cannot be expressed, defined, contained, or rationalized but assumes the fleeting existence of "jalon," marker or indication of a desire, vector, or the expression of an ever greater *precariousness* of his project and his person. Leiris' text assumes

a nakedness and vulnerability that tend to inhibit an intellectual and critical response as inappropriate and ex-
cessive in view of the fact that the text has already anticipated and accepted any conceivable objection:

> J'érige en cas de conscience d'infimes problèmes d'ex-
> pression, jouant au pur qui ne veut se souiller d'aucune
> inexactitude je passe des heures à les résoudre, et je
> m'abstiens d'aborder la vraie question. Comme s'il était
> une fin en soi, dont je ne pouais me déprendre, je
> dépense jour sur jour à etoffer et fignoler ce récit déjà
> par trop ornementé, le fourbissant, le redressant, le
> truffant de considérations qui souvent brouillent l'hori-
> zon plus qu'elles ne l'élargissent! Or ce qui compte, est
> ce mon récit comme tel ou n'est-ce pas, plutôt, le sou-
> bassement de ce récit, ce qu'il ne dit pas qu'à moitié, ce
> qui parfois (non détecté ou encore trop embryonnaire)
> ne pouvait pas même être dit?*

The only adequate reply to such vulnerability is our
own vulnerability, in this text that constitutes more of an
appeal than a communication. This evocation of an "un-
dercurrent," as Leiris makes above, constitutes, therefore,
the call or "appel" of these words, an absolutely sub- or
paraverbal aspect, and a matter certainly more of mood,
intuition, and suggestion than statement and representation. The fact that words are not exactly what the text is
saying may also account for the stubbornness with which
Leiris demolishes the structures and situations that he
has often been to such great pains to create—as if author

---

* "I make mountains out of the molehills of minute problems of
expression, playing at the pure who won't dirty himself with any impre-
cision, I spend hours resolving these problems, and I abstain from
confronting the real problem. As if it was an end in itself, that I couldn't
detach myself from, I spend day after day stuffing, finicking this tale
already so dressed up, furbishing it, straightening it out, filling it with
considerations that more often bring the horizon closer than expand it!
Now, what counts, is it my story as such or isn't it rather the undercur-
rent of the story, what it only half says, what sometimes cannot be
said?" *La Règle du jeu IV,* 199–200.

and text were always pointing to an indefinable but undeniable "elsewhere" and the function of these words were to
show the reader that this place alone, the location that
can be neither attained and occupied nor bypassed and
forgotten, is what the book is really about.

IV

C'est-à-dire on ne peut "remonter" qu'en acceptant, incapable d'y consentir, la chute, chute essentiellement
aléatoire dans le hasard inessentiel (cela que la loi
appelle dédaigneusement jeu—le jeu où chaque fois
tout est risqué, tout est perdu, le hasard de l'écriture).*
— Maurice Blanchot, *L'Entretien infini*

In the last chapter of *Fourbis* (*La Règle du jeu II*,
1955), Leiris gives us what he says is the latest version of
a text he has been working on since 1939. In that year, he
tells us, during his tour of military duty in Algeria, he had
an affair with a fascinating and beautiful Arab prostitute
by the name of Khadidja. This woman, who represents by
her name alone a sublime epiphany in the life of the author, is described as a kind of combination of the eternal
feminine principle and earth goddess. At the end of the
tale and on the eve of his departure, Leiris mythologizes
her as the Angel of Death and introduces her as a permanent fixture in the structure of his own life, representing
that point where myth and reality become fused, both the
utmost point of the penetration of the "miraculous" into
his daily life and the point from which he dates his own
prolonged but inevitable decline into death. In particular
he makes much of a certain vaginal tremor or orgasm that
he perceived Khadidja to have experienced in his embrace
and that turns out to be symbolic for him as one of the few
moments of unqualified communication and reciprocity in
his life.

---

* "That is to say you can't 'reascend' except in accepting, incapable of consenting to it, the fall, essentially random fall into meaningless
chance (what the law calls disdainfully the game—where every time all
is staked, all is lost, the chance of writing)"; 635.

In *Fibrilles* (*La Règle du jeu III*, 1966), however, Leiris sees the matter much differently. Before I explain the nature of this change, a few words are in order about the way in which history, as it occurs in the course of the writing of his book, affects Leiris' project. For one thing, the time span embraced by the work is large enough and the period under consideration so filled with momentous changes that history must *enter* integrally into its composition. This work is in large measure written by history and also at its dictates and its whims. Often, for instance, years and certainly months will pass between the end of one paragraph and the beginning of another; and Leiris will make sure that we cannot maintain even the illusion of continuity by surprising us with a series of seemingly extraneous statements about the changes in the world around him before returning to the matter at hand; he complains near the end of *Biffures* (*La Règle du jeu I*, 1948):

> Depuis le commencement de ce chapitre—phase un peu languissante de mon essai têtu de self-fabrication—il s'est produit un certain nombre d'événements. Quelques-uns de caractère public et d'autres d'ordre strictement privé. J'ai noté le débarquement des troupes alliées, puis la libération. . . . Je n'ai pas noté un deuxième voyage que j'ai fait en Afrique. . . . Bref, tout se passe comme si, dans la course que s'est engagée au cours de ce chapitre entre moi et le temps, j'étais constamment distancé et comme si ma plume s'efforçait vainement de poursuivre une actualité qui me fuit. La faute en est à la lenteur de cette plume qui peine toujours comme pour remuer des montagnes, quand je la voudrais si cursive.*

The gap between the second and third volumes of *La*

---

* "Since the beginning of this chapter—slightly sluggish phase in my stubborn efforts at self-construction—a certain number of things have happened. Some public and others private. I've noted the landing of the allies, then the liberation. . . . I've noted a second trip I've made to Africa. . . . In short, it all happens like, in the competition that's been engaged in this chapter between me and time, I was constantly

Règle du jeu is even more telling. Between the dates of publication of these two volumes (1955 and 1966), eleven years elapsed and certain historical events took place that altered Leiris' perspective considerably. For one thing, Algeria waged successfully a war of independence that, together with France's resounding defeat in Indochina, put a definitive end to France's imperial period; threatened by civil war, the country that was most euphorically united after World War II became divided. For another, the Chinese Revolution had been consolidated and was in its period of radical innovation and optimism. Leiris had been to China as an invited guest, and what he had seen there made him rethink his own methods and goals.

So it is that in this later volume of his autobiography, *Fibrilles,* he looks with eyes that are much more soberly *political* at the episode with his Algerian mistress Khadidja, which he had described in such idealistic terms in his earlier *Fourbis.* He now sees that there were imperialistic aspects to his adventure with this woman and that, however innocent his intentions, he wound up *colonizing* her with his sensibility and depriving her of any true human autonomy. Leiris further admits that the language he used to describe her probably bore very little resemblance to what she was; and he was thereby describing someone who either never existed or no longer exists.

The pretenses to relevance, accuracy, and significance of literature itself are directly incriminated in this pitiless and exhaustive self-criticism, since whatever its formal excellence (and *Fourbis* got *good* reviews), it can no longer pretend to any but the most self-serving contact with reality. Leiris' literary "immortalization" of Khadidja can protect her neither against the ravages of time nor against the changes produced by historical events:

Mais le temps n'en garde pas moins sous sa coupe le

---

distanced and as if my pen was vainly obliged to pursue an actuality that escapes me. The blame lies in the slowness of this pen that strains to move mountains haltingly while I'd like it to be so cursive"; *La Règle du jeu I,* 222.

personnage livresque dont les vingt-trois ans devraient
échapper à tout changement:avoir dépeint Khadidja
comme pour l'éternité ne l'a pas protégée—même en
tant qu'héroïne de conte de fées—contre l'action aux
mille ressources des années, puisque la perspective que
les récents événements m'ont imposée doue ce conte
naïvement vécu d'une signification qui rabaisse singu-
lièrement celle que je lui donnais en décrivant mon
merveilleux commerce avec cette fille à la fois si servile
et si fière que je ne pourrai plus, désormais, regarder
exactement des mêmes yeux.*

The irony of this situation is further compounded by
the realization that Khadidja could never even have recognized herself in the portrait that Leiris had made of her,
that is, appreciated the "work of art," excluded as she was
by birth and class from such refinements. The literary
product is thereby reduced in status to a dimension of
utter marginality and inutility, or even cosmic joke:

Pour que cette image ait une consistance dont ne suffit
pas à la doter sa formulation écrite, ne faudrait-il pas,
en premier lieu, que l'intéressée puisse s'y reconnaître
comme dans un miroir où elle se découvrirait *telle qu'en
elle-même enfin?* Or, en admettant que Khadidja soit à
même de me lire, l'histoire que j'ai racontée et la façon
dont elle y est montrée lui resteraient impénétrables ou,
s'il en était autrement, la feraient sans doute rire autant
de voir attacher une telle importance à de simples relations de fournisseuse à client que de se trouver promue
du rang méprisé de putain à celui de magicienne, de

---

* "But time still holds no less in its grip the bookish character
whose 23 years should have been able to avoid all change: having
portrayed Khadidja as for eternitv hasn't protected her one bit—even as
heroine of a fairy tale—against the thousandfold tactics of the years,
since the perspective that recent events have imposed upon me lends to
this naïvely lived story a meaning that singularly deflates the one I gave
it in describing my marvelous commerce with this girl who was at once
so servile and so proud and who I can never again look at in quite the
same way"; *La Règle du jeu III,* 227.

démon de midi ou d'ange de la mort. Ainsi non partagée et rien que subjective, cette image —idole dont la fixité n'empêchera pas sa signification de se perdre—relève de l'onirisme au même titre que les rêveries auxquelles je m'abandonne à son propos.*

Just as the earlier Leiris had seen in his affair with Khadidja the furthest point that life would allow him in his efforts for personal communication and contact with others, this slightly later Leiris now views his trip to China as the very acme of his efforts toward political relevance and universality. If the orgasm he seems to have shared with Khadidja represents for him a kind of subjective epiphany, then his permanent love affair or flirtation with the idea of world revolution may represent an objective one; and just as, upon sober reflection, literature is incriminated, if not refuted then certainly reduced in importance, by the existence of a real, living Khadidja, so this same art would be threatened, at least as practiced in the countries of advanced capitalism by modernists such as Michel Leiris, by the generalization of the Chinese Revolution. This situation is paradoxical and contradictory to the very core and may explain why many modernists are ineluctably ostracized by the very revolution they helped to bring about; Leiris cannot help but wish for and, within the limits of his capacities, help promulgate change in society that would make what he does no longer necessary: "Je vois mal comment une activité du genre de celle qui

---

* "In order for this image to have a consistency that its written formulation isn't enough to give it, wouldn't it be necessary that the interested party be able to recognize herself in it as in a mirror where she would find herself, *as she herself finally?* Now, even admitting that Khadidja would be able to read me, the story that I've told and the way it's told would be incomprehensible for her, or if it was otherwise, would doubtless make her laugh as much to see such importance attached to simple relations between seller and buyer as to find herself promoted from the scorned rank of prostitute to that of magician, demon of the desert. And so, unshared and nothing if not subjective, this image-ideal whose fixity will not prevent its meaning being lost—is fantasy of the same kind as the sexual daydreams I abandoned myself to on her account"; *La Règle du jeu III*, 229.

m'absorbe pourrait y être classée allieurs que parmi ces reliquats bourgeois—si ce n'est pas féodaux—qui appellent une rééducation."*

This literature, which Leiris so dramatically claims earlier in his autobiographical career should be an *act*, turns out to be, from a revolutionary point of view, an act of masturbation. Nevertheless Leiris remains tireless in formulating and reformulating, in a continual effort to match his political commitment to the sense of his writings, the exigencies of his style. From a theoretical point of view at least, Leiris is as close as he ever comes to certainty when he talks about the need for revolution:

> Sur ce globe il y a trop d'humiliés et d'offensés, à cet état de chose un bouleversement radical est l'unique remède, à ce bouleversement on ne peut procéder sans violence. Jugeant ainsi, je donne raison aux révolutionnaires.†

The idea of the need for world revolution is the exception, if there is one, that proves the rule of his otherwise total irony—even if such a change, as seems inevitable, would result in making the author a superfluous man. Leiris' ironic gaze is instead focused on the ambiguities of his own real commitment and the infinitesimally small contribution he sees himself making to the revolutionary cause. So he continues in the above-quoted passage, in a movement of self-doubt that his readers come to expect, to question his own sincerity:

> Mes opinions sont révolutionnaires. Mais cela ne

---

* "I am unable to see how an activity of the kind I find fascinating could there (in a revolutionary society) be classed as other than with the other bourgeois—if not flatly feudal relics—which call for a reeducation"; *La Règle du jeu III*, 34–35.

† "On this earth there are too many insulted and injured; for this state of things a radical cataclysm is the only remedy, and one cannot really have a nonviolent cataclysm. Thinking so, I approve the revolutionaries"; *La Règle du jeu IV*, 89.

prouve pas que je suis, moi, un révolutionnaire. En-
goncé dans mes soucis et dans mes habitudes, facile-
ment désarmé devant des adversaires ... je ne saurais
m'en targuer sans imposture.*

Nevertheless, the Leiris of *Frêle bruit*, the final volume
of *La Règle du jeu* (1976), seems to have made his own
stylistic and thematic adjustments to the revolutionary
cause in terms of the increasing centrality of explicitly political events (May 1968, Occupied Paris) in the texture of
his narratives and also in terms of an increase in the
expository clarity of the prose, since by now he has fallen
away from much of the elusive and involuted style of sentence structure as well as from the exhaustive inventories
and rhetorical-oneiric flights of fancy of the sustained,
lengthy blocks of writing that comprise much of the first
three volumes. This "heavy" style, reminiscent of and probably owing to Proust's and Faulkner's and similarly, in another vein, to Claude Simon's, had reached its paroxysm of
single-minded fury in the almost three-hundred-page, essentially unbroken monologue in volume 3 that Leiris so
aptly called "La Fière la Fière."† Leiris' manner in volume
4 is suddenly calm, reflective, full of typographical
caesurae, and broken in upon frequently by strange
poetry or little Cioran-like philosophical gems. His style
evolves toward the lapidary, aphoristic pole as the text
becomes dissemination, fragmentation, a chain or network of islands or forts, in attempts—"essais"—just to
catch a glimpse of a reality avowedly too overwhelming
and exigent to do very much more than to try to be

---

* "My opinions are revolutionary. But that doesn't mean that I am
a revolutionary. Bound up in my worries and my habits, easily at a loss
for words in debate with adversaries ... I couldn't call myself this without imposture"; *La Règle du jeu IV*, 155.

† Leiris' neologism incorporating *feu* = fire and *fierté* = pride for
something like a *fire* one *proudly* sets to burn in—as in an adultery
that consumes sense, health, and sanity. "La fière" also is associated
with a terrible memory from Leiris' travels, involving a woman who
throws herself into a burning lake to escape the lava behind her. Such
are Leiris' metaphors for the futility, yet inevitability, of the practice of
art in our times.

aware of it. Citing Ché Guevara's saying, "La Revolution va
vite," Leiris in this mood talks about the necessity of ad-
justing his own methods to the needs and rhythms of the
moment:

> Vitesse nécessaire de la Révolution, face à des événe-
> ments qui n'attendent pas. Rhythme auquel je devrais
> personnellement me plier, appliquant cette leçon dans
> les limites étroites de tout ce que je fais et de tout ce
> que j'écris ... Brefs et facilement isolables, les textes
> que j'amasse ici peuvent être publiés avant qu'entre eux
> et l'événement externe ou interne qui m'avait requis
> l'écart se soit par trop creusé. Gain appréciable ... ex-
> plosion d'aphorismes, phrase ou petits groupes de
> phrase qui disent beaucoup en peu de mots et main-
> tiennent à l'incandescence la matière mise en œuvre;
> peut-être, éclatement de la phrase elle-même ... ? Al-
> chimie en chambre, vers quoi—si jamais j'y parviens
> —aura contribué à me pousser cette alchimie plané-
> taire, la Révolution qui fait flamber le feu où se méta-
> morphosent les êtres et les choses.*

Leiris here is reworking, in this political arena where he
felt his presence was *required*, some of his fundamental
intuitions about the relations between individual and society as mediated and controlled by language that informed
the first dazzling pages of *La Règle du jeu.* Language, the
young Leiris had ruefully discovered, is inescapably social
in destiny. It belongs not to *me*, but to *you*, or to me only

---

* "Necessary speed of the Revolution, faced with events that won't
wait. Rhythm that personally I had to adjust to, applying this lesson
within the strict limits of all that I do and write. . . . Brief and easily
isolable, the texts I gather here can be published before between them
and the internal or external events that require my participation before
too much time has elapsed. Appreciable gain, explosion of aphorisms,
phrases or little bits of phrases that say a lot in a few words and
maintain at incandescent brightness the matter at hand; possibly, explosion of the sentence itself . . . ? Alchemy in a room, toward which, if
ever I succeed—a major impetus will have been supplied by this
planetary alchemy, Revolution that fans the blazing fire where things
and beings are metamorphosed"; "The Revolution Is Fast," 4:153–54.

insofar as it relates to you. Thus in the chapter "Reusement," which opens *Biffures*, Leiris ruminates at length on
the education involved in discovering, as a young boy, that
"reusement" is really "heureusement" (= "happily," "luck-
ily," "fortunately"). The "reusement" belongs subjectively
and personally to the individual and is meaningful to him
alone, whereas the "heureusement" represents the language that was there waiting for us before we were born, a
kind of terrorism (in Barthesan terms) that we have no
choice but to accept and undergo, whose inevitable concomitants are the imperatives of social existence and the
needs of others.

There is no such thing, of course, as a definitive victory
for this other that lays claim to language in the name of
society, not at any rate for a writer of Leiris' dynamic and
rebellious energy, incapable of accepting any enduring
compromise with the world-as-constituted. For Leiris'
imagination, which he himself calls Corneillian (*IV*:
388–89)—that is, theatrically dialectic—tends to go to extremes, but these extremes are meant more to be left behind than occupied. Leiris prefers to maintain the tension
between the "enemies" unrelaxed, unforgiving, and exigent
rather than let himself settle into any formula or comfortable *modus vivendi* or *scribendi*. Instead he wavers and
oscillates, alternately embracing and eschewing his own
most cunning articulations of the problem. Although in
what follows we deal with the personal-subjective and so-
cial-objective aspects successively, they should nevertheless be seen as operating simultaneously.

On the one hand, Leiris plunges with what seems to me
an unprecedented ambition, determination, and nerve to
the roots of his subjectivity; he explores the limits of
confession and avowal in *L'Age d'homme;* he sounds the
depths of a kind of Freudian cabala of letters, prelinguistic
sounds and early memories of tunes and toys in *Biffures*,
calling forth in great profusion, for instance in the chapter
"Alphabets," the multiple meanings hidden for him in the
most simple syllable or even the personal mysteries
cloaked and evoked by a mark of punctuation. He continues on this subjective slant all through *La Règle du jeu*,

always careful to stress the priority of what events meant to him over their purely functional or social context. Thus the memorial to Max Jacob, which he treats in *Fourbis,* triggers for him what he calls a "descent into hell" that has little to do with the social ceremony in which he participated *all the same.* Frequent also is Leiris' eccentric and arbitrary self-designation as a strange modern incarnation of a medieval alchemist or hermeticist (even in the few quotations I've made there are at least several allusions to himself in this wise) who plunges into the dark night of his own soul, there to find or refine the gold of his spirit. In *Fibrilles* ("La Fière la Fière," *La Règle du jeu III*), this subjectivity reaches its farthest extension and limit, both in subject matter and form. For the subject of this book is Leiris' attempt to take his own life, and his prose style is as elusive, demanding, and difficult as it ever gets: for the most part, interminably long sentences seem to move from point to point purely by a process of association, so that it is next to impossible to remember (if that indeed is what the reader is supposed to do) what the author was talking about a few pages or even a few paragraphs or lines previously. Leiris here is like a horse willfully trying to shake his rider, determined not to be broken into any kind of coherent sense or stable meaning.

On the other hand, and consistently all through his work, Leiris goes to great lengths also to establish the objectivity of his enterprise. He frequently interrupts himself with self-criticism, reminders, calls to order, and self-advice. During the course of this long autobiography he habitually surfaces to ask himself whether the goal he initially set for himself still makes any sense, whether he has unwittingly abandoned it, and whether indeed his work has any direction. Among the considerations he entertains most frequently is the thought of dropping the autobiography in particular and the practice of literature in general. The action of writing is seen in no sense as a given but as a decision that is made and renewed on the basis of information that ceaselessly intrudes on the attention of the writer. That writing fulfills certain subjective personal needs for Leiris is obvious enough, but he seeks equally to establish an objective necessity for it. As Leiris reminds himself and thereby his reader so frequently, he is trying to do something with his words; and he never tires of asking himself what that is, how well it has been said (and understood), and whether or not it is still worth saying:

> Quand mon projet prit corps sous cette forme . . . j'eus recours . . . à l'expression de *bifurs* pour désigner, dans mon jargon personnel, les matériaux si peu commodes à étiqueter que je voulais amasser et brasser: soubresauts, trébuchements ou glissements de pensée se produisant à l'occasion d'une fêlure, d'un miroitement. . . . Me référant au terme de "bifur" . . . j'entendais mettre plutôt l'accent sur l'acte même de bifurquer, de dévier, comme fait le train. . . . A mesure que le livre, page après page, s'alourdissait . . . l'élan initial se perdait; il n'est bientôt plus resté des bifurs que le nom . . . je perds de vue mon but ultime qu'étouffe la foison de détails plutôt qu'elle ne concourt à y mener. . . . C'est pourquoi . . . j'ai décidé, sans plus tarder, de laisser tout en plan.*

To underline the objectivity of this "decision to quit," it should be mentioned also that this self-criticism was undertaken as a reply both to critical remarks directed to Leiris by friends and also to negative newspaper reaction on the occasion of the appearance of the "Dimanche" chapter of *Biffures* in *Les Temps modernes* (1945); but also

---

* "When my project began to assume this form . . . I had recourse to the expression *bifurcations* to designate, in my personal jargon, those very-difficult-to-label materials that I wanted to gather and brew together: sudden jerks, tremblings, slidings of thought produced on the occasion of a fracture, a shimmering. . . . Thinking of the term 'bifurcation' . . . I meant rather to place emphasis on the very act of bifurcating, of deviating, as does the train. . . . As this book, page after page, grew . . . the initial élan was lost: soon there was nothing of bifurcation left but the word. . . . I've lost sight of my goal, smothered under an abundance of detail rather than facilitated by it. That is why, without further ado, I've decided to abandon the work unfinished"; *La Règle du jeu I*, 256–57, 264.

in *Fibrilles* (1966), two books and almost twenty years later, Leiris is still taking account of the critical response to his nevertheless ongoing work. The generally favorable critical response to *Fourbis* (1955) does not satisfy the exigent Leiris of *Fibrilles*. He would rather his work be rejected completely than admired for the wrong reasons. This feeling of not being understood, and thereby of not attaining his objective goals, he then goes on to describe as one of the causes for the depression he fell into after his return from his "enlightening" trip to China (his wife had cut out all these "favorable" notices and they were waiting for him), and that led him to attempt to take his own life.[7]

Thus, as we have seen, Leiris oscillates perpetually between a Scylla of subjectivity or personal fulfillment and a Charybdis of objectivity or social relevance and legitimation. There is no middle course possible for him between the two antipodes, nor is it possible for him to get too taken with one or the other, for, following the Homeric imagery, these are *dangerous* entities that forbid human entry. His object, in any case, is not to attain, master, or possess one or the other, or even to get by both of them, but to maintain their contradictions at fever pitch, at a maximally endurable level of tension and provocation, by taking them both ceaselessly and simultaneously into account. Characteristically, instead, he "cheats"[8] on one with the other. He plunges into his paradise or hells of subjectivity in order to escape the tyranny of an objective world (wherein one didn't ask to be born); but in turn he tries to interpret, justify, or redeem his personal experience (dreams, hallucinations, fantasies) in alternately mythological, psychological, and political, that is, objective terms. By oscillating incessantly from one point of view to the other he refuses to be dominated or truncated by one at the expense of the other.

Although he uses, and abundantly, the materials of madness—though he subscribes, and sincerely, to the goals of revolution—he is, by his own admission, neither a madman nor a revolutionary. He cannot be so easily defined and thus dismissed either by his readers and critics or by himself—certainly his own most exigent critic. He is, instead, fully the man of his age: this time when we no longer believe in the abstractions and ideals that consoled our ancestors, though we still use them when it suits our purposes. We no longer believe that the houses we live in will last much longer than we do, and we are certainly aware that the sky above our heads hides no heaven behind it. This movement, this dynamism, this reluctance to be trapped or confined by any system, as exemplified by Leiris' reference to the *game* in the title of his autobiography, so that *rule* comes through almost as a contradiction in terms—what does this mean except that we now play the game of life for its own sake and that we are always ready to change the rules, even to change sides, so as to keep the game from becoming more important than those who play it.

5

The Fragmentary Word of
Maurice Blanchot

The work of Maurice Blanchot in its strange intensity poses the most crucial problems for any student of literature, art, or culture as well as for anyone seriously interested in the craft of writing. Blanchot's work falls, not so neatly, into two main categories: critical and creative. The critical pieces were mainly written as reviews of recently published books for the *Nouvelle Revue Française* over a twenty-year period (from about 1945 to 1965) and have been collected over the years into six volumes, all published by Gallimard. What I call the "creative" work consists of about ten novels, récits, dialogues, and recently, collections of "fragments," which have been appearing regularly since the novel *Thomas l'obscur* was published in 1941. Blanchot is not a great respecter of "genre." His critical pieces often have a fictional, even poetic quality, and his noncritical work is often as abstract and maddeningly complicated as the texts of Kierkegaard, Husserl, or Heidegger.

For Blanchot the only works worth considering are those that explore the limits of the human adventure and therefore are ready to take up certain fundamental problems of life and death, memory and oblivion, culture and anarchy; he is, for instance, much occupied with the question of whether there is any authentic purpose for literature and art in our modern technocratic societies that increasingly marginalize if not exile entirely these forms of activity. Furthermore, what matters is not the works in themselves but the themes they invent and provoke, the experiences in which they originate, and the times to which they point the way. Blanchot is no fetishist of the written word; the important thing for him is not what exactly the author said but what he meant. Typical of this existential attitude toward literature (which he shares with Tzara, Valéry, Leiris, Bataille, and some other provocative moderns) is his judgment on the meaning of Gide's career: "Just like the best of Rimbaud and Lautréamont, the influence of his works is in the direction of the making of literature a vital experience, an instrument of discovery, a means for man to feel himself, to try himself, and in this attempt, to try to overcome his limits."[1]

For Blanchot, just as the distinction between critical and creative prose is blurred (for himself as well as in his approach to other writers), so is that between philosopher and thinker, novelist and poet. Whether he is talking about de Sade or Nietzsche, Hölderlin or Kafka, Rousseau, Breton, Mallarmé, H. Lefebvre, Foucault, or even Trotsky, the intensity and level of involvement remain the same. So little is Blanchot concerned about what "form" the individuals he talks about write in that at times it seems that he has a special sympathy for the kind of writer who leaves little or nothing behind him, citing approvingly Heidegger's judgment of Socrates as the "ultimate writer" and dwelling at length on Mallarmé's famous preoccupation with the "work as absence." In an article on the French diarist Joseph Joubert (1754–1824), Blanchot talks about this writer's lifelong preparation to put himself into the condition of being able to start writing.[2] The fact that Joubert, a man whose multifarious talents were acknowledged by contemporaries as gifted as Benjamin Constant, left nothing behind but his journals proves only that he was willing to sacrifice "the results of art to a discovery of the conditions that make art possible."[3]

Blanchot's predilection is not particularly for writers who leave "complete works" behind them (Dickens, Balzac) but for those that leave magnificent fragments for the future to puzzle over (Kafka, Nietzsche, Musil). In *L'Entretien infini* he talks about the fragmentary work being more in tune with the exigencies of the time we live in, "bypassing the conception of the work united and closed in itself, organizing and dominating values transmitted by traditional methods—it explores the infinite space of the work, with

inexorable rigor, but under a new postulate—not necessarily satisfying concepts of unity, totality, or of continuity" (510).

Referring to the German thinker Walter Benjamin, an
inveterate writer of fragments, he cites his insights to the
effect that, for the history of art, the fragment is a catastrophe, whereas for the artist himself it might be a more
adequate expression of what he really has to say than
many a finished work that he has been forced, by society
and necessity, to complete. Blanchot, as theorist of the
fragmentary, resists any intrusion by culture or society
upon the works of art. The society demands of art only
"finished products" to be stored in its silos (libraries, memory banks, museums, archives)[4] or exchanged in its mar-
kets, where their real energy and potential for affecting life
can be defused and/or quarantined—whereas for Blanchot
art is nothing if not incomplete and problematic. It supplies no answers; in fact it only asks more questions; for
society this art, which comes across as pure question "and
questions the very possibility of art, can only appear as
dangerous, hostile and coldly violent."[5] Society and its culture are interested only in limited and finite works that are
easy to digest or at least to classify, and are thus opposed
to the finest of the "new art," which is "exigence infinie à
laquelle l'expérience artistique nous demande de répondre,
expérience qui ne peut s'accomplir que dans des œuvres
de fragment, lesquels suffisent à ebranler de leur présence
tout avenir de culture."[*] The message of the work of art is
thus seen to consist not in itself, nor even in any moral,
philosophy, or idea it purports to propose, nor in any
stylistic quality[6] or textual integrity, but instead in its capacity to challenge its audience to question their lives.

This is not to imply that Blanchot dismisses all traditional approaches to these problems, as far as they go; he
admires, for instance, the ingenuity of Georges Poulet's
studies in the metamorphoses of the circle as a literary

---

[*] "Infinite exigency that artistic experience demands that we respond to, experience that can only be accomplished in fragmentary
works, that by their presence alone are enough to shake the whole future of the edifice of culture"; *L'Entretien*, 511.

figure but is only suspicious of its relevance to the "new art," which can have no use for circular forms because its center is at once everywhere and nowhere—in other words, absent. Blanchot then goes on to wonder what will happen to man the day he has to renounce the hypothesis of a "curved universe"—or any other way to define it optically or systematically. The question such a day will surely pose will be whether or not man is capable of a "radical interrogation," which is tantamount for Blanchot to asking the question that recurs incessantly in his work—whether man is capable of literature.[7]

Just as Blanchot finds an early example of the modern writer's preoccupation with the "fact of writing" in the anguished self-consciousness of J.J. Rousseau's pen,[8] he locates the quintessence of this "philosophy of the fragmentary" in the German romantics—particularly those who wrote for the short-lived but influential *Athenaeum Review* (1798–1800). Blanchot characterizes romanticism as the exigence and experience of contradictions, with a distinct vocation for disorder. It was that age that promoted the mixture of writer and philosopher that Blanchot sees as having become a commonplace in twentieth-century art. In that time "la littérature annonce qu'elle prend le pouvoir."*[9] Failure and success in worldly terms become inverted for the world of art; what Morse Peckham has eloquently characterized as the "success of failure" and the "failure of success"[10] Blanchot was to use elsewhere to argue that, contrary to Sartre's well-reasoned attack, Baudelaire's success lay precisely in the pathos of his social failures (even to live up to his own ideals); and Blanchot pleads similarly and at great length for those two magnificent "misfits," Lautréamont and de Sade.[11]

The German romantics invented an art whose equivalent was the "nontransitive word"—a word without an object[12]—an art that is useless for society and culture in the terms we describe above. The attitude of these artists makes of literature a question, not an answer. They dream of a total novel that approaches the condition of poetry

---

* "Literature announces that it's taking power" (*L'Entretien*, 519).

and that can only be conveyed by the exigencies of the
fragment—because only the fragment can take into account the "interruptions," breaks, cracks, "fêlures,"[13] and
lacks that constitute an artistic consciousness. Blanchot
cites A. W. Schlegel as not being discouraged by the incomprehensibility of those fragments to his contemporaries:
"Future centuries will know how to read them";[14] and
Novalis talks of the fragment as "seed," this same fragment
that in its discontinuity can alone express the irony (that
we are most complete when most incomplete) inherent in
the romantic attitude. The fragment is not to be confused,
of course, with such other literary forms as aphorism and
maxim, to which it is both closely related and totally opposed, because these forms represent a historical, often
political need for unity and coherence, that is, an attempt
to close the fragment in upon itself, "finish" it, make it
useful and even quotable socially. Nor is, of course, the
fragment to be taken too literally. Fragmented, whatever
their stylistic continuities and massive lengths, are the
works of Musil, Beckett, and Leiris, because of the "jagged
edges" or uncompromising refusals of these efforts to fit
into any conceivable explanatory paradigm. What makes a
work fragmentary is not its length (or lack thereof) but its
resistance to incorporation by the world around it or to
come.[15]

The hero of and heir to, and father of, the fragment is of
course Friedrich Nietzsche, whose works float like icebergs
in the seas of Western thought; for Blanchot, who is suspicious of System in any form, the great betrayal of Nietzsche was the posthumous publication of the *Will to Power*,
which was nothing less than an attempt to convert a fragmentary writer into a systematic philosopher, in obedience
to the whims and dictates of political expediency. Thus the
contradictions, paradoxes, and oscillations, that make up
the very pulse and life of the work, were flattened out,
ironed over, and selectively misread or ignored, as a
power- and production-oriented culture uses the death of
the artist as an excuse to convert him into material for its
mills.

Nietzsche, as Blanchot reads him, saw clearly that the

contradictions of progress were also the risks and existential predicament of humanity—that is, "man is choosing to produce a world where the man of knowledge is no longer permitted to subsist as such and where it would no longer be allowed to him to work according to the objectivity of knowledge, but according to the arbitrary meaning of the new world."[16] Nietzsche saw that a certain point of no return had been reached for humanity and that mankind, as we think we know it, had ceased to exist.

To bring this issue closer to the present, Blanchot cites the dialogue between Ernst Jünger and Martin Heidegger, published under the provocative Nietzschean title *Crossing the Line*, on the occasion of both the writer's and the philosopher's sixtieth birthdays. Fragmentary writing is seen as corresponding to the exigency of a rupture that demarcates the new age from the old. In discussing Jünger's *The Wall of Time, Essay on the Atomic Age*, Blanchot emphasizes the qualitative changes introduced into the very nature of life by modern technology: "la bombe est un avertissement visible de la menace invisible que toute la technique moderne dirige contre les façons de l'homme."*[17] The underlying purpose and value of our technology, Blanchot says in a later text, is not to make life easier for us (which everybody is right in saying it does not do), it is to ensure that we can never feel complacent, secure, "at home" in the world again.[18]

The break demanded by fragmentary writing implies a separation from traditional thought—the major defect of which was its tendency to freeze into systems that give us the illusion of understanding and dominating existence. Blanchot is thus anti-intellectual, both abstractly (opposed to classical and scholastic modes) and concretely (opposed to purely materialistic and technocratic concepts). This iconoclasm is exercised in the name of a higher destiny demanded for a creature that it is far from certain will be man (at least as we know him)—and in the name of art: "La coupure exigée par l'écriture est coupure

---

* "The bomb is a visible warning of the invisible threat that modern technology directs against man's ways"; *L'Entretien*, 403.

avec la pensée quand celle-ci se donne pour proximité im-
médiate, et coupure avec toute expérience empirique du
monde."*

Here Blanchot is close to being a revolutionary with
his pen. He has certainly shown elsewhere that he
would shed no tears over the disintegration of modern
society and its power structures.[19] Traditionally art has
been monopolized by elitist elements in society. Max
Weber, among others, has argued convincingly that the
oppressed and alienated masses do not have the leisure or
opportunities to develop the inclination for such pursuits,
whether "mystic" or "artistic," which will always be the
pastimes of an aristocratic elite.[20] The millennial dream of
a "universal art" is destined to remain just a dream.

The fact is, though, that the imbalance and inequality
of this situation have provided a source of permanent instability in history—an instability that has been accel-
erated in our own revolutionary times to the point that the
privileges of the elite to enjoy their art "in peace and quiet"
are visibly threatened. For Blanchot this is not a problem;
the end of traditional art and culture, the sinking of what
Allen Ginsberg calls "the whole boatload of sensitive bull-
shit," would evoke no complaints and call forth no re-
grets—as indeed it should not, for what will pass will be
the art of "finished products" whose function it was to
supply answers and justifications for the cultural and social hegemony of those in power.

The *ars nova*, on the other hand, can not be threatened
by this cataclysm because its real existence is not in the
museums, concert halls, schools, and libraries but in the
minds and spirits of its creators; for Blanchot there is a
strict analogy between revolution and this kind of art, in
the sense that both imply a radical break with the past.
The new art, far from being elitist in character, would demand as its precondition the end of human alienation. In
the meantime we are cut off from even an approximate

---

* "The break demanded by writing is break with thought (when the
latter tasks itself for immediate proximity) and break with all empirical
experience of the world"; *L'Entretien*, 391.

knowledge of what real writing would be. The closest we can get to it would be graffiti or something like a cry in the night—as simple, elemental, obvious, and necessary as throwing a bomb: "cri du besoin ou de la protestation, cri sans mot sans silence, cri ignoble ou, à la rigeur, le cri écrit, les graffities des murailles ... *'car en effet je m'étais rendu compte que c'était assez de mots, assez même de rugissements et que ce qu'il fallait, c'étaient des bombes.'*"21*

The idea here is that writing exists in some mental realm of pure anticipation outside of its concrete form in language and certainly exterior to any alienated embodiment in print (104).22 For Blanchot, as for Heidegger, the poetic word is something rare, elusive, but paradoxically omnipresent and undeniable, an energy that percolates under and around existence but is, and must be, mostly invisible, authorless, and endless (in terms of practical finality): "Poetically man dwells," claimed Heidegger, citing Hölderlin; without poetry man would not be human, life would not be humane; and the democratizing force of this "elitist" idea stops our self-destroying logical powers in their tracks, baffles us into a knowledge that is, as it was for Walt Whitman, an action: the poetic is at once the everyday and the exceptional—but poetry is as rare and as necessary as is the awareness that the everyday *is* the exceptional.

The references to "graffiti" and "cries in the night," as well as the unidentified citation that calls probably from some wall to the simplicity of violence, lead us ineluctably back to the fragmentary (both cause and result of the bomb): these nothing-if-not-transitory expressions are ideal fragments because, unlike aphorisms and maxims, they are forms that are impossible to socialize or control. Graffiti by its very nature must appear as a kind of spontaneous guerrilla warfare, explosions on the walls we pass. Putting aside all arguments as to the relative aesthetic

---

* "Cry of need and protest, cry wordless but without silence, ignoble cry, or, at the limit, written cry, graffiti on the walls ... *'for, in effect, I realized that there'd been enough words, enough howling too, and what we needed was bombs'*"; *L'Entretien*, 392–93.

worth, which would be class-biased in any case, it is clear
that graffiti interferes with the morale of an orderly
citizenry on its way to and from work. It touches the
untouchable, marks the unremarkable, turns the system
against itself, and opens up the perspective of there being
another dimension than blind obedience. It is provocative
to the utmost extent, because at the same time that it
poses embarrassing questions to the powers in place, it
answers these questions itself by proposing to all and
sundry the unspeakable heresy that the time to live is
now. It points out blatantly and permanently (hard to
erase) the gap between the system's stated goals and the
paucity of its realizations.

The power of the fragment is thus founded on its ability
to express certain profound incompatibilities in the nature
of things—first of all between man and his power to
communicate (his inability to express himself) and also between the universe that we live in and the "world where
writing [which for Blanchot means nothing less than *freedom*] calls us."[23] These incompatibilities, to which Nietzsche was certainly susceptible, play a part in the theme of
"difference" as expressed by Derrida, as well as in the philosophy of the absurd as pronounced by Camus ("the
absurd rises from the unreasoning silence of nature in the
face of human demands"). Another way of expressing this
would be to invoke the concept of the "limit-experience,"
which Blanchot borrows from his friend Georges Bataille.[24]
The fragment thus conveys or invokes the limit-experience
in the sense that it involves the perennial conflict between
what is thought possible and what is possible. It attempts
to answer the question, by continuing to pose it, of what
man is really capable of, and what his real limits are. The
fragment, as limit-experience, is the "answer which man
receives when he has decided to put himself radically into
question," *L'Entretien*, 302.

A fragment is the kind of statement that is neither an
affirmation nor a negation. A negation, for Blanchot, is
only another form of affirmation, and Blanchot's ideal literature is fragmentary in the sense that it neither affirms
nor denies: "The guiding thread through this process is

that with literature we are dealing with a statement that is not reducible to any unifying process" (*L'Entretien*, 594–95). Like the deity in the negative theology of the mystics Boehme and Eckhart, literature can be conceived of only in negatives—we can say only what this literature is not, but we can no more identify literature with this negation than the mystics could positively find their god in his own absence (*L'Entretien*, 595).

That these attempts to talk about the experience of literature are strictly modern, Blanchot would be the first to admit. In *L'Espace littéraire*, for instance, he traces the evolution of the art of writing from classical antiquity, when it was the "parole des dieux" ("the word of the gods"), to the Renaissance, when it was "parole de l'absence des dieux" ("the word of the absence of the gods"), to the eighteenth century as "parole juste, équilibré de l'homme" ("the just and balanced word of man"), then to the nineteenth and twentieth centuries when it becomes "parole des hommes dans leur diversité, puis parole des hommes déshérités, de ceux qui n'ont pas la parole, puis parole de ce qui ne parle pas en l'homme, du secret, du désespoir ou du ravissement" ("word of man in their diversity, then word of the disinherited, of those who have no word, word of what doesn't speak in man, of the secret, of despair or violation"), asking himself inevitably, "que lui reste-t-il à dire?" ("what's left for it to say?"; *L'Espace littéraire*, 314).

What history has performed has been a progressive stripping of the work of art of any and all functions. If we search around "the bottom of the pot," so to speak, to find some way of conceiving of art in our time, we find only an art that stands for and by itself—and that inhibits any attempt to say it is something else. "This is what we have been left with, for now!" (*L'Entretien*, 595).

This reduced, nihilist vision of literature is also conveyed in the novel *Thomas l'obscur* (*Thomas the Obscure*), which reads as an allegory of art and human communication in general being stripped to the bare essentials—which presumably remain. The written text dates back to 1931 and publication to 1941. The second edition, that of 1950, is changed only by deletions,[25] as if to say that we can add nothing new to art, except by cutting away to get down to essence.

The characters of this book are not personalities so much as mere names. Thomas, the hero? of the novel, reminds one nevertheless of the independent, ruthlessly logical artist-type that Joyce projected in Stephen Dedalus of *A Portrait of the Artist as a Young Man* and *Ulysses*, and Anne, a mutation of the hero in search of an authentic death such as Rilke propounded in the *Notebooks of Malte Laurid Brigge*, wherein the young exile in Paris complains that no one "dies their own death anymore—they die the death belonging to their disease."

The doctor, and any expert upon whom we call to explain to us the inexplicable, to objectify our maladies,[26] is entirely useless in explaining, retarding, or otherwise dealing with the death of the patient, Anne, although it is comforting to the relatives to have him there: "Le médecin se pencha et crut qu'elle mourait selon les lois de la mort, ne voyant pas qu'elle était déjà parvenue à l'instant où en elle les lois mouraient."*

There is no way to grasp concretely the reality of what is going on in this book. Thomas goes for a swim, true, but is that what is happening when it is said "tout se fût borné pour lui à continuer avec une absence d'organisme dans une absence de mer son voyage interminable"?† Every definition that is advanced is instantly retracted or infinitely refracted. Anne literally "disappears" under Thomas's gaze (chapter 3): *as* he looks at her, her aspect changes from solid and attractive to shadowy and evanescent. The words that Thomas looks at in chapter 4 are reading him back and seem like "a series of angels opening up on the infinite up to the eye of the absolute" (28). There is also a matter of

---

* "The doctor leaned over her and believed she was dying according to the rules of death, but he did not realize that she had already reached the point where in her the very rules had died"; *Thomas l'obscur*, 2d ed., 96.

† "It all came down for him (Thomas swimming) to continue in the absence of his body in an absence of sea his interminable voyage"; *Thomas l'obscur*, 11.

a thinking rat and a speaking cat that have suspiciously human concerns. Blanchot is obviously doing everything in his power to keep our sympathy, understanding, or even attention from settling on any tangible object.

Blanchot is particularly tricky with pronouns and likes to play with narrative levels and voices, always lurking with an unexpected "I" and "he," "we," "they," and "you" when the reader is least ready for it, a little like schizophrenics who refer to themselves as impersonal objects —though this habit of Blanchot's of mixing up the pronouns isn't given full vent until *L'Attente l'oubli* of 1962.

As Michel Butor has it in an important short article "L'Usage des pronoms personnels dans le roman" and to which, not surprisingly, Blanchot explicitly refers the reader of *L'Entretien infini:* "Dans le roman, ce que l'on nous raconte, c'est donc toujours aussi quelqu'un qui se raconte et nous raconte. La prise de conscience d'un tel fait provoque un glissement de la narration de la troisième à la première personne."* Likewise, Thomas, who is a writer, is having a bad case of "pronominal slippage": "the words *He* and *I* start their carnage in his senseless person" (*Thomas l'obscur*, 29). If the "he" is inauthentic because it hides an "I," then the "I" is no more satisfactory since it also sends us back to the "he": in Rimbaud's glorious formulation, "I is another." We are caught in a maze of infinitely reflecting mirrors, and the variety of routes and approaches Blanchot takes merely convinces us more surely that there is no way out of this labyrinth, as there was no way into it.

The trouble with the third-person narrator of traditional fiction is that this "person" is always a more or less transparent lie—since whatever happens is always only the account of a person who claims "I saw it" but who disguises the claim in order to give it more authority. On the other hand, the "I" of the "sincere" writer, whether keeper of journal, or teller of eyewitness account, is in no

---

* "What we're told in the novel is not only what someone is telling us but that someone is telling about himself. Bringing such a fact to awareness provokes a slide of the narration from the third to the first person"; *Répertoire 2*, 62.

better shape, since we are manifestly trying to resurrect a "subject" that was unsatisfactory in the first place, like Beckett's unnamable "I go on saying I knowing it's not I," or Blanchot's almost-blind speaking cat, "Je dis moi, guidé par un instinct aveugle, car depuis que j'ai perdu la queue toute droite qui me servait de gouvernail dans le monde, je ne suis manifestement plus moi-même."*

So we go on using the only words we know, victims of some kind of hereditary echolalia, unsatisfied with the education we have received but not able to do much more than continue repeating by rote the lessons we have learned.

Such a dilemma must have led Butor to make his unusual experiment with telling a story exclusively in the second person (*La Modification*), as it accounts for the general lability and interchangeability of the pronoun (as well as the name) in Beckett's *Unnamable*, Joyce's *Wake*, and Sollers' "experimental" fictions. Here, with Blanchot, as utterly as anywhere we confront that phenomenon so widespread in modern literature and consciousness: *a dissolution of the concept of identity*, or fragmentation of the self into myriad irrecoverable shards. We are here in some kind of threshold landscape or inscape, or *outside* of same, where subjects and objects are neither themselves nor something else but merely "neuter."[27]

The beings who dwell in this end-of-the-world territory come off like mutants or clones, objects left to carry on by themselves by a creator who has long since left and will not be heard from again. They are robots that are no longer entitled to say "I"; and we may say that the only difference between people is that some have realized what has happened to them (Thomas, Anne) and some have not (Anne's relatives, the doctor, or Louise, in the first version of the novel of 1941, who tries to add Thomas to her "collection"). Since Blanchot is not at all foreign to the image of the bomb as marking a qualitative rupture between past and present, I think it is apt also to cite Herbert Marcuse,

---

* "I say no, guided by a blind instinct, for since I've lost the straight tail that served me as rudder in the world, I'm manifestly no longer myself"; *Thomas l'obscur*, 37.

theorist of "one-dimensional man," who assured audiences he lectured to that "the bomb has dropped and we are the mutants."

For Blanchot the pathos of a situation, equally incapable of acceptance as of denial, may be what he is trying to express in his frequent references to apocalypse, which certainly form an important segment of his critical and creative vocabulary: about Anne it is said that "son impatience se confondait avec l'espoir de participer à un cataclysme général où, en même temps que les êtres seraient détruites les distances que séparent les êtres."* This is a nothingness that involves a mood more despairing and nihilistic than any Pascalian abyss could possibly be. The "bet" that Pascal urges us to make is that there is, in spite of all the evidence to the contrary, a sense to the universe. Blanchot's people run the risk of there being no universe at all; but even if that is so, our instincts and conditioning oblige us to continue asking the questions that belong to a time and space that no longer exists—as if we don't have words yet to describe what we are experiencing, or as if words were only serving us provisionally until we come upon a better way of saying what we mean. Thus Anne wonders aloud to Thomas, "Who are you really?" when it is obvious to her immediately that the question not only cannot be answered, it cannot even be asked, or what is really important is what you are saying about yourself by asking the question, "Anne qui existait encore et qui n'existait plus, suprême moquerie à la pensée de Thomas."† If there is a theme to this novel, it is surely our inevitable insignificance to each other as well as our total uselessness to ourselves. We cannot even call this situation "ironic," or refer it to "the laughter of the gods." The gods are not amused, not only because they do not exist but because the enormity of the destruction we have wrought in the twentieth

---

* "Her impatience was confused with the hope of participating in a general cataclysm, where, at the same time as the individual beings there would be destroyed the distance that separated them"; *Thomas l'obscur*, 55.

† "Anne who did not yet exist and who no longer existed, supreme mockery of Thomas's mind"; *Thomas l'obscur*, 70.

century, alike in our environment and in ourselves, has
bereaved us of the standards, values, and norms upon
which such irony was based. The Enlightenment was the
last to laugh, as the romantics were the last ironists.

So it is that our situation cannot even be called "pathetic"; it is instead *meaningless:* Anne understands at
last that it is best to say nothing, "à quoi bon—ce mot
aussi était le mot qu'elle cherchait,—Thomas est insignifi-
ant. Dormons."* Thomas's grand monologue on death in
chapter 11 makes even this resolution seem premature
and unwarranted.[28] Everything Blanchot gives us he takes
back immediately. There is clearly no peace (answers) to
be had, either in life or in death, no way of unifying our
thoughts and doubts around any single center, thought,
idea, or conclusion; and the conclusion that we can come
to no conclusion is equally forbidden to us.

The two stories, or conte and récit, published in *Le
Ressassement éternel (The Eternal Recapitulation)* by Éditions de Minuit in 1951 were written in 1935–36. The hero
of the first tale, "L'Idylle," an anonymous man who is given
the name of Alexandre Akim—mostly for the sake of classification: "Ce nom étranger lui convient aussi bien qu'un
autre"†—has been arrested and detained for vagrancy in
a kind of country club–work camp, distinctly related to
similar institutions in Kafka. Vagrancy, nomadism, lack of
permanent address—all very artistic qualities for Blanchot—are all anathema for the bourgeois order of things,
for obvious reasons: armies, schools, factories, stores cannot be staffed with vagrants. So the basic house rule, in
fact the only real rule and, in case of infraction, punishable
by a beating so severe it always results in loss of life, is that
the prisoners are not free to wander. A prisoner is free to
leave only if he marries, that is, if he enters another institution that assures him a stable identity for society.

The model for this kind of escape from one prison to
another is the marriage of the keepers of the institution,

---

* "What's the use—this word also was the one she was looking
for—Thomas is unimportant. Sleep"; *Thomas l'obscur*, 98.

† "'This foreign name suited him as well as any other';" *Le
Ressassement*, 9.

who are a husband-and-wife team. Akim insists on thinking of married life in general and the relationship of his keepers in particular as an idyll; he is unable to see the harsh life-and-death struggle going on beneath a deceptively calm exterior. He himself decides to marry, not only to escape his prison, but because he believes in the happiness of his keepers. He lets himself be lulled into a false confidence on the night before his wedding, and he wanders away from the prison, is apprehended, and punished according to house rules. It is as if Akim, who has been described as "un étranger ... il ne deviendra jamais un homme d'ici,"* is constitutionally incapable of living anywhere, that is, as an artist he is considered a permanent menace to the established order—an order that must extinguish him to preserve itself.

The second story of *Le Ressassement éternel*, "Le Dernier Mot" ("The Last Word"), introduces us to a world in which the structures of power have been definitively destroyed. Our first-person narrator wanders into a city deprived of any permanent orientation. In particular, the central symbol of permanence, memory, and authority— the library—has been or is about to be abolished. The iconoclasm is close here in time as well as mood to the surrealist rage that inflects the astounding tone-poems-in-prose that Tzara composed in the mid-thirties, *Grains et issues* and *Personnage d'insomnie*, especially in the attention that Blanchot pays to the "breaking up" of the language and the subsequent promise or prophecy of semiotic anarchy. For language here is in disarray: "Il y eut un temps où le langage cessa de lier les mots entre eux suivant des rapports simples et devint un instrument si délicat qu'on en interdit l'usage au plus grand nombre."†

The last word—the ultimate sound—is not a noun, since the substance on which it is based is no longer there

---

* "A foreigner, he'll never become a man from here"; *Le Ressassement*, 46.

† "There was a time when language ceased being able to connect words in simple, clear ways and became so delicate of an instrument that they prohibited its use to the great majority"; *Le Ressassement*, 105.

but is instead something as evanescent and fragmentary as a prepositional phrase or an article. Blanchot's narrator thus explores the linguistic and symbolic depths involved in our everyday, apparently not-so-innocent use of phrases such as "jusqu'au," "il y a," and especially "ne pas."* Furthermore the narrator alone is bewildered by the anomaly, the sheer strangeness of a world in which words have lost their resonance and meaning and the social institutions that are supposed to supply a space for communications are crumbling; all the others see this "limit-situation" as perfectly natural, as if they had been living so long on the brink of nothingness that it has become nothing special to them.

As the tower in which the narrator has taken refuge is crumbling to its foundation, by dint of the social assaults it is no longer able to contain, the narrator alone is worried (through the voice of a young woman who somehow starts articulating his disaffection) by the finality of this event. His hosts continue to maintain, even while they and their world are being swept into destruction, that there is nothing extraordinary taking place, nothing to be concerned about.

Blanchot's curious first-person narrator continues his adventures in a short story first published in a journal in 1948 under the ambivalent title *Un Récit?* (the question mark is Blanchot's) and reprinted in book form by Fata Morgana in 1973 under the hardly less strange rubric of *La Folie du jour* (*Madness of the Day*). Blanchot's hero, now finally nameless, is patently imprisoned—he is being kept against his will, ostensibly in an institution, where he is frequently challenged and interrogated. He is especially annoyed at being bothered because he has not been putting what are called his talents to some obvious social use:

They said to me (sometimes it was the doctor, sometimes the nurses), "You're an educated man, you have

---

* "Jusqu'au" = until; "il y a" = there is; "ne pas" = not at all; *Le Ressassement*, 105.

talents; by not using abilities which, if they were divided among ten people who lack them, would allow
them to live, you are depriving them of what they don't
have, and your poverty, which could be avoided, is an
insult to their needs." I asked, "Why these lectures? Am
I stealing my own place? Take it back from me." I felt I
was surrounded by unjust thoughts and spiteful reasoning. And who were they setting against me? An invisible learning that I myself searched for without success. I was an educated man! But perhaps not all the
time. Talented? Where were these talents that were
made to speak like gowned judges sitting on benches,
ready to condemn me day and night? (*Madness of the Day*,
13–14)

The fragmented consciousness obviously on display
here does not satisfy the authorities—either medical or
otherwise—who demand that the narrator constitute himself into an authorial entity, an "I" capable of taking responsibility for his actions and giving sequence and coherence to what he has to say. Later it becomes clear that the
narrator is being treated for having "lost the sense of history," in other words having lost the beliefs in sequence,
coherence, and totality that constitute and are mainstays
of the society we live in.

For the authorities, though, there are no excuses; the
story they are dedicated to preexists any decision one
might make about it, and it is the one they are determined
to hear. This "story" must have a beginning, a middle, and
an end—and it must be capable of a "summing up," pref-
erably with a detachable moral. These are people in power,
whose power is derived precisely from the unswerving
allegiance they swear to their ideas—which they treat as
absolutes. For them there is no such thing as disagree-
ment—there is only treason. The reason for them (and everything has a reason for *them*) that the narrator will not
tell them the story they want to hear is not that he is
unable but that he is unwilling. The function of the
"experts" they assign to his "case" is to break down his resistance by using the sophisticated techniques of bilateral

interrogation alluded to below to get him to tell them *their* story—that is, to pretend that there is such a thing as history, in which men are born, live, and die—and that this, and this only, is what existence is all about:

> I had been asked: Tell us *"just* exactly" what happened. A story? I began: I am not learned; I am not ignorant. I have known joys. That is saying too little. I told them the whole story and they listened, it seems to me, with interest, at least in the beginning. But the end was a surprise to all of us. "That was the beginning," they said. "Now get down to the facts." How so? The story was over!
> I had to acknowledge that I was not capable of forming a story out of these events. I had lost the sense of the story; that happens in a good many illnesses. But this explanation only made them more insistent. Then I noticed for the first time that there were two of them and that this distortion of the traditional method, even though it was explained by the fact that one of them was an eye doctor, the other a specialist in mental illness, constantly gave our conversation the character of an authoritarian interrogation, overseen and controlled by a strict set of rules. Of course neither of them was the chief of police. But because there were two of them, there were three, and this third remained firmly convinced, I am sure, that a writer, a man who speaks and who reasons with distinction, is always capable of recounting facts that he remembers.
> A story? No. No stories, never again. (*Madness of the Day*, 18)

The point that Derrida makes about the conclusion of this "story" is applicable to Blanchot's work in general and certainly to many of the most advanced elements of modern art. He notes "an essential *unfinishedness* that cannot be reduced to an incompleteness or an inadequacy."[29] The fragmented and unfinished quality of this art can in no way be explained as a deterioration either of ability or of will but is an intentional decision whose concomitant is the blurring of the separations upon which traditional art was based. The author invites the reader to finish, or better yet to continue, the work that has only been started, by leaving the work open, by refusing to "toe the line" or close the circle—by refusing to create the kind of work that can be digested by the culture and by insisting in sticking irremediably in the same culture's throat! The fragment that cannot be incorporated by a culture cannot be definitively rejected by it either, that is, relegated to that ghetto outside of time, history, and discourse that society reserves for such phenomena as manifest insanity and blatant sabotage that directly affront its order. The fragment instead has cunningly mastered and utilized the discourse of power (as Blanchot above very definitely *starts* his story) to the degree that order therein recognizes too much of itself to be able to expel the fragment totally without committing a kind of suicide too; like the wayward relative grudgingly supported by many a disgruntled family, the fragment survives and endures by means of intimidation.[30]

L'Attente l'oubli (*The Wait, the Oblivion*), published in 1962 by Gallimard, carries all these tendencies involved in this philosophy of the fragmentary as far as Blanchot, or anyone else that I know of, has taken them. In its lucid incoherence and acosmic ability to disorient, it stands as a kind of miniature *Finnegans Wake*. Here the fragment truly comes into its own, for the work is made up entirely of fragments. The characters (unnamed, naturally) are a "he" and a "she" about whom next to nothing is known except that he is some kind of writer and she is some kind of reader. In addition there is a dubious narrator who usually prefers the impersonal third-person singular but who also falls back at times into first or even second person, so that it is intentionally unclear whether it (the narrator) is talking about the characters, itself, to itself, or to us. The function of this "nonnarrator" is doubtless to destroy, or "deconstruct," any sense that is in danger of being made.

"Who is speaking?" (7) "she" asks "him" after reading a few of his lines, and this is a question like many others that is not meant to be answered, perhaps not meant to be asked. What was it that brought them together, the narra-

tor asks, was it chance? (8) and this question likewise remains without answer. Blanchot's favorite grammatical
construction is of the contrary-to-fact conditional type: "Il
aurait voulu avoir le droit de lui dire. . . ."* What's happening between the characters (l'événement) is not a fiction, but that doesn't mean it is true either: "Plus tard il
pense que l'événement consistait dans cette manière de
n'être ni vrai ni faux."† A hotel room where a conversation
takes place is totally nonspecific—it is any room, anywhere. The city they are in, the windows they look out of
are totally neutral too. It is as if the reader is waiting with
the characters (the reader is surely *one* of Blanchot's characters) someplace or anyplace and is hearing a word being
spoken without knowing for sure who exactly is speaking
and why. When the impersonal? narrator states, for instance, "Avec quelle mélancolie, mais quelle calme certi-
tude, il sentait qu'il ne pourrait plus jamais dire 'je,'"‡ the
reader may well wonder who or what really is speaking,
may wonder further, if this be the narrator, how he ob-
tained access to this rather specific bit of information and
whether indeed the third person here is not some kind of
feint to describe the inevitable first-person singular that
one just cannot bring oneself to say—in other words,
whether there isn't an author hiding somewhere behind
the ruses.

This narrative discontinuity is further enhanced by
numerous disturbing devices. In some of the fragments a
first-person narrator appears who calmly (it seems) commences to talk about himself—with no quotation marks,
or any other indication of shift in time, as when it is suddenly said: "Quelqu'un en moi converse avec lui-même.
Quelqu'un en moi converse avec quelqu'un."§

---

   * "He would have wished to have the right to say to her . . .";
L'Attente l'oubli, 11.
   † "Later he thinks that the event consisted in this way of being
neither true nor false"; *L'Attente l'oubli*, 13.
   ‡ "How sadly, but with what calm certainty, he sensed that he
would never again be able to say 'I'"; *L'Attente l'oubli*, 34.
   § "Someone in me is talking to himself, someone is talking with
someone"; *L'Attente l'oubli*, 46.

Whoever this last "quelqu'un" is supposed to be the reader can only guess, and in fact is probably only supposed to guess. The fact is that nothing is more shocking, in life or in art, than to hear a first-person voice being expressed where none was expected, as if our tools suddenly started to talk to us, or as if a stranger on a train were to say to us, without preamble, and inexplicably, "As I was saying."

Just as in Brecht's theory of theater, which I have referred to so frequently in these pages, the audience is invited to distance itself from the hypnotic and therefore noxious effects of the spectacle and to think of how what they are seeing connects with life outside the theater, so is Blanchot's reader *forced* outside[31] the text, if only to wonder if the explanation he is searching for might not lie outside this or any text. When, for instance, Blanchot introduces the refrain, "*Fais en sorte que je puisse te parler,*"* he writes it in italics. This of course alerts the reader that something special is going on, but what is it that the reader is supposed to be *particularly* aware of? This phrase has in fact just been dropped on the page as if it fell out of the sky and landed in the book. There is no narrative preparation for it and absolutely no clue to who is talking. It is as if *the book was talking,* an eerie effect similar to that which Beckett achieves in the unidentifiable rant that constitutes *The Unnamable.* The mystery is compounded as the "*fais en sorte que je puisse te parler*" is repeated three times in three pages—each time in italics—as if the reader were a tourist who was lost in a strange city and had circled the same block three times to see the same meaningless (to him) sign. By now we have been lost long enough to know our way around, but do we? Persevering to page 57, the obstinate reader then is relieved to find this same phrase supplied now comfortably

---

* "So act so that I can talk to you"; *L'Attente l'oubli,* 24. This probably is a subversive development of Kant's categorical imperative: act so that what you do can be considered a universal rule of conduct. We may register all the difference between a classical and modern temper in the evolution from Kant's universal moral *rule* to Blanchot's existential amoral *demand.*

with quotation marks and introduced as something that "she" has said frequently to "him."[32] The narrator then assures us in his dubiously reliable third-person style that "il ne pourrait plus jamais oublier cette prière,"* where-upon the reader will perhaps wonder what makes it a prayer and how this narrator who does not seem to know what he will say next is suddenly omniscient enough to know that "he" will *never again* forget it.

A little later on the reader seems to be directly ad-dressed by the narrator: "N'est-ce pas ainsi que vivent les dieux? Solitaires, uniques, étranger à la lumière dont ils brillent. Ils me dérangeaient peu"† ... and by the end of this passage Blanchot introduces a "we" that presumably includes author, narrator, reader, characters, and all of extant humanity: "Les anciens dieux, les anciens dieux, comme ils sont proches de nous."‡ The assumptions of this last sentence, aside from the incredible arrogance of the repetition—as if that were to make this absurdity any more acceptable—are, strictly speaking, remarkable: as if we were suddenly on the most intimate footing with some-one we just met, who knows our most intimate feelings and is entitled to speak of us in conjunction with himself. The narrator becomes suddenly our best friend of the mo-ment with whom we have perhaps just taken shelter from the same stormy text under cover of the same porous roof.

Elsewhere the narrator addresses himself familiarly as "tu" and seems to blend it in with the "he" it? has created, as in the fragment on page 73: "Ce que tu as écrit détient le secret ... et toi, c'est seulement parce qu'il t'a écharpé que tu as pu le transcrire."§ Finally what seems to happen in this work is that certain words acquire a peculiar density and resonance that make them independent of the "secrets"

---

* "He would never again be able to forget this entreaty."

† "Isn't this how the gods live? Solitary, unique, strange to the very light with which they shine. They didn't bother me much"; *L'At-tente l'oubli*, 66.

‡ "The old gods, the old gods, how close they are to us"; *L'Attente l'oubli*, 67.

§ "What you've written contains the secret ... and you, it's only because you've missed it that you've been able to write it down."

they transcribe. Words like "attrait, don, oubli, commencement, attente, douleur."* These words acquire a life of their
own, almost like a modern cabala,[33] and seem to use humans more than they are used: "Elle parle, parlée plutôt
que parlant, comme si sa propre parole la traversait
vivante et la transformait douloureusement en l'espace
d'une autre parole."† This is not to say that the words of
L'Attente l'oubli can be understood or "tamed." Just like
children who are one step ahead of their parents' attempts
to control them, Blanchot's words are always up to new
tricks just when you think you are beginning to figure out
the old ones.

Blanchot's method is neither that of accretion nor of
palimpsest; the snake sheds its old skin before it puts on a
new one; and the new one is for all practical purposes the
only one it has ever worn. The meaning, the message, the
center is there—but it is unfindable in that you'll never be
able to put your finger on it: "Il cherche, tournant et
retournant avec, au centre, cette parole et sachant que
trouver c'est seulement chercher encore par rapport au
centre, qui est l'introuvable."‡ Blanchot's butterfly will
never be "pinned and wriggling on the wall" to satisfy an
obscene science's obsessive need to classify. *His fragment
will always fly away as there is nothing to hold it down.*

The fragment, as Blanchot conceives it, and as he indefatigably argues in a recent book, *L'Écriture du désastre* (*Writing of Disaster*, 1980), is neither a negation nor an affirmation. Fragmentary writing comes into play when language,
"having exhausted its power of negation, of affirmation, has
put ... knowledge to rest" (80); it is a "writing outside of
language, nothing else possibly than the end (without end)
of knowledge, and of myths and of utopia. . . . "

---

* "Attraction, gift, oblivion, beginning, sadness."

† "She speaks, spoken rather than speaking, as if her own words
passed through her living flesh and transformed her sadly into the
space of another word"; *L'Attente l'oubli*, 150.

‡ "He's searching, turning and returning with, at the center, this
word—and knowing that to find is only to seek again in relation to the
center that is the impossible-to-find"; *L'Attente l'oubli*, 132.

He who has said *no* to being, essence, system, history has only shown that he believes firmly in the permanence of his own negation as well as that of the structure he attacks: "Dire non, c'est dire avec éclat que le non est destiné à préserver."*

The *disaster* that fragmentary writing conveys is not an event that happens in historical time. We customarily date the modern epoch from the Copernican and Galilean hypotheses that unseat man from a central place and role in the cosmos; but although no longer central, man still existed in rapport with an enduring structure and was to some extent sheltered by a certain relation or lack of relation to what he perceived to be the truth. The disaster of which Blanchot speaks strikes at what is left of certainty after the discoveries of the Renaissance abolished man's centrality. Blanchot cites as symptomatic of our common disaster Bataille's stunning formulation "The sun no longer exists." That is, we who have been moved around in the cosmos have now shuffled off of it entirely. *Disastrous* is the adjective Blanchot uses to describe our contemporary nonrelation to any cosmos. *Dé-s-astre* brings forth the idea of being separated from the astral, from the stars and heavens: and fragmentary writing takes place then under no sky, on no earth, and outside of historical time, just as the *récits* of Blanchot have evolved over the years to a stripped or *dépouillé* condition that estranges them from all tangible root, contingency, circumstance, or location:[34] "fragmentaire sans fragment ce reste à écrire qui, à la façon du désastre, a toujours précédé, en le ruinant, tout commencement d'écriture et de parole."†

The fragmentary word neither affirms nor denies; its existence is unnecessary, implausible, unproved, unfindable, untraceable. It neither takes place nor does it fail to take place. There is no authorial "I" to take credit for it, to begin it, or to bring it to any conclusion. The fragment neither

---

* "To say no is to say with insistence that the no is destined to endure"; *L'Écriture du désastre*, 102.

† "Fragmentary without fragment what's left to write, which, like a disaster, has always preceded, in ruining it, all beginning of writing and the word"; *L'Écriture du désastre*, 199.

begins nor ends: "Tout commencement est recommence-
ment."* You don't write it, it lets itself be written, though
there is nothing automatic about it. It is like a disaster
that "ruins everything while leaving all exactly the way it
was" (7); for the fragment, theories are fine and necessary
(including the theory of the fragment) but also profoundly
interchangeable. Likewise, fragmentary writing does not
militate against any particular law but just observes with
a little humor: "Le dessein de la loi: que les prisonniers
construisent eux-mêmes leur prison. C'est le moment du
concept, la marque du système."†

Unlike the aphorism, the fragment neither evolves nor
is it perfectible. You cannot succeed with a fragment. The
fragment uses words as if they were a form of silence; what
counts, as when we speak to each other in friendship or
intimacy, is an undertone, what Blanchot and also Tzara
call a "cri"[35] or appeal underlying everything we say, for all
the sense these wandering words make is read into them
by the insistent reader or critic who has his own dialectical exigency (God) or ideology to satisfy. The sense of
Blanchot lies more in the French "sens" as direction, not a
meaning but a movement. To say you can't succeed with
fragments, that they come from and go toward no unity, is
also to say you can't fail with them either: "Put no trust in
failure, that would only betray your nostalgia for success"
(25).

Where literature, culture, art, and philosophy stop, and
where progress can push no further, that is where the
fragment suddenly comes up against us. The fragment
does not contend with or try to modify the dominant disciplines and ideas (it is not "teachable" and therefore can
never assume a place in any syllabus, program, or curriculum). It lets the dominant disciplines and ideas gradually
exhaust themselves in their increasingly obvious futility.
What we are incapable of saying, explaining, or expressing
by any theoretical structure—the reality and impossibility

---

* "To start is to start over."
† "The strategy of the law: that prisoners build their own prisons.
It's the moment of the concept, the mark of the system"; *L'Écriture du
désastre*, 76.

of death, the nonrelation between our ideals and our practice and between our dreams and our waking life, the
horrors of Auschwitz, the bomb, and the Gulag that we're
just starting to be able to talk about, and that no system
of knowledge, no dialectic can justify or rationalize without
demonstrating its own complicity— here the fragment has
something to say (for the fragment the bomb has *always*
just dropped) and contribute, because it doesn't con-
ceptualize these events; it merely listens to them and
thinks about them in sadness: "Apprends à penser avec
douleur. . . . Douleur elle désunit, mais non pas d'une
manière visible (par une dislocation ou une disjonction qui
serait spectaculaire): d'une manière silencieuse, faisant
taire le bruit derrière les paroles."[*]

The fragmentary writer does not oppose (he may even
support) all that Systems or Revolutions can do. He lets
them have their say, and when they have finished, takes
over what is left, what remains. He writes not out of a will
or a desire to write, or for gain, fame, glory, distinction, or
out of deep sorrow or overwhelming joy. He treats his writing as a sign, on the contrary, that his will has failed him.
He *falls* into writing more than he rises up to it, so that
what he says is merely a reminder of what cannot be said.
Like a Narcissus who does not recognize himself in his
own image, the fragmentary writer cannot see himself in
his own productions. He will of course admit to an examining magistrate, "I wrote that," but inwardly he does not
believe it or knows that it makes no difference. He is not
corroborated, not strengthened and made more secure by
what he has previously put down on paper. After all, however well received, these were just things he was *forced* to
say at the time. His old phrases then may even work
against him: "Elles réintroduisent une assurance à
laquelle on croyait avoir cessé d'appartenir, elles ont un
air de vérité, elles disent: tu a pensé cela il y a longtemps,
tu es donc autorisé à le penser de nouveau, restaurant

---

[*] "Learn to think with sadness. . . . Sadness separates, but not
visibly (in a dislocation or a disjunction that would be spectacular):
silently, to silence the noise behind words"; *L'Écriture du désastre*,
219–20.

cette continuité raisonnable qui fait les systèmes, faisant jouer au passé une fonction de garantie, le laissant devenir actif, citateur, incitateur, et empêchant l'invisible ruine que la veille perpetuelle, hors conscience inconscience, rend au neutre."*

He writes then "against the grain," reluctantly, having no confidence either in the power of words (or their nonpower) or the possibility or advisability of the "other" (reader, culture) responding to them. Paradoxically, he can be a writer only in the sense that he is not a *writer.* "On ne peut que devenir écrivain sans l'être jamais: dès qu'on l'est, on ne l'est plus."† Just as no man is a prophet in his own land, the fragmentary writer is forever exiled from the land of writing; and it does him no good to lose that "I" so precious and so bothersome to us in the West, the *ego* that Montaigne, Schopenhauer, Stirner, Gide have alternately glorified or excoriated. In the *nouveau roman* of Sarraute, Simon, Pinget, Robbe-Grillet, as well as the "ready for anything" explorations and divagations of Sollers and his "tribe," remnants of that "subject" that so much is made of losing are easy enough to find in the debris, if only in their characteristic styles; but Blanchot's disaster is more nearly allied to the double-bind frustrations of mad Artaud: "le moi ne se perd pas parce qu'il ne s'appartient pas. Il n'est donc moi que comme non appartenant à soi, et donc comme toujours déjà perdu."‡ Responsibility for this state of affairs is primordial and innate. Though praise and blame are to be eschewed,

---

* "They reintroduce an assurance that one has ceased to possess, they have an air of truth about them, they say: you thought that a long time ago, you're therefore authorized to think it again, restoring the reasonable continuity that makes systems, making the past fulfill the function of guarantee, making it become active, citing, inciting, and preventing the invisible ruin, outside of consciousness-unconsciousness that a perpetual wake, in complete neutrality, renders"; *L'Écriture du désastre,* 97.

† "You can become a writer only be never being one: as soon as you are you're one no longer"; *L'Écriture du désastre,* 101.

‡ "The self isn't lost because it wasn't *there* in the first place. There is only a 'me' insofar as it isn't there and therefore is always already lost"; *L'Écriture du désastre,* 105; italics mine.

since there is no freely choosing subject to fix them upon ("all faults are faults of position"), we are born responsible for a situation that we did not create. The fragmentary writer, who like Blanchot has been contemporary with the unspeakable horrors of the twentieth century, who has *lived through the war,* has the responsibility somehow to disseminate his attitude that life cannot go on as it was. Without pretending to be able to explain these events, we have had to admit that a kind of turning point has been reached; we don't hold our heads up quite so high as before, as humanity seems a creation more damned than blessed and more to be pitied than damned.

We moderns can go nowhere, neither into life (it is too late for that) nor death (we have already died—at Auschwitz and Hiroshima), only repeat, monotonously, insistently, unchangeably, a litany of regret, an inaudible cry —a testimony not even meant to be read or heard, except by inconsequential accident, the way we see graffiti from a passing train or catch a glimpse of a stranger's face in pain. This is what our fragmented lives and writing mean . . . and not *even* that.

6
The Endless Question:
Finnegans Wake, 1, 6

I

Book 1, 6, of *Finnegans Wake* (126–68) starts with a brief introductory passage that sets our scene in (a kind of) space and time. Shem then begins his interrogation with a question to end all questions, a question so long, involved, abstruse, and absurd that it is a question in name only. The voice and mood here are in an epic register; but what is it that is being enunciated, celebrated, announced in this avalanche, this rain, this thunderstorm, this earthquake of words? The *reading* here is some of the easiest in the *Wake*. The clauses, connected by semicolons, that stretch over these thirteen densely packed pages all relate back to the same interrogatory subject. Those infamous Wakean sentences that never end and seem never to have begun, that crawl like long snakes around our consciousness, are less conspicuous here. Joyce's phrases instead now are short, abrupt, often staccato and naturalistic; fairly plain English even peeks through now and then:

> business, reading newspaper, smoking cigar, arranging tumblers on table, eating meals, pleasure, etcetera, etcetera, pleasure, eating meals, arranging tumblers on table, smoking cigar, reading newspaper, business; minerals, wash and brush up, local views, juju toffee, comic and birthday cards, those were the days and he was their hero. (127)

It is not as if there isn't still plenty to wonder about; for one thing, the sheer diversity of the utterance is never more dazzling and awe-inspiring; but lists, even abstruse, surreal, and endless ones like this, make for comparatively easy reading. Lists tend to be selective, exhaustive, mono-logical, and exhausting—as well as comforting. We habit-ually put things we want to acquire or do on lists and thereby assume that reality can be controlled and things accomplished; and we habitually resort to lists in moods of confusion and dissatisfaction. Particularly serviceable is the kind of list that *covers everything,* or has ambitions to do so, as if we will eventually hit the target if we just keep firing. Such is the list that Shem here supplies; its com-plexity and diversity are compensated for by the terrible simplicity of a question that is sufficient unto itself and is its own answer. Thematically, all the descriptive items here refer to the archetypical conglomerate and nexus of the Father; and this list is, in fact, a halcyon biography that mixes elements pell-mell from many disparate realms, including (among an infinitude of others) history, politics, mythology, geography, war, perversion, and religion—as if the Father were somehow the sum total of all these ava-tars. Also, a consistently maintained tone of epic enco-mium surrounds this larger-than-life creature and bal-ances in the larger scale of the *Wake* the comical-caustic denigration of an earlier list "of all the abusive names he was called" (71–72).

Joyce's literary precedent in thus "mythifying" his hero is, of course, Rabelaisian hyperbole. HCE (Here Comes Everybody)

> lights his pipe with a rosin tree and hires a towhorse to haul his shoes; cures slavey's scurvy, breaks barons boils; called to sell polosh and was found later in a bedroom; has his seat of justice, his house of mercy, his corn o'copious and his stacks a'rye; prospector, he had a rooksacht, retrospector, he holds the holpenstake; won the freedom of new yoke for the minds of jugo-slaves; acts active, peddles in passivism and is a gorgon of selfridgeousness . . . (137)

By the use of a familiar and time-honored style like the "gargantuan" above, Joyce seems to be facilitating the forward progress of his reader, just as elsewhere in the *Wake* he makes every effort to slow him down or even stop him completely in his tracks. The "what" with which the question has begun (126: "What secondtonone myther rector and maximost bridgesmaker was first to rise taller") provides a certain minimal direction and structure for the numberless clauses that follow; the forest may become deep but the way back is clearly marked, so one advances boldly into these thickets. However experimental Joyce gets within the clauses in vocabulary, mutant and invented words, and sheer anomaly of the diction and its referents,[1] he sets limits on how lost the reader can become, for the end of each clause always throws him back to the controlling structure of the initial interrogation. We are, of course, here as always in *Finnegans Wake,* in the position of a reader who is in the process of learning how to read in a foreign language, but now the learner's task has been explicitly facilitated, insofar as he has been supplied prior access to at least one solid level of an argument—in the same way that a book, movie, or broadcast in an unfamiliar language is likely to make more sense if we have some idea beforehand of what is going to be said.

Our hypothetically obdurate reader knows already—through a few skirmishes with the nine lines introducing the chapter and perhaps through the help of Campbell and Robinson's *Key,* Tindall's *Reader's Guide,*[2] and other commentaries that, on one level at least, something very basic and familiar is taking place, something that has a theatrical nature and setting: "Who do you no tonigh, lazy and gentleman?" (126), namely, one of the fundamental rituals of our culture—the examination and/or public interrogation: "this nightly quisquiquock." The test, the examination is a ritual at once threatening and comforting; the threat lies in one's being put on the spot to answer, and *well,* for one's time; the comfort is in the assumptions both that one's knowledge counts and that there are answers to the questions that life poses. At this point in the *Wake* the "reassuring" aspects of the ritual dominate.

Whether the reader has made it this far into the text or is just looking for a reasonable place to browse, the binary and dyadic structure (inherent in the question-answer format), even if it turns out to be only a semblance, mockery, or parody of one, must seem like an oasis of stability and substance in the *Wake*'s ocean of limitless referentiality. Reinforcing these more or less dependable but certainly welcome hints at a controlling structure for the chapter, Joyce, so scrupulous about removal of scaffolding after completion of the work,[3] has made a point here of letting the numbers stand. We may not know what the questions or answers are, what they mean or why they are being asked and answered; we may not even be able to tell, at times, a question from an answer, or we may forget in the digressions, amplifications, and divagations of the text that there are questions being asked and answered; but we always know which number it is, we know how many are behind us and how many we have to go.

Whatever the complexity, though, of the later interrogations and responses, here in the first of the questions Joyce is making the reading flow as much as it ever does in the *Wake*. That typically obscuring tactic of the run-on (non)sentence, whereby Joyce so frequently "loses" his reader by dint of erasing his tracks in a kind of illimitable confusing present, is absent here where the clauses all refer so compellingly to the initial question.

The comparative clarity and consistency of the grammar here is paralleled by an analogous reliability in thematic referentiality. HCE is the constant subject of concern, preoccupation, and focus, and his numberless avatars and manifestations all point to a figure that the reader grasps and accepts (in the sense of Coleridge's "willing suspension of disbelief") as being somehow larger or other than life; he is therefore not subject to correction by our merely human criteria of time and space, common sense, and logic. HCE is at home everywhere, in all times and places; the totality of the visible and invisible world and all possible realms of spirit, psyche, and imagination are subject to invasion by his energy, power, and influence:

as far as wind dries and rain eats and sun turns and
water bounds he is exalted and depressed, assembled
and asundered; go away, we are deluded, come back, we
are disghosted; bored the Ostrov, leapt the Inferus,
swam the Mabbul and flure the Moyle; like fat, like fat-
like tallow, or greasefulness, yea of dripping greasefulness; did not say to the old, old, did not say to the
scorbutic, scorbutic; he has founded a house, Uru, a
house he has founded to which he has assigned its fate;
bears a raaven geulant on a fjeld duiv; ruz the halo off
his varlet when he appeared to his shecook as Haycock,
Emmet, Boaro, Toaro, Osterich, Mangy and Skunk;
pressed the beer of aled age out of the nettles of
rashness; put a roof on the lodge for Hymn and a coq in
his pot pro homo; was dapifer then pancircensor then
hortifex magnus; the topes that tippled on him, the
types that toppled on him; still starts our hares yet
gates our goat; pocketbook packetboat, gapman gun-
run; the light of other days, dire dreary darkness; our
awful dad, Timour of Tortur; puzzling, startling, shocking, nay, perturbing; went puffing from king's brugh to
new customs, doffing the gibbous off him to every
breach of all size; with Pa's new hef and Papa's new
helve he's Papapa's old cutlass Papapapa left us; when
young-headed oldshouldered and middlishneck aged
about; caller herring everydaily, turgid tarpon overnight; see Loryon the comaleon that changed endocrine
history by loeven his loaf with forty bannucks; (136)

Joyce here is throwing the paint on his canvas in large
blobs of color, giving the brush a few brisk turns, then
looking back to his palette for a new hue. Now in the
throes of his riotous first question we are in the midst of,
as Lessing never dreamed it could be, writing as an art of
space.[4] A characteristic of the modernist text has certainly
been an emphasis on a spatial, as opposed to a temporal,
pole of writing—and a corresponding focus, as in the
nouveau roman, on the descriptive as opposed to the narrative functions of the text. The effect of this displacement
has been to de-thematize, de-psychologize, and de-moral-

ize writing by locating it in a dimension of pure autonomy and intransitivity, where it no longer has to *mean* but can simply *be*.[5]

Seeds of narration live on though, in their modest, insistent way. Diachrony is not utterly forgotten nor completely transgressed, for stories, like tenacious grass in ruptured paving, have a way of peeking through this hyperbolic, synchronic edifice:

> heavengendered, chaosfoedted, earthborn; his father presumptively ploughed it deep on overtime and his mother as all evince must have travailled her fair share; a footprinse on the Megacene, hetman unwhorsed by Searingsand; honorary captain of the extemporised fire brigade, reported to be friendly with the police; the door is still open; the old stock collar is coming back; not forgetting the time you laughed at Elder Charterhouse's duckwhite pants and the way you said the whole township can see his hairy legs; by stealth of a kersse her aulburntress abaft his nape she hung; when his kettle became a hearthsculdus our thorstyites set their lymphyamphyre; his year-letter concocted my masterhands of assays, his hallmark imposed by the standard of wrought plate; a pair of pectorals and a triplescreen to get a wind up. (137)

The staccato exigency of his overwhelming question make it impossible or unnecessary for Shem to do any more than hint at stories yet to be told or ones that lie beneath the surface and never can be told but whose existence is just meant to be sensed in a rudimentary way. Certainly one of the most pervasive effects that Joyce achieves here lies in this skill of his to evoke the existence of powerful and perdurable currents of narration that run beneath the surface of his description and occasionally erupt like geysers into full view. Joyce, like Mallarmé, values suggestion over definition. He would rather hint at yet-to-be-discovered recesses than tell us what never happened as if it did. For Joyce, as for Mallarmé,[6] "facts" are the grossest of fictions (frequent in the *Wake* is the neologism "ficfact"),[7] and there is more truth for him in the wildest of rumors than in the most compendious and apparently exhaustive of academic treatises. This accounts for the tremendous respect shown in the *Wake* for gossip, hearsay, and the kind of snatches of information and scandal that one gleans haphazardly from sources like advertisements, newspaper headlines, propaganda, folksongs, jokes, and all such imponderables.

Shem's strange monologue in the form of a question invites a more comfortable reading than does the rest of the *Wake*, for however wild the words and referents get, the reader knows who is talking and about what. But what Joyce gives us with one hand he always takes away with the other, for in another sense, reader participation is repelled by the relentless, unilateral rush of the thirteen pages of delivery. The monolith of this first question is meant to be gaped at in astonishment, amusement, confusion, and disbelief rather than related to; it is an astounding tour de force that cannot be "digested" any more than can be a pyramid; nothing here is real (for long) or natural; everything is exaggerated, uncanny, unsuspected, and extreme. It would take a god (no merely mortal reader) to identify with this infinitely refracted panoply that comprises HCE; and certainly he is not, or not only, a character in a book but a living symbol, "the word made flesh," a catalyst, inspiration, a source and focus of energy, a perpetual and compulsive process of production, and a sublime mockery or parody of everything he is reported to be, who

> with one touch of nature set a veiled world agrin and went within a sheet of tissuepaper of the option of three goals; who could see at one blick a saumon taken with a lance, hunters pursuing a doe, a swallowship in full sail, a whyterobe lifting a host; faced flappery like old King Cnut and turned his back like Cincinnatus; is a farfar and morefar and a hoar father Nakedbucker in villas old and new; squats aquart and cracks aquaint when it's flaggin in town and on haven; blows whiskery around his summit but stehts stout upon his footles;

stutters fore he falls and goes mad entirely when he's
waked; is Timb to the pearly morn and Tomb to the
mourning night; and an he had the best bunbaked
bricks in bould Babylon for his pitching plays he'd be
lost for the want of his wan wubblin wall?
      Answer: Finn MacCool! (138–39)

This machine-in-perpetual-motion incarnates and ex-
emplifies a principle of constant flux and dynamism that
underlies *Finnegans Wake*.[8] If to judge is to "fix" things in
time and space, then HCE is impossible to judge, almost
impossible to conceive or think about.[9] HCE won't stay
long enough in one place for us to make up our minds
about him or conceive what he is, was, and will be. For
here the temporal dimension and with it the laws of cause
and effect are utterly elided.[10] There is never any cause, or
any sufficient one certainly, why HCE is one place rather
than another, does what he does, and is what he is; the
rapid alternations, contrasts, shifts in color, register, and
tone ensure that the only solid idea a reader can maintain
is that of many different HCEs. Above all there is no
standard of truth or reality to appeal to or rely on through
his peregrinations and metamorphoses—most of which are
couched anyway in terms of reported gossip, hearsay, and
other unreliable sources. We are, to employ David Hayman's neat formulation, "doubly distanced"[11] from our
hero, first because we know of him only what is said,
second because these reports, scattered, contradictory,
rhetorical, and fragmentary, float in a kind of gravity-free
space of language, disconnected from any single unquali-
fiable anchor of meaning. HCE ultimately is just a magnificent collection of images, guaranteed by no reality, cause,
purpose, or source —just simply there, as a mountain of
words resting on thin air or a sunset over a nonexistent
sea. Human existence and the communication with others
that commonly gives it meaning tend to be reduced or
expanded, in this perspective, to versions of the purely
mythical or literary, like an invented letter that alludes to
a love affair that might have been: "Dear Hewitt Castello,
Equerry, were daylighted with our outing and are looking

backwards to unearly summers, from Rhoda Dundrums" (135).

The existence of time in HCE's world of signs undergoes a mutation[12] that corresponds to his "liberation" from contingency, since here is a character who moves and acts in a dimension that is far removed from any allegiance to practical exigencies. Here indeed is a creature who was never born, nursed, reared, or educated but burst fully grown (at no specific moment) as if from the forehead of Zeus. Along with any rational sense of a slow evolution in time, of precedence and "before and after," HCE similarly explodes the laws of cause and effect. It makes as much sense if not more to say that the past is caused by the present as the other way around, since HCE rewrites history to suit Joyce's rhetorical needs of the moment. Similarly, the future becomes the already-has-been. The recent, the long ago, the far-into-the-future are compressed here into a single tense that the *Wake* likes to call the "pressant."[13] This apparently is a kind of dreamlike time that liberates the subject from the trammels and limits of his own and others' contingency, and wherein he assumes a godlike mobility. He relates in this dimension equally to and with his own past and future avatars, as well as indifferently to the dead, the living, and the yet unborn—as this dream-logic, exceptional in the life of the normal man, becomes the very rule of his world. In the *Wake* the dream is never over.

Above all, the subject in this oneiric landscape is not exposed to that inherently human quandary of choosing to pursue one direction at the expense of another. There is no "road not taken" here. Intrinsically and perhaps tragically human is the situation where choice becomes destiny. Deciding on any particular activity is tantamount to excluding others. Even to think, to concentrate on any matter, is to define everything else as momentarily irrelevant: "conclure, c'est exclure" ("to conclude is to exclude").[14] Now characteristic of HCE is a tendency to refuse this exclusion: to think and act and yet be infinitely available for all other thoughts and actions; to do, feel, be, think, sense, and know everything; in a word, to accomplish an impossible project of including all within one's purview.

HCE embodies this godlike exemption from the limitations and quandaries of mere *human* existence, that is, of ordinary waking life, since for him the exceptional, the miraculous, the uncanny have become the rule. Birth and death, both his own and others', those perpetual parameters of life, become for HCE mere words, figures of speech that can be altered or erased to meet the desires of the moment. Everywhere the limitations of reality and language yield to the onslaught of his unqualified being; not only is he larger than life, he is other than real, as he

> changes blowicks into bullocks and a well of Artesia into a bird of Arabia; the handwriting on his facewall, the cryptoconchoidsiphonostomata in his exprussians; his birthspot lies beyond the herospont and his burial-plot in the pleasant little field; is the yldist kiosk on the pleninsula and the unguest hostel in Saint Scholarland; walked many hundreds and many score miles of streets and lit thousands in one nightlights in hectares of windows; his great wide cloak lies on fifteen acres and his little white horse decks by dozens our doors; O sorrow the sail and woe the rudder that were set for Mairie Quail!; his suns the huns, his dartars the tartars, are plenty here today; who repulsed from his burst the bombolts of Ostenton and falchioned each flash downsaduck in the deep; a personal problem, a locative enigma; upright one, vehicule of arcanisation in the field, lying chap, flood-supplier of celiculation through ebblanes; a part of the whole as a port for a whale. (135)

HCE will not be "pinned down" and defined not only because he is perpetually being re-defined, re-explained, and re-presented but because the language that captures him is in a permanent state of mutation and evolution. The language acts like a sieve that lets everything through but sense. We cannot say therefore that we ever know HCE unqualifiably one way or the other; nor can we ever say that we have even approached knowledge of him, for though the imagery may seem occasionally fathomable, though contradictory and immediately brought into question by the next flight of words, the very orthography pushes us away, as if the words themselves were subject to a kind of slippage of meaning and referent, were denied the glue that makes them stick to objects in the so-called real world, leaving behind a kind of shell, remnant, or residue of meaning, though conveying the kind of heavy emotional charge characteristic perhaps of psychotic discourse: "ace of arts, deuce of damimonds, trouble of clubs, fear of spates" (134).

It is as if this language were a body whose integument was attacked by a virus or some other infectious and discoloring mechanism that has altered its appearance visibly and irrevocably but left enough of the original intact to leave it teasingly recognizable. The Joycean onslaught on language itself thus is not even totally unqualified. Joyce destroys but not utterly. The "ace of hearts, two of diamonds, three of clubs, and four of spades" still lurk visibly behind the newly created entities, enriched now with a few more layers of intimation and suggestion. Joyce has moved the word then to a point where it no longer means exactly what it used to, nor does it mean or not mean exactly anything else either. This is perhaps the sense of the famous "operation" that Joyce performs upon the living body of language and from which all of us involved in the study and practice of literature are still experiencing the fallout.[15] He has disturbed, and profoundly, the link between signifier and signified, making it seem tenuous, alterable, and ambiguous, making us unsure what we really mean when we think we are talking about things; he has loosened and stretched that tie, replacing definition and substance everywhere with connotation and suggestion, moving language massively from the pole of prose to that of poetry, and in the process blurring the distinction between the two: "So?/Who do you no tonigh, lazy and gentleman" (126).

The above are words that are neither transparent for any definite message nor sufficient unto themselves. They occupy an indeterminate realm that is the Joycean terrain par excellence, where words cannot make up their minds what they say or cannot say and where all is hesitation, ambiguity, and uncertainty. The question that Joyce poses is at once endless and unanswerable. Any answer that is supplied comes through as mere formality or as a further extension of the question which, properly speaking, is infinite. Is indeed there any sense through this interminable first question, which eventually is cut off rather than ends, that our two-word answer, "Finn MacCool!", which we have surely anticipated and consulted, is going to solve anything? All that can be known "for sure" merely adds to our ignorance, as on a map where all the indications lead away from our destination—*which can be shown on no map.*

In this quasi-mystical perspective, which may remind one distantly of the "negative theology" of Boehme and Eckhart, the things we think we know turn out to be obstacles and ignorance. Our "knowledge" is a negative rather than a positive quantity, a "no," that is, a negation and denial, fruit of our impatience and frustration, rather than "know"-ledge. We can get closer "tonigh"(t), but that doesn't mean we'll know any more when dawn breaks. We can slide up and down and back and forth across the slippery and nonresistant surface of Joyce's endless attempts to circumscribe, present, hide, reveal, and veil HCE, but we will never come to *know* him, for the one rule we cannot violate here is the absolute proscription of any stability or fixation.

There is no point of rest in the Joycean cosmos, no central place,[16] or strategic post, no privileged point of view from which the rest can be surveyed. The text itself, far from pretending to the status of sacred object, was and is subject to constant correction, emendation, and reinterpretation. HCE "like a heptagon crystal emprisoms trues and fauss for us; is infinite swell in unfitting induments" (127). We must be satisfied instead with the multifarious images and the corresponding concept of language whereby "true" and "false" are no longer absolute standards but merely words among words and as such subject to the same mordant acid of mutation and evolution that affects the languages as a whole. What is left of the "false" when "fauss" is put in its place, or of "truth" that has become merely "trues"? Is it more or less, better or worse? We can't say for sure and even if we could we probably would change our minds eventually, as time works its changes upon the reader also. All we know is that "trues" and "fauss" are other than true and false and have perhaps invaded each other's domains[17]—and that when we look into this "heptagon crystal," certainly another attempt of the *Wake*'s at self-description,[18] we are more likely to be fascinated by the changing play of light, pattern, and color than enriched by any solid contribution to our stocks of knowledge. Furthermore, once we look into this crystal, we are subject to the rules of the prism ("emprisoms"), which privilege no abstract prior entity but change the world according to the exigencies of the prism's structure. The Father, then, seen through the prism of the language of this first indefinitely refracted question, is likely to emerge as a paradoxical, ambiguous, and tenuous being.

If the Father has been, historically and traditionally, the locus of all stability and certainty, the surety of an origin and that we come from and are going to somewhere, then what is manifest here is a massive dislocation of this image. The Father can no longer be relied on; he has been fractured into a million shimmering shards. If, furthermore, the Father is identified with sense, structure, authority, and law (*grammar*, in short), then all of these are threatened too. Joyce has effected an Einsteinian revolution in the meaning of the figure of paternity. The Father as lawgiver, norm, standard, and judge is no longer possible to locate; he has become a vector of historical change, a victim of "progress," evinced and exploded by the pressure of the contradictions he was not able to master—he has passed in sardonic apotheosis into the centerless vacuum of limitless space; for the Father's position, always untenable, has become impossible; the contradiction of his role lay in the difficulty in conciliating his political and social function as father figure with the weakness to which all flesh is heir. Hence the Joycean obsession with the strangely haunting case of the Irish leader Parnell, ruined by sexual scandal—as shown, for instance, by the massive presence of the word "hesitancy"[19] (a misspelling of which was convoluted evidence of the Church's plot against Parnell) in myriad allusions and versions: HCE "is un*hesitent* in his unionism and yet a *pigott*ed nationalist" (133).*

As certain unforgettable pages of *A Portrait of the Artist* make clear,[20] the fall of Parnell left all of Ireland a confused and disillusioned orphan. In a climactic early scene of *Portrait,* Stephen Dedalus's individual sense of abandonment and loss, affected by bitter quarrels in his family about the case, is transmogrified in a feverish dream into a universal vision of pathos and emptiness.[21] The Telemachus motif that underlies the structure of *Ulysses* thematically also has much to do with this nostalgia for a vanished absolute; but here on the terrain of the *Wake* we are no longer in the realm of wishful thinking, or dreaming at the limit. *Finnegans Wake* will no longer make sense out of a world that doesn't make sense to begin with; it is no longer searching for a standard to go by, for a god to replace the one that has died, or for a kind of modern absolute. *Finnegans Wake* brings no new answers to the age-old questions but instead shows these questions for what they are—basically senseless, obsolete, and functionally *unanswerable.*

Past a certain point of development the rhetorical device of amplification,[22] so intrinsic to the creation of *Finnegans Wake,* turns out to be a technique of annihilation. Saying too much about something may be a surer way of reducing it to ashes than saying too little or even nothing (when we say little or nothing there is still implied that something might be said, if not by us then by others, if not now then sooner or later). By saying as much as can possibly be said and more, Joyce is reducing the object of his lucubrations to dust; and nowhere is this negative process more comically active than in his celebration of the Father of question one. By maintaining the concentration of his

---

* Pigott played a signal role in the case against Parnell; italics mine—PB.

focus, piling haphazard rumor upon improbable event, upon wild and striking metaphor, figure, analogy, and contrast, what ultimately is circumscribed turns out to be a nullity—as if to prove the point that if you keep talking about the same thing long enough you will wind up talking about nothing, or not knowing or caring what you are talking about (even if that still mattered). For Joyce insists on stretching this question far beyond the point where it or any question can any longer make sense; he is not developing and describing his character, as is the traditional fictional practice, for later use and cogitation. He is getting rid of HCE once and for all (though nothing ever happens *once and for all*[23] here), burying him with adjectives so that not a trace of reality is left.

This rhetorical destruction of the father figure is paralleled by Joyce's preoccupation in the *Wake* with the theme of patricide. The murder of the father is certainly one of the major recurring motifs in *Finnegans Wake*, of which the assassination of the Russian general, "caught with his pants down,"[24] is the single most exploited avatar; and the story of Oedipus,[25] archetypical parricide, is as relevant for the *Wake* as Hamlet was for *Ulysses*. What is left, then, when Shem is finished with his father at the end of question one, is a kind of desert, an emptiness, or vacuum, that our mythical answer "Finn MacCool" doesn't do a lot to fill. In a sense, though, maybe the boards have been cleared for action, at least provisionally. Now that the father has definitively "shot his load," been described out of existence and neutralized, he is no longer a factor in the Joycean equation. His rules, laws, authority no longer need to be taken into account. The destruction of the father by the language he himself created is the necessary precondition for the creation of a new cultural idiom. The figure of the father has been "de-mythified," so that when he enters the game again (though he is conspicuous for his absence for the rest of the "questions" chapter) it is as just another contingent individual in a world or family of such.

We therefore interpret these thirteen unrelenting pages of alternating rant, apostrophe, encomium, ridicule, cele-

bration, nursery rhyme, bric-a-brac, etc., as tantamount
to an intentional deconstruction and deflation of the figure
of the father. Nietzsche's wry remark[26] near the beginning
of *Twilight of the Idols* about the negativity inherent in the
Socratic quest for total knowledge might apply as well to
these overwhelming pages. When we have said all that can
be said about something, then we are *done with it.* It is
perhaps hostility toward the phenomenal world that informs our drive for (complete) knowledge of it, especially
where this knowledge is, or pretends to be, exhaustive.
Intellectual and cultural history and tradition turn out to
be only some, among other (e.g., military, commercial, religious), symptoms of aggression.

II

Question ten shows us Joyce at just about his most
comically sensual and seductive. This is "intimate" writing
replete with onomatopoeic sounds of sexual foreplay, full
congress, and the orgiastic grunts and groans naturally
associated with such acts. The *Wake*'s style in language is
indeed ideally suited to convey such effects, since, like sex,
it undercuts the normal communicative patterns of everyday discourse.

Our introductory question here is mere pretext for
unlocking the mechanism of the text. It operates, in typically Wakese obliqueness, more by suggestive intimation
than by bold direct statement: "10. What bitter's love but
yurning, what' sour lovemutch but a bref burning till she
that drawes do the smoake retourne?" (143). Shaun seems
to start his answer off in the form of an address to his
sweetheart-and-sister; polysemy is temporarily minimized
as he speaks here in words that very nearly resemble plain
English:

> Answer: I know, pepette, of course, dear, but listen,
> precious! Thanks, pette, those are lovely pitounette, de-
> licious! But mind the wind sweet! What exquisite hands
> you have, you angiol, if you didn't gnaw your nails, isn't
> it a wonder you're not achamed of me, you pig, you

perfect little pigaleen! I'll nudge you in a minute! I'll bet
you use her best Perisian smear off her vanity table to
make them look so rosetop glowstop nostop. I know her.
Slight me, would she? For every got I care! Three cream-
ings a day, the first during her shower and wipe off with
tissue. Then after cleanup and of course before retiring.
(143–44)

Without much, or any, warning, and without our being
able to say precisely where it happens, we notice by a shift
in gender that the sex and identity of the speaker have
altered: "He is seeking an opening and means to be first
with me as his belle alliance" (144). We have been warned
in the introductory nine lines of the chapter (126) that
others are likely to answer Shem's questions in Shaun's
place; and we are accustomed already, in the briefer preceding questions, to having the twelve disciples (cus-
tomers), the morphios (28 houris), even old Kate and Joe
(servants in a saloon) speak in his name. In the world of
Finnegans Wake, as in what we have called the "literature
of deconstruction" in general, an individual, a subject, is a
permeable and unstable entity liable to be "possessed" by
other (momentarily) more insistent beings with more
urgent things to communicate.[27] In this case the consciousness of Izod comes very quickly to dominate and
direct that of the brother. Instantaneously he becomes
putty in her hands, listener-reader-voyeur—the entranced
and ineluctably stimulated audience to a re-*living* of her
sexual life:

Poo! What are you nudging for? No, I just thought you
were. Listen, loviest! Of course it was *too* kind of you,
miser, to remember my sighs in shockings, my often expressed wish when you were wandering about my
trousseaurs and before I forget it don't forget in your
extension to my personality, when knotting my remem-
brancetie . . . I'll always in always remind of snappy new
girters, me being always the one for charms with my
very best in proud and gloving even if he was to be
vermillion miles my youth to live on, the rubberend Mr

Polkington, the quonian fleshmonger who Mother
Browne solicited me for unlawful converse with. (144)

The tone of the entire answer to the tenth question is
consistently maintained on this level of lovers' small talk.
Joyce, always interested in the transforming effect of
powerful emotions upon language, here studies the ways
in which sexual arousal commutes language into an adjunct of desire. These are words whose meaning is clearly
only a matter of context and situation. They are meant to
evoke and reproduce the events they describe, performing
thereby the traditional function of erotic-pornographic
prose, from Petronius to Cleland, de Sade, Klossowski,
Bataille, Henry Miller, and D. H. Lawrence, to engage, involve, compromise, and to make culpable the reader. Language, at any rate, in the context of a sexual act, can only
demonstrate the contingency and interchangeability of
words. There is obviously something going on here that the
words merely point to or indicate without pretending to express, describe, or contain, for here the contained clearly
overflows the container:

Ha! O mind you poo tickly. Sall I puhim in momou.
Mummum. Funny spot to have a fingey! I'm terribly
sorry, I swear to you I am! May you never see me in my
birthday pelts seenso tutu and that her blanches
mainges my rot leprous off her whatever winking
maggis I'll bet by your cut you go fleurting after with all
the glass on her and the jumps in her stomewhere!
HaHa! I suspected she was! Sink her! May they fire her
bor a barren ewe! So she says: Tay for thee? Well, I
saith: Angst so mush: and desired she might not take it
amiss if I esteemed her but an odd. If I did ate toughturf
I'm not a mishy-missy. (144–45)

The sexual metaphor is one that translates everything into
its own terms; it allows no difference, but renders all the
world a scenery or decor for its performance; the sexual
act, of course, does not exist ontologically separate from
the culture of signs and signals in which it is embedded,

but it interprets these as being preliminary, accompaniment, or aftermath of itself. It refuses to recognize the sacrosanct dignity of our most precious cultural products and rituals but treats them all, from popular song to classical opera, as so many *pretexts*. Thus sex is the kind of tyrant that establishes equality by fiat, being profoundly suspicious of hierarchy and its accompanying claims to privilege and status; it stands not in awe of Mozart, Beethoven, Shakespeare, but sees them as so many "dirty old men" trying, like anyone else anyway they can, to seduce, in the literal sense of the word, their audiences.

Izod, who incarnates the purely sexual as closely as any character in the *Wake*, thus notices and perhaps produces sex everywhere; she spares no one and nothing as she levels all of life to its common denominator. Especially suspicious in Izod's eyes is the pedagogical-academic situation, wherein the pretense to knowledge and the assumed need of the student for a "guiding hand" supplies student and teacher with scene and opportunity.[28] Joyce explores elsewhere and plentifully in the *Wake* such classic examples of the "détournement" of the pedagogical into the sexual as Paolo and Francesca[29] and Heloise and Abelard. In Izod's world, as we witness and participate in it here, there is no such thing as an innocent desire to acquire or impart knowledge. The pedagogical-academic-exhortatory posture is incriminating in its very nature. The book, the poem, the "lesson" (to borrow a figure from Adamov and Ionesco)[30] is just so much foreplay for the main event and purpose:

> Of course I know, pettest, you're so learningful and considerate in yourself, so friend of vegetables, you long cold cat you! Please by acquiester to meek my acquointance! Codling, snakelet, iciclist! My diaper has more life to it! Who drowned you in drears, man, or are you pillale with ink? Did a weep get past the gates of your pride? ... Pore into me, volumes, spell me stark and spill me swooning ... More poestries from Chickspeer's with gleechoral music or a jaculation from the garden of the soul. Of I be leib in the immoralities?

O, you mean the strangle for love and the sowiveall of
the prettiest? Yep, we open hap coseries in the home.
And once upon a week I improve on myself I'm so keen
on that New Free Woman with novel inside ... For
creepsake don't make a flush! Draw the shades, curfe
you, and I'll beat any sonnamonk to love. (145)

This sexual motif thus undercuts and deflates the seriousness of all "high" culture, art, and politics. The morally
strident Swift accordingly is remembered solely for his
lifelong infatuation with younger women: "How vain that
hope in cleric's heart / Who still pursues th'adulterous art"
(146), invoked habitually by permutations of the names of
Stella and Vanessa.[31] Likewise, what peeks through of
Parnell's political career in the *Wake* is only the adultery
that brought him down and the trial that cleared his name
but broke his spirit, as evoked so frequently in the syn-
drome of "hesitancy" and "pigottry."[32]

Joyce, indeed, has an unerring eye for weakness in
human nature, for the corresponding gap between ideal
and reality—and a perpetual delight, almost an obsession,
in discovering the foibles in the lives of the great. One
could almost say, as Sartre says about Flaubert,[33] that he
was eager to confirm an essentially cynical view of humanity. Biographical details confirm that Joyce often shows
very little trust in the motives and actions of others, even
those closest to him.[34]

Indeed, the reduction of all experience to the sexual
that Izod effects is tantamount to cynicism in action. For
just as cynicism refuses to recognize the claims to honor,
disinterest, holiness, and any abstract ideal, so Izod's consistently sexually intimate tone tends to undermine belief
in these too. The state of sexual excitement that she provokes by assuming it in her listener is enough in itself to
reduce all history, philosophy, literature, and religion to
that timeless moment when the urgency to climax is the
only meaning there is in the world. So that when the
teacher opens his mouth it is not exactly to ask a question
or express an intellectual reservation. All such scholarly
attitudes are nullified as Izod repeats and rehearses with

her teacher the lesson she has learned so well:

> Now open, pet, your lips, pepette, like I used my sweet
> parted lipsabuss with Dan Holohan of facetious memory
> taught me after the flannel dance, with the proof of love,
> up Smock Alley the first night he smelled pouder and I
> coloured beneath my fan, *pipetta mia*, when you learned
> me the linguo to melt. Whowham would have ears like
> ours, the blackhaired! Do you like that, silenzioso? Are
> you enjoying, this same little me, my life, my love? Why
> do you like my whisping? Is it divinely deluscious? But
> in't it bafforyou? *Misi, Misi!* Tell me till my thrillme
> comes! (147–48)

Beckett's famous observation, "*Finnegans Wake* is not about something. It is that thing itself,"[35] could well apply to the above. A reader who could stay immune from the seductive power of these images and sounds would be incompletely human. Joyce has a way of seducing his reader along with his characters, of luring one, as in certain "climactic" scenes in *Ulysses*, into sub- or preverbal situations where pretensions are collapsed and affectations assaulted.

This practice may amount to a radical critique of the traditional separation of reader from text-and-author, similar in intention to the kind we are going to see Sollers operate with, in the next chapter, in his novel *Drame*. All of this puts a certain pedagogy and academia in a not always so comfortable position. The work is no longer worshipped, studied as monument, but enters our lives, and in this case, maybe our beds, as an intimate friend with whom we have an ongoing relationship. The work points to no meaning but participates in a process of which it is merely a part. The joke in the *Wake* is always on those who think they can reify this dynamic process by abstracting a message, explanation, or some other guiding idea from the work, always on the preacher, pedagogue, or author who likes to pretend that he is not already participating in the process he describes:

> Shshsh! Don't start that, you wretch! I thought ye knew
> all and more, ye aucthor, to explique to ones the signifi-
> cant of their exsystems with your nieu nivulon lead. It's
> only another queer fish or other in Brinbrou's damned
> old trouchorous river again. (148)

All of this is not to imply that Joyce's exclusive focus on
the sexual in the tenth question is equivalent to an epic
celebration of the sexual impulse, à la D. H. Lawrence perhaps, which would amount to a reification in itself.[36]
Joyce, instead, presents the sexual as a perfect model of a
process that abrogates and undermines the separation
and hierarchy of traditional attitudes—in the sense that it
dissolves and renders nugatory all identities, certainties,
and absolutes.

With Joyce we never stay on a terrain that we have
come to know, but instead always pass on.[37] This is why,
concurrent with rhetorical devices and styles that force us
to focus on any particular area, there are always compen-
sating mechanisms at work that help us forget where we
have been; and we call this quality in the *Wake* precisely
the self-erasing,[38] which operates here by the selfsame
mechanism of amplification by which an area is exhaustively explored. As we have seen with the interminable first
question, an extensive development in any one direction
can be tantamount to a kind of closure. As we experience
through the limited consciousness of Izod all the permutations and ramifications of the sexual instinct and explore,
if not submit to, its mysterious power that has reduced, in
Joycean terms, the great men of history to the status of
thralls and makes all "serious" human activity a mere
mask for its workings, we are left as readers in the
numbed and drained state that might appropriately follow
a sexual act in real life. If, after the first question, we are
finished with a certain kind of father because an over-
supply of information has made us despair of ever separat-
ing fact from fiction, life from avatar, here also a mono-
maniacal passion spends and erases itself in the very
process of its realization. The "nevers" and the "alwayses"
cancel each other out in Izod's passionate conclusion, in a

rhetorical explosion so utter that it leaves no residue of meaning, no memory behind:

> Never that ever or I can remember dearstreaming faces, you may go through me! ... Or ever for bitter be the frucht of this hour! With my whiteness I thee woo and bind my silk breasths I thee bound! Always, Amory, amor andmore! Till always, thou lovest! Shshshsh! So long as the lucksmith. Laughs! (148)

III

Jones's halcyon lecture in answer to question eleven is as madly comic a piece of writing as Joyce ever produced, perhaps as exists in English literature. This lecture is a non- or antilecture if there ever was one. The speaker, Jones, is some sort of psychoanalyst (allusion to Freud's English biographer) as well as bigot, academic, and pedagogue—with all the tics and eccentricities of these respective and inclusive trades. Speaking in Shaun's name, by process of substitution whose workings we analyze above, he has delivered a resounding "no blank ye" in response to Shem's question, whose gist was whether he would befriend his own down-and-out brother. The rest of his long answer is given by way of amplification and justification of this initial "no." He musters his arguments from every conceivable source to support his position that is already unalterably taken. Prominent in the panoply of his proofs or nonproofs are the doctrines of Marcel Jousse, a French philosopher in whose work Joyce took great interest,[39] and according to whom primitive man communicated by gesture rather than by word: "The speechform is a mere surrogate" (149). Underlying Jousse's teaching were apparently his suspicion that language is an inferior form of communication and his corresponding Rousseauistic mistrust of progress and civilization. According to him, the gift of words represented for humanity a very equivocal advance at best; words only became necessary because we lost the power to communicate through authentic and powerful gesture. Jones, the speaker, a man of words if ever there was one, thus paradoxically deflates and deemphasizes the significance and meaning of his own argument and indirectly of all argument and rationality by allusion to a philosophy that discounts the verbal to begin with.

If words are an inadequate form of communication then the supposition is that you cannot do very much with them, nor can words or those that live by them, the class of intellectuals, be taken very seriously. It becomes functionally a matter of indifference what *exactly* the lecturer is saying, since, in the final anaysis, he is only an ape, grinning, grunting, and grimacing before others of his kind. Thus words from the mouth of our speaker, Jones, tend to drop their meaning and to resemble mere noise. In Jones's hilarious parodic version of some of the basic disputes of Western culture, what creates this irresistibly comic effect is precisely this supercilious attitude toward language. For if language is to be reduced to the status of a mere adjunct or surrogate of gesture, then there are no limits to the uses you can put it to. Propagandistic discourse has known this trick for at least a century; and the motto of all totalitarian regimes, as Hannah Arendt would have it, might very well be: "There is no such thing as truth."[40] Such an attitude toward words makes them into more or less freely floating signifiers whose only meaning is their *effect* on their audience, a form of advertising whose purpose is to modify the opinions and behavior of those addressed (Jones is exquisitely and constantly aware of the presence of his audience). These words are, as it were, free of gravity or anchor in any real world; they show no respect or allegiance to any enduring notions of meaning or significance. All you can do with them is to make fun of them; the more abstract your language, the greater the comic effect, since you are exploiting a gap that is all the greater between the pretension of the word and the little or nothing it ostensibly renders. Thus Jones's target of predilection is quite naturally the intellectual and the type of words he is likely to use:

Talis is a word often abused by many passims (I am working out a quantum theory about it for it is really most tantumising state of affairs). A pessim may frequent you to say: Have you been seeing much of Talis and Talis those times? optimately meaning: Will you put up at hree of irish? Or a ladyeater may perhaps have casualised as you temptoed her *à la sourdine*: Of your plates? Is Talis de Talis, the swordswallower, who is on at the Craterium the same Talis von Talis, the penscrusher, no funk you! who runs his duly mile? Or this is a perhaps cleaner example. At a recent post-vortex piece infustigation of a determinised case of chronic spinosis an extension lecturer on The Ague who out of matter of form was trying his seesers, Dr's Het Ubeleeft, borrowed the question: Why's which Suchman *talis qualis?* to whom, as a fatter of macht, Dr Gedankje of Stoutgirth, who was wiping his whistle, toarsely retoarted: While thou beast' one zoom of a whorl! (Talis and Talis originally mean the same thin, hit it's: Qualis.) (149–50)

The targets of Jones's ridicule are the absurdity, fatuousness, and pretension of the Western intellectual tradition,[41] which takes its chimeras, wishful thinking, and fancies, its *reason* for reality, and then proceeds to manipulate and corrupt them with the good conscience and "innocence" afforded by the separation it assumes as unquestionable between the thinker as human being and his thoughts. It is precisely Jones's role to deprive Western thought of its good conscience; for him thought is always conditioned, if not vitiated, by its source. He has denied from the outset that words and the systems we form with them can have any cogency or meaning apart from the needs and drives that inspire them in the speaker, thinker, or theorist himself. Words, deprived of any referential reliability, serve only to reveal, more properly, to *expose* their user. The intellectual is defined as obsessive neurotic or paranoid psychotic because he insists that his words have a natural relation to reality. Just as the cynicism of Izod in question ten elicits the sexual component in every supposedly "higher" activity, so here the *ad hominem* attitude of Jones uncovers the disturbed

mental case behind every glorious contribution to humanity's stock of knowledge. Implicit in Jones's attitude is a
critique of Western science, based as it is on a strict isolation of knowledge from its source, so it can become both
an object of study and a means of experimentation and
manipulation. In Jones's world, on the other hand, there
is no such thing as an enunciation separated from its
source. For Jones the detective is always himself the primary object of his investigation:

> (I should like to ask that Shedlock Homes person who
> is out for removing the roofs of our criminal classics by
> what *deductio ad dominum* he hopes *de tacto* to detect
> anything unless he happens of himself, *movibile tectu,*
> to have a slade off.) (165)

The theory is always contaminated by the theorist, whose
complexes, ambition, egoism, and blindness qualify, as
well as very commonly vitiate, the theory.

In terms of information the clarity of the message is always obscured by the "noise" surrounding it, with which it
exists in a permanent state of dialectical tension. In Jones's
lecture the interference is subject to a double articulation,
first of all arising from the mentally aberrant state of the
speaker (and of those he speaks from *his* point of view)
and second from the resistance and distraction of the audience. The message thus is always all but drowned out by
the interference, like a radio emission that barely comes
through despite static. Jones, though ostensibly oblivious
to the way all his personal digressions and *ad hominem*
libels and digs impede the delivery of whatever it is he has
to say, is preternaturally aware of the potential for
rebellion simmering in his classroom, just as speakers in
the *Wake* generally are sensitive to and try to anticipate
and guide their reader-listener's reaction.[42] Whatever the
obscurity and/or relevance of his address, permeated as it
is by the purely personal and evidently extraneous, Jones
remains determined, as Joyce in a larger sense certainly
was, *not to lose his audience:*

> As my explanations here are probably above your understandings, lattlebrattons, thou as augmentatively uncomparisoned as Cadwan, Cadwallon and Cadwalloner, I shall revert to a more expletive method which I frequently use when I have to sermo with muddle-crass pupils. Imagine for my purpose that you are a squad of urchins, snifflynosed, godlingnecked, clothyheaded, tangled in your lacings, tingled in your pants, etsitaraw etcicero. And you, Bruno Nowlan, take your tongue out of your inkpot! As none of you knows javanese I will give all my easy free translation of the old fabulists parable. Allaboy Minor, take your head out of your satchel! *Audi*, Joe Peters! *Exaudi* facts! (152)

What this reminds us of is the fact that a repressive or at least intimidating power structure is always the more or less hidden precondition for "peace" in the classroom; before someone can be heard, the potential for disruption must be eliminated and a social space cleared for the reception of the message.

Jones's lecture is threatened from within by intrusions from his personality, so that it becomes at points a kind of intellectual striptease, and from without by an audience that is always on the verge of escaping from his control. The lecture creates and defends the space in which it occurs, and the *effect* of its delivery is very much in the direction of a laying-bare of this mechanism. Although he articulates thematically for his listeners some of the most familiar controversies of the Western intellectual tradition, he surrounds his points with such a bewildering barrage of interference that the purported message becomes secondary to a host of other factors.

Levy-Bruhl, the eminent French anthropologist and a respected and revered figure on the contemporary intellectual scene, thus becomes a natural target[43] for Jones and the brunt of a wildly suggestive and digressive passage, where information and interference are mixed so inextricably it is in the end impossible to tell one from the other:

Professor Loewy-Brueller (though as I shall probably
prove his whole account of the Sennacherib as distinct
from the Shalmanesir sanitational reforms and of the
Mr Skekels and Dr Hydes problem in the same connection differs *toto coelo* from the fruit of my own inves-
tigations—though the reason I went to Jericho must remain for certain reasons a political secret—especially as
I shall shortly be wanted in Cavantry, I congratulate
myself, for the same and other reasons—as being again
hopelessly vitiated by what I have now resolved to call
the dime and cash diamond fallacy) in his talked off
confession which recently met with such a leonine
uproar on its escape after its confinement *Why am I not
born like a Gentileman and why am I now so speakable
about my own eatables* (Feigenbaumblatt and Father,
Judapest, 5688, A.M.) whole-heartedly takes off his
gabbercoat and wig, honest draughty fellow, in his
public interest, to make us see how though, as he
says: 'by Allswill' the inception and the descent and
the endswell of Man is *temporarily* wrapped in ob-
scenity. (150)

The distortions of the name of Levy-Bruhl, as they appear
here and on the following page ("Professor Levi-Brullo, F.D.
of SexeWeiman-Eitelnacky finds ... Professor Llewellys ap
Bryllars, F.D., Ph. Dr's showings") tells us much about the
lecturer's feelings about academia, titles, and research but
very little about the anthropologist. What comes through
here is not any thematic content of the words themselves,
which refer too wildly to be tamed by the organizing force
of any mere abstraction, but the posture, or "gesture," of
the lecturer. His words form no timeless structure but are
almost pure contingency, for they could be replaced by
others that would work as well. It is as if these words
worked by themselves, informed by an attitude but set free
like a machine that has been coded in a certain way. If the
words call attention to anything it is to their speaker and,
indirectly but surely, to their writer; and to the trail they
have left behind.

7

The Strategy of Interruption:
Philippe Sollers' *Drame*

"*Drame* is a novel that can be read as a poem."
—Roland Barthes

"The words in *Drame* refer to no known reality, but instead to each other."
—Leo Pollman

I

There are two principal characters in Philippe Sollers' novel, *Drame*: (1) an "il" or "je," who represents a writer or narrator, often in the act of writing and/or reading the book, preparing to write it, or reflecting on or reacting to the action; and (2) a "tu," which most often refers, as with Blanchot's *L'Attente, l'oubli*, to a woman-and-reader. There are also some other people that serve as a kind of background or distant audience: nameless individuals going to work, indistinguishable and interchangeable, and whose command of the language consists of a few banalities; or anonymous heads gathered around the bed of an accident victim. There are also a few other shadowy beings that emerge from paintings that are described: for instance, a melancholy man across the river from a nursing mother. But these and any other people described in *Drame* are only permutations or temporary expressions of the writer-reader's fugitive identity, so that essentially we are only concerned with a "me" (or "he") and a "you" (woman and/or reader).

What takes place between "you" and "me" is sexual, literary, philosophical, political, or frequently merely some

151

kind of silence or silent communion (although an exhaustively *commented* one). "You" are alternately my sounding board, constant critic, contact with reality outside of myself, obstacle, detour, and correspondent. Your purpose, as much as any, is to *interrupt* me before I go mad or too far.

Interruption is the very essence of Sollers' style in *Drame*. Without interruption, the words become an endless monologue, a rant; our author, articulate and prolific to an almost miraculous degree, has no trouble thinking of words to follow the ones he has written: "Mais du côté 'parole,' il découvre l'absence de limites: cela peut se décrire sans fin, cela peut se décrire sans fin en train de se décrire, etc."[*]

Some of the techniques whereby Sollers keeps his text in a perpetual state of deviation and obstruction are: parentheses in which exceptions are presented or conditions described, or that begin but do not end or end but did not begin; irregularities in register, tone, even punctuation; cutting a textual flow off in mid-sentence, -word, -phrase, -syllable or in the middle of a conversation or thought; self-quotation from the current novel or Sollers' earlier books; the application of quotation marks to seemingly familiar words ("my life" is a favorite) to ask what they *really* mean—with not even the shadow of an answer; evident and sudden pastiche of other authors' styles and ideas (Bataille, Proust, Faulkner, Robbe-Grillet, Blanchot ...); the schizoid tension of having the first- and third-person singular so thoroughly interchangeable; the gratuitous location of events in time, indifferently past, present, or future, or indeterminate conditional—so that the tense of the verbs as well as the meaning of the adverbs acquires the status of sheer formality; citation of other authors, often obscure and enigmatic (traditional mystics like Boehme and Swedenborg); instructions that emanate from the text on "how-to-read-me" or self-criticism by the writer on questions of literary theory and practice relating to this

---

[*] "But on the 'word' side, he discovers that there are no limits: this can be described endlessly in the act of being described, etc."; *Drame*, 98; *Event*, 49.

text, others, or to culture, literature, or just about anything and everything else in general; ambiguous and untrustworthy use of analogies, "painted" scenes, metaphors that are immediately denounced but never renounced. It must have been these techniques, along with a host of others, that led Henri Peyre to judge severely that "the book diabolically attempts to bewilder, astonish and remain impenetrable to the reader."[1]

Efforts to simplify or rationalize these processes of interruption seem vain, even when they enjoy the sanction of their author. Sollers considerately tells us on the back cover, for instance, that his novel is divided into the sixty-four squares of the game of chess, which is supposed to represent "time projected into space"; and other commentators, as well as Sollers in an interview, have suggested the sixty-four hexagrams of the *I Ching*, a Chinese text of divinatory wisdom, as an equally valid correspondence.[2] According to this scheme, the "odd" chants would be narration, standing for, as in Greek drama, the judgments of a chorus that sees things from an objectively social point of view. The "even" chants would be personal discourse, representing an individual. The qualities of the narrator of the "odd" chants, however, seem just about identical to that of the speaker in the "even" chants, so we are dealing here more with an interpenetration. Whether or not we agree that the two entities can be distinguished, it seems obvious that they have complete access to whatever the other is thinking or/of writing, and for all practical purposes the reader has to see them (as well as himself) as parts of a single process.

However futile the apologies for them may be, this organization of alternating chants serves the larger purpose of Sollers' strategy of interruption, for aside from the multifarious devices of interruption that, as we observe above, the text employs so ubiquitously, it also avails itself of this structural method of insuring discontinuity and abrupt change: the chants, of unequal length, tend to run no more than two or three pages, and often less, so that whatever narrative tangent we are on, we may be sure that it will shortly be altered.

Complicating matters further is the fact that Sollers' is the kind of text that only *seems* haphazard, accidental, and gratuitous; in reality it forgets nothing it has uttered, so that not only is the reader kept in a state of unrest due to the structured alternations but is also inevitably going to be exploring the text in all directions, especially backward, looking for hints of things that may have been dropped but now mysteriously reappear. Lest things appear to be too predictable in their very contingency, Sollers occasionally "pleases" his reader with a passage of lovely prose poetry, or lets a description run on for a page or two.[3] Once we even seem to get an orgy. These are, however, rare treats, isolated in the text like those moments are in life.

As demonstrated by the obviously ineluctable return of the word "d'abord" ("in the beginning"), with which it opens, this is a text where the word "finish" has no place and where another aesthetic or ethic than that of the "beautiful" is in control. Accordingly the text affords neither space nor station to *appreciate* what we have read, nor are there discrete, self-contained segments that we can admire or reflect on separately. For every word here is conditioned and qualified by every other word and is therefore never part of a chapter that can be thought of as finished, but instead is perpetually liable to explanation, interrogation, and mutation. We don't start and finish one of these chants the way we might a segment of traditional fiction, perhaps returning later, if our memory is good enough, to "finish up where we left off." We are instead reading these chants simultaneously and in all directions and dimensions. The fact that they are separated on the page, *that* is the fiction.

In the world of *Drame*, therefore, one doesn't finish what one has to say, utter a statement, give voice to an opinion or prejudice, or express an emotion that is meant to be appreciated in isolation from whatever else is happening. For one thing nothing here is ever *completed*; for just as in ordinary conversation we frequently don't wait for our interlocutor to finish a thought, phrase, or even word before responding, so do these chants habitually end and/or start with an abrupt hiatus of some sort: three dots, a "however," a dash, or some other device that indicates that nothing is going to be concluded or decided, although it may be taken up again later from a changed perspective. The model for this style may be the interview or other event in the media—where also the content of the message, as we have been aware of at least since McLuhan, must yield to the structural exigencies of the means used to communicate it, and where whatever one has to say is subject necessarily to truncation, distortion, exploitation, and abortion by whatever else must urgently be emitted. For here, as in *Drame,* one ends not when one concludes but when one's time at the microphone, so to speak, has elapsed; and the philosophy of such a "mediated" world might well be that *there is always something happening somewhere else that is more important* and therefore claims with greater priority and insistence our attention and care.

Adding then to the interruptions structured by the alternating chants are the many times our text is fractured, fragmented, broken in upon, as listed above, by observations about environment, light, or weather, undocumented citation, self-quotation, double or one-sided parentheses or other typographical anomaly (for instance, leaving a blank space where a word should end a sentence, but dutifully including the period),[4] descriptions of paintings or scenes that are immediately relegated to a merely linguistic existence, figures introduced by teasingly imprecise statements like "it seemed as if" that pile one upon the other with the obvious message that none is to be indulged (in). The repertoire of Sollers' discontinuity is endless and far-ranging. We even get some punctuationless prose, perhaps in anticipation of later exciting and controversial developments in Sollers' writing—and, of course, self-examination, recrimination, observation, measurement, calculation ad infinitum.

One of the devices that Sollers uses most consistently to dam the flow of the narrative, to "stop literature in it tracks," as it were, is to examine commonly used words for meaning that might escape the casual user. Such a style,

which Heidegger and Derrida employ in philosophy, we
have named in our introductory chapter the "etymological"
or "molecular" outlook in literature, whereby the writer
holds up to anxious doubt and scrutiny the very words he
is *forced*, like everyone else, to depend upon—and we have
discussed this tendency in its various modalities in other
writers in our "network of the literature of deconstruction"
(Tzara, Beckett, and Blanchot, in particular). The typical
formula for this "molecular" interpolation in Sollers'
Drame: x does y; but what is "*x*" and what is "*y*," and what
does it mean "to do"? Nothing else can transpire evidently
while these simplest notions remain unexplored. Everything comes to a stop while hermeneutics takes over:

> "... Et ce langage: faux, borné par rapport à notre pré-
> sence que je regarde au-delà des vitres se jouer en bas
> maintenant dans les reflets lumineux de l'eau sur la
> pierre, incessamment débordante, la même, renouvelée
> ... Rien ne ressemble moins à un roman que notre his-
> toire, et pourtant c'est bien le seul roman dont j'aurais
> envie de te parler (celui que personne ne pourrait écrire,
> celui qui s'écrit en nous devant nous). Le seul qui serait
> gagné sur ce que nous pourrions, cédant au mensonge,
> appeler, comme dans les romans, notre vie."5*

And later our narrator considers suicide, but what stops
him is that he can't decide who this "I" is that kills itself,
just as he hasn't been able to conceive what his life is that
makes it "mine":

> ... Se tuer? Mais qui se tue, s'il se tue? Qui tue soi?
> Qu'est-ce que "qui" là-dedans? (il ne peut pas se tuer

---

* "And this way of talking: false, hemmed in by its relation to our
presence that I watch beyond the window panes now playing in the
luminous reflections of water on stone, incessantly overflowing, the
same, renewed. . . . Nothing is less like a novel than our story, and yet
it is certainly the only novel I would want to talk to you about (the one
nobody could write, the one that is written within us in our presence).
The only novel that might be gleaned from what we might call our life,
as in novels, were we to give in to lies"; *Drame*, 27; *Event*, 10.

puisqu'il n'est pas ce qu'il est, puisqui'il est en définitive
négligeable quant à ce qu'il est; et il aime son ignorance
... *

II

What is it, then, that "happens" in this book? What
is the event that Sollers talks of on the back cover?

Le mot *drame* est ici employé dans son sens le plus
ancien, non pas celui d' "action"—encore moins celui
d'intrigue psychologique—mais plutôt celui d' "histoire,"
d' "événement."†

The reader, of course, is allowed to grasp, in a rudimentary way, that certain things take place. An accident is
referred to a few times, and sexual contact, or a metaphor
thereof, is not infrequently evoked between the "je" and
"tu." At one point the presence of a third person of indeterminate sex seems to call forth the description of an orgy;
and our heroes seem to do a lot of walking and as much
talking and reading. They read passages that sound like
they could be from or about his book; and their talk is
often incomprehensibly banal, or obscure, enigmatic, and
oracular. They certainly talk in circles, never really deciding anything, and they walk similarly, always leaving and
returning to those same fixed points that are never really

---

* "Kill himself? But who's being killed, if he's killing himself? Who
kills self? What is this "who" in there? (he can't kill himself since he
isn't what he is; since he actually has very little importance to what he
is; and he loves his ignorance"; *Drame*, 91; *Event*, 46.

† "The word *drama* is here meant in its oldest sense, not that of
action—even less psychological plot—but rather that of 'story', 'event'";
Drame, back cover. *Event* is, indeed, the title of the novel in its recent
translation by Bruce Benderson and Ursule Molinaro and is also a kind
of code word for the kind of *différance* introduced by deconstruction, as
in Derrida's introduction of it to America in 1967: "Perhaps something
has occurred in the history of the concept of structure that could be
called an 'event' ... " (quoted by Melville, *Philosophy Beside Itself*, 3).
Significantly what *takes place* between the characters in Blanchot's
L'Attente, l'oubli, neither fact nor fiction, is *the event* (see p. 114 above).

described. They spend a lot of time in their room, looking out the window frequently, as if it were somehow important here to go to the window as a contact with reality, talking maybe about what they think, saw, or "what's on the other side of words," and particularly privileging their *dreams.* Going out seems to be another deeply meaningful gesture, fraught with terror and suspense, although the world as they see it seems to be a pretty drab affair, at least in its civilized aspects: crowds of people mechanically and somnambulistically going about their daily business (of which our heroes have *none*), as if they were hypnotized subjects of some nameless controlling force.

This is a world of rampant anonymity, as in the ultimate fictions of Blanchot; nothing here has a name of its own, as pronoun has supplanted noun in some inexplicable but undeniable sidereal revolution whose outcome is that person, place, object, and phenomenon have become just so many classes or types. And the topography of this limit-landscape is certainly a simulacrum of the environment, insofar as there is one, of Blanchot's *L'Attente, l'oubli,* which we described earlier.

Occasionally, however, a more substantial detail peeks through. We find that somehow a port city is involved, and much is correspondingly made of "port" as synonymous with a kind of lost identity or security that is now forever unattainable; and nameless boats, winds, seas, and mountains enter occasionally in descriptive passages that, as shown above, interrupt or redirect the flow of the text. All these elements, together with the night and day, the varying qualities of light, and panoramic views of the earth as seen from a plane, seem heavily laden with a symbolic or psychological meaning that nevertheless remains vague and imprecise. We feel the importance of these things by virtue of the attention lavished upon them, without ever being sure as to what exactly they are supposed to mean.

The anonymity or complete absence in the text of proper names and nouns further compounds this indeterminacy. We don't know where we are except that we seem to be in a city with a port, in a hotel room from which we can see the mountains and the sea—we look at workers, merchants, machines (plenty of cars), even each other; everything has a dual existence and a lack of existence, equally something and nothing—anything. Even the words in which the book is written are once called an echo, but this would be paradoxically an echo of an echo, where one is incapable of finding any sound that was first. This is a post-Platonic world of simulacra, of copies of no findable original, that is, copies of copies that Jean Baudrillard, Gilles Deleuze, and others have used as metaphors for modernity—a world of which representation is impossible since it is *already* and only semblance.

Sleep, dream, night, waking (veille), city, sea, even sex —all of these seemingly substantial entities are there, but only as part of an autonomous universe of signifiers. They lead, come from, and refer endlessly only to themselves and each other. They are ""rien qu'une agonie sans fin reprise au vol par un autre, et un autre, et un autre encore,""* the almost automatic substitution of one passenger, pedestrian, car, book by another-yet-the-same—each a mere station or relay on a spiraling road that goes nowhere *inside* of some incomprehensible destiny or rendezvous rather than anything solid or identifiable in its own right.

By a frequent incursion of the words "problem" and "failure" we are also given to understand that there are problems to be solved or failed at. But we are allowed neither to solve these problems nor to abandon them. At that very moment when the narrator is ready to abandon, a way of egress, a possibility is inevitably suggested: "... "une langue se cherche, s'invente"... ."† "Comme si la véritable histoire ne pouvait pas être dite (il la sent pourtant en lui pas à pas, immuable). Comme si le véritable projet se dévoilait enfin avec l'abandon du projet."‡ This

---

* ""Just an endless agony recaptured in flight, by someone else, and someone else, and someone else""; *Drame*, 30; *Event*, 12.

† " "A language in quest of itself, inventing itself" "; *Drame*, 147; *Event*, 77.

‡ "As if the real story could not be told (however, he senses it in him at every step, immutable). As if the real project were finally being revealed with the junking of the project—"; *Drame*, 115; *Event*, 59.

"true story" is no longer a story, with all that the words connote in terms of representation for amusement or edification, but simply the affirmation that something is happening, the event itself, the *drame* being sheerly the struggle with questions that can be neither answered nor abandoned.

Nothing then can be *told* here, but there is something to be done, recognized, inspected, learned, but only from the inside—as words that learn of the larger text to which they have no choice but to belong. Mention is made occasionally of "following the thread": "Où trouver le fil? Comment le tenir? Où, la coulisse? Où, l'arrière-plan permettant le recul?"*

These are questions without answers and they are meant to be; but what is most endemic, precious, and salutary in our Western tradition are not the *things* that we find or create, which commonly work against us anyway, but the *seeking* attitude, between the lines, as it were, of the texts we read and are—this thread that is, as it should be in all good work, invisible.

Drame is part of a literature not of answers but of questions, not of solutions but of problems.[6] We are led ineluctably to treat whatever answers we stumble over only as a starting point of further doubts and questions, in this text of the perpetual "D'abord":

"Il devrait suffire de tenir le fil. Mais c'est justement là l'opération la plus difficile, la plus trompeuse—car comment etre sûr, comment savoir si l'on est dans la continuité juste ou seulement dans son envers chaotique et glacé? Sur une page fictive, la multitude des livres viennent présenter leurs versions contraires: comme si la bibliothèque s'était contractée pour finir en une courbe tangente à cette page toujours reblanchie (impression, projection, disparition par effleurements successifs, et c'est exactement cette ombre qu'il faudrait

---

* "Where to pick up the thread? How to hold on to it? Where are the wings? Where is the background that gives enough distance?"; *Drame*, 72–73; *Event*, 35.

retenir, faire passer devant le regard entraîné dans une glissade sans efforts et sans fond). Roulé dans les mots. . . . S'ils viennent en premier lieu (et tu es parmi eux, transparente, tu marches à travers eux comme un mot parmi d'autres mots), je sais qu'il y aura en moi, pour leur répondre, une réserve indéfinie, des croise-ments, des vies "tout autres" un instant perçues en correspondances dans leur champ d'action . . . Rien qui ne puisse avoir un sens, indiquer un sens."*

We are dealing here with a kind of meta-metafiction that not only contemplates itself but also contemplates itself contemplating itself. This is one large, abstract, and cold step beyond the other experimental ventures we have looked at that still retain some recognizable semblance of content and message. While those texts like to think about themselves, they do not make this cogitation their sole subject and preoccupation; the reflection is ancillary to other factors, like revolution for Tzara, the development of a language adequate to modernity for Joyce and Leiris, or the sheer tedium of existence for Beckett. Of the writers we have been concerned with, Blanchot is certainly closest in mood and style to Sollers, and unquestionably Blanchot, at a certain point at least, was an enormous influence on him, as he was for Sollers' generation; but, nevertheless, a humanism, a solitude, a density and concern are in Blan-chot's texts that are missing in Sollers'. With Blanchot's

---

*   " "Holding the thread ought to be enough. But that's exactly what is the hardest to do, what is most deceptive—since how can you be sure, how do you know whether you are in the right sequence or merely in its frozen, chaotic mirror image? On an imagined page, the hosts of books come to present their opposite versions; as if the library had shrunk in order to end in a curve tangent to that eternally re-whitened page (imnpression, projection, series of light erasings, and it is pre-cisely this shadow that would have to be kept, brought past a gaze be-ing pulled into an effortless, groundless sliding). Rolled into the words . . . If the words come in the first place (and you are among them, transparent, you walk through them like a word among other words), I know that I will answer them by being filled with a limitless store, cross-breedings, lives that are "totally other" seen for a moment corresponding in their field of action . . .""; *Drame*, 80–81; *Event*, 40.

texts we are *left* with something, if only, as in his important essays on Kafka, an image of the *possibility* of the
proud isolation of an artist who is not of this world, nor of
any other one;[7] but here, in *Drame*, and in the other limit-
texts of Sollers and his *Tel Quel*-and-after colleagues, abstraction and cogitation have abolished all retreat and
consolation, meditation has caught up to life; in these
texts author, action, story, character, scene, insofar as
they exist, are present only because they give the text
something to chew on.

Drame then is a book that reflects ceaselessly upon itself and its own possibility, feasibility, and relevance as
well as upon literature, art, and "culture" in general. This
is also a book that tells us how to read itself, that ultimately seems to read itself, or to be read somehow automatically, and that spends many metaphors searching for
an always elusive adequate picture of itself. The real book
is confronted at every turning with the ideal book it is
anticipating or recovering from, that first and last text that
cannot be identified with any actual volume: "I dream of a
book as vast as the sea" (115).

This is no book that we learn to write when we learn
the alphabet. By the time the alphabet comes along we are
already past masters at writing and reading, being read
and written. If we agree with Deleuze, and I think we
must, that the interpenetration of art and everyday life is
the crucial moral-aesthetic dilemma of our time,[8] then the
direction of this book is toward the merging of reality with
this text in particular and with all texts in general.
Reading becomes synonymous with any other kind of contemplation or regard, whether it be toward our bodies,
those of others, our cities, habitations, faces, pasts, and
futures—all are subject to our *reading*, that is, to our
interpretation and *modification*.

III

The word, for Sollers, as we have shown for other
moderns whose texts relate to his, has lost its ancient
privileges; it is no longer the location of any absolute

standard or value. As in *Finnegans Wake* or Beckett's *Trilogy* we no longer really know what words *mean*. The word has been fractured, dissolved, "disseminated," as Derrida observes about a slightly later book by Sollers, *Nombres*[9]—if anything, more coldly mathematical, rigorous, and self-calculating than *Drame*. The word can no longer be located, admired, or despised, followed or rejected—but only looked for, surprised, and ultimately seen through and beyond. The inevitable concomitant of Sollers' discourse, as well as other modern discourses that move on and through the word, is a radical critique of separation that must approximate the twentieth-century text to revolutionary action—and we have seen how Tzara and Blanchot make this connection: the modern writer who "knows nothing" (whose very words, as with Beckett, belong to *someone else*) is a functional equivalent of the proletarian who has nothing. An inherently elitist culture that masks its everyday brutality behind a facade of museums, libraries, galleries is deemphasized in favor of a culture that suffuses our every waking and sleeping moment and recognizes no separation of rank, title, or even talent. We are all now, as the beats once announced in their inimitable, fervent, and sincere way, "in the same soup together": sports, politics, culture, city, workers, ads, soap operas, our latest interests, infatuations, fantasies, schemes, trips on drugs or planes, amusement-park rides, outer-space ventures, recessions, philosophies—all merge and melt into a homogeneous mass of indefinable contours and infinite suggestibility and ramification; and Sollers' later magnificent and remorseless punctuationless texts, *H* and *Paradis*, are especially meant to convey this dynamic confusion of our all-leveling culture in the throes of gestation, this primal ooze or sticky stew where, whatever our delusions of status, separation, accomplishment, and value, we all simmer as one; and where is the word in all of this, where is that text, once graven in immortal stone, that we are all supposed to live by and for? For we now live in a world of limitless commandments that contradict and undermine each other incessantly, a world of which Rousseau's schizoid ambivalence and Kierkegaard's existential anguish were among the first intimations and Sollers' infinitely refracted style of thought and writing one of the most original modern concomitants.

In *Drame*, therefore, it would be presumptuous to define where exactly art ends and life begins. Honored formulas like "art is long, life short" would have no place here. Mordant interrogation of these words would commence at once, with obvious results—the utter negation of the enunciation—and even that medieval slogan, so dear to Joyce, "let paradise perish, so that the book may live," would make no sense here. Sollers' art (nor the ultimate Joyce's) is not that of the privileged moment or monument around which the rest of life crystallizes; like *Finnegans Wake*, it is probably closer to madness, or to a defense against it, than to a traditional event- or personality-centered aesthetics. If the madman is he who can and does find meaning everywhere (which is why he must be sequestered, since he doesn't know where to "go") then Sollers' narrator is perilously close to mad, or that is his pose and mask: "Mais en fait, n'importe quoi peut devenir limite, point critique. . . . Pas un coin de tableau qui ne puisse s'ouvrir";* as in this expression, we can no longer maintain the posture of disinterested contemplation where the painting opens up to *include* us. This same perilous frontier of sanity, this side of which only we know who we are, is brushed by the narrator when he looks out of the window from what theoretically should be a privileged space of contemplation of the "other" only to recognize his own shadow. The writer no longer stands apart from what he describes, as he continues to do even in a minimal and ambiguous way in the earlier fictions of Sollers. For here the waking mind of the narrator is as subject to incursion and occupation as that of his dreams. Theories of intertextuality would understate the dimensions of this uncertainty and porosity and perhaps constitute an academic recuperation of the anguish. The narrator's room, his mind, his writings are equally subject to the duress and

---

* "Actually, anything at all can become the limit, the critical point . . . Not a corner of the picture that can't unfold"; *Drame*, 36; *Event*, 15.

challenge of constant interchange and inspection from whoever and whatever is out there.

Our text not only conveys these attitudes thematically, it also manifests them stylistically, as frontiers, limits, separations (writer/reader; me/he/you/us) are blurred, occluded, abolished. Finally we won't know *what* we're reading, *if* we're *reading,* or if *we're* reading; but we may very well wonder what reading is.

Our wonder won't get the chance to lapse into an attitude, or anything that resembles an idea or conclusion, as Sollers rather teases the reader with the exceptions that can be taken to any point of view than allows him to occupy any one of them. Furthermore, a book that is its own perpetual critique just about precludes criticism, disarming it and rendering it in advance nugatory and superogatory, since it methodically removes in advance the very basis on which thoughts about books are formed. It attacks and rectifies itself before it can be corrected and judged by others. This amounts to a continual dislocation of the reader from any position of security, knowledge, and certainty. And more than one reader has expressed dissatisfaction, dismay, and even reprobation at this state of affairs.[10] The reader has become just another figment of the imagination, another fictional character, someone of indeterminate contour, often interchangeable with the writer (invention of the reader), but no one whose independent position would give weight to the judgments he happens to pass.

The reader, demoted, as has been the writer, from any position of authority, control, or command, thus enters into Sollers' strategy of dislocation and discontinuity. This strategy is obviously meant to keep the author, his writer, woman friend, reader, book, story from ever really finishing a train of thought or arriving anywhere. It must be discrete individuals that complete thoughts, pictures, statues, buildings, and books, although we shouldn't underestimate the role of compulsion in the process. The other side of the coin from completing the things we start is being obstructed from doing so. The interplay between the ongoing project and whatever is interrupting it is seen

as having neither end nor resolution. The situation, unsatisfactory as it is, remains incapable of solution. The questions it poses are permanent and unanswerable. The book
in the end has no result, or none that you could point to
and name: ""il n'y a pas de résultat, peu importe ce qui
arrive (on l'aura voulu). Somme nulle, volume détruit par
le feu"";* what is necessary, instead, is a perpetual state of
expectation and tension, of receptiveness and suspension
of prejudice and conditioning.

This is a self-consuming experience that erases itself in
the very process of enunciation and combustion, so absolutely is Sollers determined to give his reader/writer *nothing* to hold into. We may remark on a molecular level, for
example, the dissolution of "il faut" in the following:

> "Il faut dépenser le plus possible, immédiatement. Ne
> rien garder pour soi, pour ailleurs. Arracher la suite.
> Oublier cet "il faut." Se tenir simplement dans la vibra-
> tion transparente qui permet de voir et d'entendre et de
> dire à la fois ce qui vient et précède en violence chaque
> histoire immobile, sous les yeux, ici."†

The erasure of the "il faut" above is an apt microcosm
for this self-erasing text, as *Drame* spends itself entirely,
impossible to remember really, to save as to store. It is like
the classical "arts of memory" in reverse, an "art of forgetting"; for Sollers has attacked those very mechanisms
by which things are remembered, classified, and kept for
later use. His tendency to cancel out his enunciations by
process of indefinite development, dialectic, or reflection
inhibits recall, as does his refusal to decide (for us) what is

---

* ""Or rather: there is no result, what happens matters little (that's
what you wanted). Sum zero, volume destroyed by fire""; *Drame*, 156;
Event, 82.

† ""You *have to* expend as much as possible, immediately keep
nothing for yourself, for somewhere else. Tear out what follows. Forget
this "you have to." Simply stay in the transparent vibration that allows
seeing and hearing and telling all at once what comes and glaringly
comes before every motionless story, under your very eyes, right here"";
Drame, 147; *Event*, 77 (italics mine—PB).

or is not important, that is, to assign priority to any single moment in the process. For the other moderns we have discussed, much the same point could be made, in that they employ styles that inhibit our ability to grasp and retain the material. We have examined, for instance, Joyce's annihilation of the figure of the father by the self-same process of endless amplification and adumbration that celebrates him, and we have shown also how Leiris' "life" becomes a problematic and shadowy entity that is difficult to locate beyond the brilliantly expounded paradoxes that inhabit it. But with Sollers the devastation is more total and the landscape correspondingly more devoid of landmark, because here we are dealing with subjects and objects that never existed in the first place and therefore do not even leave us that consoling trace or two, evidence of their passage.

IV

Since nothing here is sure or certain, the reader tends to lose track of things even before they have been properly acquired. What is this "problem," for instance, that is announced so frequently in this text and so enigmatically?

> Problème: pousser la reconnaissance le plus loin possible, supprimer le malaise qui ne cesse de l'envahir. Problème: avoir vu le piège mais perdu ses limites. ... "Problème: pour être sans limites, ressembler à un mot."*

Equally baffling is the recurrent notation "manqué" ("failed") after the enunciation of the "problem." Without ever really coming to grips with what the problem is, we are to assume that one has failed in solving it; yet we cannot rest easy even in failure, as it opens the way, equally

---

* "Problem: reconnoitering as far afield as possible, suppressing the feeling of uneasiness that keeps taking hold of him. Problem: he's seen the trap but lost sight of its limits." ... ""Problem: being limitless, being like a word""; *Drame*, 12, 130; *Event*, 2, 67.

obscurely, to that perpetual further attempt. The problem,
thus, without losing anything of its air of cogency and urgency, escapes articulation and totalization. We are told
that the problem is always there but never really in front of
us, and a hint is dropped that somehow vested interests
may be involved: ""Jamais le problème en direct. ...
L'organisation générale fonctionne pour nous empêcher de
le poser.""* Sollers' grammatical formulation for this kind of
quasi-real but insistent thought is a conditional that he
may have learned from Blanchot but that is also massively
present in *Finnegans Wake*.[11] The conditional is so well
suited to the modern self-erasing works because, especially in its contrary-to-fact forms, it denies while affirming
itself:

> On dirait qu'une dramatisation s'est communiquée aux
> dessins du monde, légère d'abord, comme un geste à
> demi conscient des avant-pays du réveil, puis de plus
> en plus affirmée, précise (quoique dépourvue d'un sens
> explicable et unique), traçant ses figures elliptiques
> dans toutes les directions, écrivant, en somme, écrivant
> pour lui, l'écrivant lui-même en dehors du temps. ... Si
> le plan général lui échappe comme acteur (à moins qu'il
> se laisse aller à mentir, à rejoindre des passages prévus
> d'avance, ce qui d'ailleurs le renseigne pour ainsi dire
> négativement), il sent bien, malgré tout, qu'il s'agit de la
> même histoire, et peut-être, d'une seule immense his-
> toire qu'il pourrait contenir, veiller, réciter ...[†]

These lines by their very nature escape definition or cer-

---

* ""The problem never presents itself head on. ... The general
organization keeps us from posing it""; *Drame*, 53; *Event*, 25 (slightly
modified).

† "It is as if the world's design were infused with a dramatization,
lightly at first, like a half-conscious gesture at the promontory of waking, then becoming more and more precise, definitive (although still devoid of an explainable, unique meaning), tracing its elliptical figures in
all directions, writing, then, writing for him, writing himself outside of
time ...If he as an actor cannot understand the overall plan (unless he
lets himself slip into falsehood, join together already predetermined
passages, which, moreover, supplies him with virtually negative infor-

tainty. What do they say, indeed, that is not as soon re-tracted, qualified, or conditioned? What do they announce that is a matter of fact, or even observation, rather than of conjecture or appearance? They belong to a text that is in effect one continuous condition, which creates a suspense that is never lifted and a mystery that can never be solved.

The reader, who from the beginning has been deprived of the mechanisms and justifications he uses to order the raw flow of information, is forced back upon himself. The book he has under his eyes is a constant confession of a failure that can never even be regarded as definitive, a per-manent autolaceration and critique that undermines anal-ogously the pretenses and illusions of art and culture in our bourgeois society for which, as Barthes points out so memorably, writing is merely decoration.[12]

No writer is to be trusted, and "good" writing, making the "beautiful" its object, maybe least of all. Sollers thus seems to be debunking even the best of fictional practices by the most accomplished masters. He aims his barbs at Proust, Simon, Faulkner, and doubtless a few others as he considers and then eschews the temptation simply to "tell the story"; much like Blanchot's narrator's refusal to accommodate his interrogators (discussed earlier in con-nection with *La Folie du jour*), *Drame* will stand aloof from such "cooperation":

> Il pourrait évidemment résumer ou exagérer la situa-tion: un homme, une ville, une femme—ce qui arrive, ce qui se fait—, procéder à une narration elliptique qui aurait l'avantage de profiter de mille détails concrets en même temps que d'éléments personnels. Il pourrait ré-courir à une fable commode: présentation spectaculaire sur fond de légende, digressions de plus en plus ambiguës, menées souterraines, démenties, détours ... (C'est ainsi probablement qu'on écrit un livre. Mais il s'agit bien d'écrire un livre. ...) Ce n'est pas la fausse

---

mation), he is despite everything well aware that he is dealing with the same story, and perhaps with a single immense story, which he would be able to hold inside, watch, tell about ...."; *Drame*, 72; *Event*, 35.

évidence des premières constatations, ni une invention
privilégiée qui peut maintenir la question à ses yeux.*

The process whereby masters even of unconventional fiction lend credence to their creations is thus laid bare, or at
least stripped of its aura. Sollers' purpose here is evidently
to discredit other fictional practices as severely as his own,
and thereby to undermine even a temporary belief in what
we read and in the very possibilities of the medium.

The reader, unable to find authority in the written
word, is forced to look for it elsewhere. It is not that Sollers
is incapable of hypnotic, seductive, compelling prose that
fascinates in a more traditional manner. His writings
previous to *Drame* as well as his recent novels in the style
of Céline (*Femmes* and *Portrait du joueur*) prove the contrary;[13] and some of his effects and descriptions in *Drame*
do involve the reader for a few paragraphs or pages in the
kind of "spell" that art has traditionally aimed to exercise.
But Sollers shows always, and in short order, that he has
mined these structures with the explosive charge of
mordant self-criticism; and he detonates these charges
without hesitation or remorse:

> "Et ce langage: faux, borné par rapport à notre présence
> que je regarde au-delà des vitres se jouer en bas mainte-
> nant dans les reflets lumineux de l'eau sur la pierre,
> incessamment débordante, la même, renouvelée."†

---

* "He could of course sum up or exaggerate the situation: a man, a
city, a woman—what happens, what is done—, go on to an elliptical
narration that would have the advantage of a thousand concrete details
as well as personal elements. He could resort to a convenient fable: a
spectacular presentation drawn on a legend, more and more ambiguous digressions, obscure twists, denials, detours . . . (Probably how a
book is written. But isn't this all about writing a book . . .) Neither the
false evidence or initial observations, nor an ingenious imagination can
keep the question before his eyes"; *Drame*, 60–61; *Event*, 29.

† " "And this way of talking: false, hemmed in by its relation to our
presence that I watch beyond the window panes and now playing in the
luminous reflections of water on stone, incessantly overflowing, the
same, renewed" "; *Drame*, 27; *Event*, 10.

Nor will Sollers allow us the illusion that we are some-better off for having struggled through the text, for this is a book that we don't get through in the sense that we know what it's about and feel that we've *read* it—although we might feel that it's *done* something to us: "main ouverte, rien à saisir."* This is a book that denies itself to its reader as soon as offered. Instead we have been shown ""Ce qui passe au fond dans les livres, et les porte, les rapproche, les ouvre comme malgré vous, les inquiète sans fin: voilà le sujet et le dernier acte.""† This "What happens in all books" cannot be named, since what is named is not what happens. Therefore we find that "silence" is evoked very frequently in *Drame*, yet in keeping with his determination of depriving the reader of any orientation, even a negative one, Sollers submits both word and concept to the kind of interrogation they were not meant to survive:

"... silence que rien, aucune violence, aucune négation ne sauraient atteindre puisque dans chaque cri il est à l'intérieur du cri, dans chaque refus ce qui se refuse. C'est en lui, par lui mais toujours apparement sans lui que l'ensemble a lieu, le mot "silence" est à peine la trace de son reflet ..."‡

We are confronted, in *Drame,* not only with the complete illusoriness and unreality of the world of referents that we take so much for granted but also with the futility and vanity of our attempts to lessen our confusion by resorting to the comforting fictions of words. Words, as

---

* "Hand open, nothing to grab"; *Drame,* 84; *Event,* 42.

† ""What ultimately moves through the books, and supports them, compares them, opens them as though against your will, endlessly disturbs them: this is the subject and the final act. Even if the contest ends abruptly in silence. Even if for the moment it is impossible to go any farther""; *Drame,* 157; *Event,* 83.

‡ ""... silence that nothing, no force, no negation could reach, since in every cry it is inside the cry, in everything withheld it is what is holding back. In it, because of it, but apparently always without it, everything takes place, the word "silence" is barely the trace of its reflection ...""; *Drame,* 65; *Event,* 31.

signs, are always wide of the mark. They can never over-
take a referent that, as in Zeno's paradox, is always ahead
of them. Above all, there is no longer any standard by
which to judge when the goal has been reached; such
decisions currently always involve the arbitrariness of
manifest power and self-fulfilling prophecy. The junction
of sign and world is at worst a typical abuse of power and
at best a temporary expedient; meaning, therefore, is always elusive and totality an illusion: ""On ne comprend
pas ce qui a été dit, ceux qui parlaient ne comprenaient
pas la totalité de ce qu'ils disaient.""* *Drame*'s punctilious
awareness of its own inadequacy is correspondingly
conscious of the failure of all language and all thought.

By reminding the reader so persistently of its own dubious claims to significance or relevance, of the futility of
its own machinations, and of its fortuitous, haphazard, accidental, finally *unlikely* and contingent existence as a
consumed physical object, the book makes it less feasible
for the reader to "lose" himself in the reading. The reader
is reminded of and thrown back upon the ambiguity and
precariousness of his own individual existence and the
corresponding fragility of the cosmos in general. We are reminded of what it is in the interests of power to hide from
us, namely, that there is nothing natural or inevitable
about the way we have organized our world, that we are
only signs among signs[14] that, together with their supposed referents, can so readily be changed: "(il vérifie en
somme qu'il n'y a pas de 'sujet'—pas plus que sur cette
page)."†

This work that reads itself, that tells the reader literally
how it is to be read, "neither too near, nor from too far
away" (74) and that it is only a book, is showing us the
mechanism of its functioning—that which underlies the
operation of all texts. The book itself functions to maintain
our awareness of the problematic and arbitrary nature of
its existence at a peak level. In order to do this it has to

* ""What's been said isn't understood, the speakers didn't
understand everything they were saying""; *Drame*, 100; *Event*, 51.

† "(he realizes, in other words, that there is no 'subject'—no more
than on this page)"; *Drame*, 121; *Event*, 62.

remind us continually not to fall back into traditional and discredited modes of thinking and reading: we can never be reminded often enough that the word is not the thing, since this is the kind of lesson that runs so counter to our social programming that we tend to forget it as soon as we learn it. *Drame* is a kind of school in a new kind of thinking, and what this school teaches in myriad ways is a more sensitive appreciation, use, and reading of the world and the violence we work upon it, as well as the violence worked upon us, in even the most casual gesture and word.

Drame never stops teaching us to be dissatisfied with the descriptive powers of our language and our manipulation of and by a reality that we can only *pretend* to be outside of:

> ... il voit par exemple des chevaux dans une prairie en pente, et c'est un matin sec et bleu qui l'enfonce en pleine stupeur, lui, l'herbe, les rafales de vent. ... Il voit les chevaux, il ne peut les penser (il ne sait plus penser, rien que des glissements dans un glissement latéral). Les mots: "des chevaux courent dans la prairie" ont beau s'appliquer à la scène, il reste en retrait, vide, vidé de paroles, et les mots ne sont plus qu'une répétition inutile ... (cependant il les suit du regard en train de courir, de s'arrêter—signes vivants, trop vivants pour lui).*

Another style that Sollers uses to distance the reading from the text is the extensive introduction of the vocabu-

---

* "... he sees horses, for example, in a sloping meadow, and the dry, blue morning smashes him into pure dumb amazement, he, the grass, the strong gusts of wind. ... He sees the horses, he can't conceive of them (he doesn't know how to think any more, nothing but slidings into a lateral sliding). No matter how much the words: 'horses are running in the meadow' are applied to the scene, he is still distanced from it, empty, empty of words, and the words are no longer anything but a useless repetition seen by a useless double (yet he follows them with his eyes in the act of running, stopping—live signs, too alive for him)"; *Drame*, 103; *Event*, 52–53.

lary of games and game theory. The two most recurrent metaphors for this are chess and the Chinese divinatory device of the *I Ching*. The text of *Drame* is often referred to as " l'échiquier," "damier," and the process of writing it as the "jeu."* A game, by very definition, is that which can be crucially important one moment and a matter of indifference the next. Games can be adopted or dropped without scruple depending on changing circumstances. One owes nothing to a game. Games provide alternate and varying ways of deciphering and perceiving the world; and one game leads naturally into another, or changes with respect to rules, playing style, and temperament of the player. Our involvement in a game is always somewhat of a fiction; we are never as seriously concerned as we look, aware as we are of the unreality of it all. Our societies revel in games because there they can parade unashamedly the lack of finality that inhabits them. For in the game, especially in its modern avatar of "spectator sports," the goallessness and irrationality implicit in our society is made manifest and even subject to celebration. The game is the very image, furthermore, of a system in which the sign refers only to other signs and that transforms external reality into an adjunct of itself. Above all, you don't have to *believe* in a game in order to play it, although one pictures all too easily a game that one is obliged to play whether one likes to or not: ""On ne peut cesser de lire, même en retrait, ici, derrière le front et les yeux ("oublie, rappelle!"), on ne peut éviter le jeu. . . .""†

The text mirrors also the impermanence of the game. The book that has been read, like the game that has been played, is not there anymore, although inevitably one starts to play (read) all over again:

Il a perdu ce qu'il a écrit, sans recours. Ce qu'il a écrit est resté dans la mer. Au moment où il se décide à aller

---

* "L'échiquier" = chessboard; "damier" = checkerboard; "jeu" = game. See chap. 7, n.2.

† ""You can't stop reading, even from this distanced position, here behind the forehead and the eyes ('forget, remember'), you can't avoid the game""; *Drame*, 156; *Event*, 82–83.

le rechercher, il s'éveille. C'est ici. Rien n'a commencé, à
vrai dire. En face, le mur blanc est éclairé, comme
chaque jour de soleil. . . . Il ouvre un autre livre.*

Like the game of chess, where the game can be over
with many or most of the pieces still on the board, the
book can have accomplished its purpose without having
(been) finished, without comprehensiveness. So too we find
Sollers sardonically listing and apologizing for his omis-
sions, indirectly mocking the realists and naturalists who
are commited to include and account for everything:

Il s'aperçoit qu'il n'a rien dit de son passage le long des
quais (un remorqueur devant lui traversait la rade).
Rien, non plus, de cette suite déclenchée en marge:
l'étang vert, les insectes, les herbes—l'océan, la côte, le
vent, les rochers—les champs loin des routes—l'ob-
scurité des collines—les chantiers—les hélices dans
l'eau, les reflets bougeant sur les coques rouillées—le
sable et l'accumulation de sel sur les bords—la tempête
et le ciel vertical comme poussant la mer dans le noir et
leurs mains froides se touchant alors rapidement dans
le noir—texte surchargé, bref—†

Sollers' text-as-only-a-game works well with a critique
of our modern systems of pervasive power and total

---

* "He has lost what he wrote, without recourse. What he wrote has
stayed in the sea. Just when he decides to go look for it, he wakes up.
It is here. Nothing has actually started. Across the way, the white wall
is illuminated by every sunny day. . . . He opens another book"; Drame,
143–44; Event, 75.

† "He notices that he has not said anything about his passing
along the docks (a tugboat in front of him crosses the basin). Nothing
either, about what follows unleashed in the margin: the green pond, the
insects, the grasses—the ocean, the coast, the wind, the rocks—the
fields far from the roads—the darkness of the hills—the dock-
yards—the propellers in the water, the shifting reflections on the rusted
hulls—the sand and the coatings of salt on the sides—the storm and
the sky as vertical as if it were pushing the sea into blackness, and
their cold hands touching that way quickly in the blackness—dense,
short text—"; Drame, 149–50; Event, 78.

control. For Sollers, evidently, much of our malaise arises from our very seriousness, that is, our inability to release our ambitions of completeness and totality. We accordingly either say (and do) too much, in our efforts toward exhaustiveness, or not enough, because we have been satisfied that we have said it all. Sollers does not need to tell the "whole story" because for him there is no "whole story" to tell. Nor does there ever come a point when everything coheres, crystallizes, makes sense around any single aspect. There is no "message" here; at most, he is trying to share an attitude, but nothing that can be reduced, clarified, communicated. Sollers' prose is, in the sense that Barthes meant it, profoundly and intransigently intransitive;[15] and, accordingly, that moment when a hitherto difficult writer is finally understood marks not his success but his failure:[16] all understanding is misunderstanding. There is nothing to say except that there is nothing to say, or that everything we can say is so infinitely beside the point.[17] This is a kind of antilesson, or lesson to the effect that there is no lesson.[18]

V

Nevertheless the presence of the reader is duly noted, just as the dutiful students' attendance is noted by teachers who are at once reluctant and obliged to go on lecturing. Although communication is absent, there is a certain kind of communion here, as barriers have been effaced and pretensions reduced. The writer, no longer having anything to say, can now just *be* with the reader, both caught between the covers of the same book: ""...il est entendu que je n'ai rien à te "raconter,"—nous n'en avons pas le temps—, il nous suffit d'être ensemble, ici, maintenant. . . .""* Lest we feel that we have reached some kind of plateau, or even achieved something, the image even of this minimal relationship or communion between

---

* ""... of course, I don't have anything to 'tell' you—there's no time—, it's enough for us to be together here, now""; *Drame*, 102; *Event*, 52.

reader and writer does not survive the sentence that gave it birth. It turns out to be just another passing thought, soon to be fractured by the disintegrating power of the text as it continues to qualify, explain, modify, and in this case even *sexualize* the encounter:

"... (et comment y être, en effet, sinon en silence ou encore sur un autre plan par l'appel brusqué de ce que tu sais: l'intérieure douceur de la peau et morsure en passant par la peau, contact réduit à un fil, point de rupture, visage obscurci, ta main et l'appel pour qu'on ne vienne pas, distance maintenue la même entre toi et ce que tu vois: d'une part cet égorgement bref d'animal surpris autrefois et de l'autre les deux face à face se touchant à peine et l'une se laissant tomber peu à peu et s'arrêtant ou plutôt arrêtant sa bouche là longuement et faisant apparaître comme sien l'autre visage de plus en plus défait et mal supporté sans crier—) dans l'air de nouveau présent, ouvert—"*

In Sollers' prose there is no resting place, no point of view or perspective that we can attain or where we can stay. With Sollers we never get to finish what we start but are always interrupted and carried on in a relentless motion, always "de nouveau" pushed back into the moving current of things. We grasp perhaps at a passing branch to slow things down a bit, but with another gust of wind we are gone. Just as in cinema[19] the rapid changes in perspective preclude and defy an audience's calm reflection, Sollers' text inhibits rational judgment. One is reminded of

---

* "... (and how to be there, actually, if not silently or else on another plane by the brusque appeal of what you know: the inner sweetness of skin and bite passing by it, contact reduced to a thread, breaking point, face in the dark, your hand and the appeal not to come too early, same distance maintained between you and what you see, on the one hand this brief throat-cutting of the animal surprised before and on the other the two face to face hardly touching and one letting herself fall little by little and stopping or rather stopping her mouth there for a long time and making appear as his the other face more and more unknit and unsupported without crying—) in the air that is present, open, once again—"; *Drame*, 102; *Event*, 52.

the existential imperative, the "leap" or interruption that Kierkegaard never ceased stressing against the futility of thought ever reaching a conclusion (merging into action) on its own premises alone. Logic is inherently and discouragingly endless, as one thought rises indefinitely out of another. Against Hegel, apostle of logos, Kierkegaard urged the necessity of the irrational, the intrusion, the interruption that alone can help us descend from thought to life.[20] Sollers' strategy is very much in the nature of this Kierkegaardian leap; and one of the most important words that function in this manner is the "cependant" ("however") whose overwhelming exigency frequently concludes or opens the chants. This introjection and others like it, "all the same," etc., characteristically do not wait until the thought, much less the sentence, has been completed before the text is reformulated or reorganized on another tangent.

This "leap" into discontinuity and abrupt change of focus and perspective naturally alters with circumstances and subject. If "he" is sleeping, he suddenly wakes, and we find he was dreaming and we with him. Or if "he" is awake, he talks of sleep and dreams wherein we naturally expect that new rules will apply. The important point is not so much the nature of the hiatus as its suddenness and inevitability. We are reminded that, in the end (of which there is none), whatever we are seeing, thinking, hearing, wondering, doesn't matter very much, that in the nature of things there is always something happening *elsewhere* that requires our more urgent attention.

The process that Sollers circumscribes is that of a perpetual attempt to come to grips with a world that is forever fugitive. The metaphor of the sea, which Sollers uses occasionally in *Drame* as an equivalent of the text, is singularly appropriate in this connection—as a phenomenon that escapes all of man's attempts to codify, dam, or arrest it:

Il pense à un livre qui ne s'arrêterait pas plus que la mer ("l'homme conçoit une pensée, elle passe de là au souffle, le souffle le passe au vent . . .")—et pendant qu'il la touche, en effet, tout continue et commence, recom-

mence, respire at se respire en lui: ce qui est détaché,
ici, en surface, ne peut rien enfermer, chaque phrase
s'éteint dans une autre phrase qui la contient . . .*

This book that has been erasing itself as we read it finally disappears altogether, because it has merged with a
universal ebb and flow, a cosmic rhythm that is ceaseless
and unrelenting and useless to deny. The story here, as for
Joyce of the final pages of *Ulysses* and of *Finnegans Wake*,
is reduced to the one affirmation we all utter whether we
articulate it or not: the yes:

> "Précédant et acceptant ce qui vient et ne comptant
> plus, et saisis par notre vie depuis début à travers son
> obscurité voulue, et disant oui à qui surgit reparaît
> s'écoule—lignes couleurs—et il y a cette joie qui se
> passe du mot joie et c'est de son histoire qu'il s'agit
> malgré la fatigue et l'horreur imprégnant serrant chaque
> scène sa racine invisible son sens—Oui encore à cela?
> Oui. A cela encore? Oui. Il n'y a plus de fin si nous
> cessons d'être une fin."†

Drame thus incarnates a world of perpetual change,
confrontation, mutability, and incessant, irresoluble paradox. Whichever way we turn, the book points us immediately in the opposite direction. It would be correct to say
that it sends us in circles if we ever could know we had

---

* "He thinks of a book that would go on as long as the sea ('man
conceives of a thought, it passes from there to breath, breath passes it
to the wind . . .')—and in their contact, in fact, everything goes on and
starts, starts afresh, breathes, and is breathed through him: what is
released, here, on the surface, cannot enclose anything, each sentence
dies away in another sentence that contains it"; *Drame*, 115; *Event*, 59.

† "'Preceding and accepting what comes and without counting
any longer, and captured by our life from the beginning through its
intentional obscurity, and saying yes to that which emerges reappears
flows away—lines colors—and there is this joy that comes from the
word joy and it is a matter of its story despite the fatigue and the
horror impregnating constricting each scene its invisible root its
meaning—Yes to this, too? Yes. To this, too? Yes. There is no more end
if we stop being one'"; *Drame*, 138; *Event*, 72.

gotten back to our original starting point; but then we
don't really begin this book, we plunge in, as into the sea,
and then who can say when we started swimming; the
essential thing is to stay afloat. Although we don't go in
circles, we don't advance either. Myriad are the ways in
which Sollers evokes this impossibility to progress, from
the figure of the reader who, whether he knows it or not, is
still on the same page, to that of the writer whose
manuscript is gone, to that of a sign that would have to
mean more than it can in order to relate to any referent:
"(Le signe 'etc.' est d'ailleurs ici dérisoire; il faudrait in-
venter celui qui signifierait l'incessant, l'innombrable,
quelque chose comme l'abréviation du vertige insérée dans
le dictionnaire général.)"*

Whichever way we turn we are confronted endlessly
with the same situation: nothing we can say, write, or do
can change things very much; but by hiding behind the illusions of traditional fiction (story, character, moral,
and/or historical progress, etc.), we are not advancing
things either, only postponing the recognition of our hopelessness (as in the illusions of "postmodernism," as if there
were something for it to come "after"!). It is certainly not a
question in *Drame*, as it may have been for the *Nouveau
Roman*, of "seeing things as they are" but of realizing that
we are incapable of seeing things at all, much less describing what we have not seen. All our precious words,
our priceless art, our clever sciences do not amount to
very much more than a perpetuation of the ultimately
harmful illusion that we know more than we do and that
we are less helpless than we are. *Drame* is an attempt to
"break the habit" of such narcotic illusions by undermining the separations and hierarchies on which they are
based. Without making exorbitant claims about its ability

---

* "... (the sign 'etc' is absurd here; something that would signify
the incessant, the uncountable would have to be invented, something
like an abbreviation for vertigo wedged into the complete lexicon)";
Drame, 98; *Event*, 49–50.

to affect or change a world mostly beyond its reach (as beyond the pale of art in general), we may venture to say that the achievement of Sollers with *Drame* is to have written a novel whose end is not a foregone conclusion.

8

A Deconstructed Epiphany:
Des Forêts' *Le Bavard*

Tutto a causa del cosidetto peccato originale che,
salvo interventi contrari della grazia, porta l'uomo ine-
lutabilmente al male e alla perfidia, anche se si tratta
di un homo cosi altruiste e moralmente elevato.[*]
— Dino Buzzati

One does not write because one has something to
say but because one *wants* to say something.
— E. M. Cioran

Le Bavard of Louis-René Des Forêts is a complex
and subtle work that poses, in crystalline and deceptive
simplicity, some of the basic questions of our time about
culture, art, the value of language, the possibility of truth,
and the increasingly equivocal if not culpable relations,
KDin our times, between author and character as well as
author and reader. This work is quintessentially and teasingly post-Nietzschean—in the sense that it confronts us
with a world that has been emptied of the transcendental
structure or meaning that has been the basis for community and communication. Such a "wasteland" we have
entered (but not left) in the texts of Blanchot and Sollers,
and it is very evidently the landscape in which Beckett's
remnants of character are "at home"; but here, with Des
Forêts the *Destruktion* (in Heidegger's comprehensive sense
of an *undoing* of the metaphysical postulate that traditionally guaranteed and grounded our being—the once

---

[*] "All because of the so-called original sin that, unless grace inter-
venes, conveys man ineluctably toward evil and perfidy, even if we're
dealing with someone whom we think of as unselfish and highly
moral."

necessary fiction of the primacy-authority-tyranny of a logos-word-grammar-order emanating from an unquestioned and unquestionable Platonic-Christian realm of absolute self-sufficiency or Idea) is more insinuated than overtly expressed and engaged. This *Destruktion,* or *deconstruction,* to employ Derrida's contemporary version of the action, operates more deceptively and slyly (and maybe in the long run more effectively) in Des Forêts; it "hides," perhaps, as just the problems or situation of a unique and bizarre person—so that the reader tends to be stripped of the defenses he may have been able to muster against more self-conscious statements of other more openly iconoclastic texts. Here we can read more innocently, just "for the story," as it were—but the realization, I think, is all the more devastating, inescapable, damaging, and undeniable for having been *deferred,* that what is being projected is not merely the existential anguish or malady of an individual but the universal predicament of humanity in our "advanced" societies of the West.

For on its most immediate and literal level, *Le Bavard* is the confession of an individual (nameless) who is suffering from a strange kind of malady. That is, he has been frequently seized by a paradoxical desire, which first came upon him one day when, having the "cafard" (or "blues"), he decided to deal with his ennui by going to the beach. Significantly, the malady first attacked him after he had enjoyed a brief period of calm and felicity by the water's edge: while lying on a cliff overlooking the ocean, he was suddenly seized by the desire to speak, or more precisely, to gab ("bavarder"). So irresistible was this desire that he almost, like Demosthenes, began addressing the ocean, although we should not confuse this desire to speak with any concrete purpose, as of praise or elegy, such as in the famous "vieil océan" passages in Lautréamont's *Chants de Maldoror.* The reason this desire is paradoxical is that, although during this first and subsequent crises our narrator is possessed and driven by the will to speak, the fact remains that *he has nothing to say.*

The second onset of this malady occurs while he is celebrating one evening with some friends in a dancing bar. He has been dragged reluctantly into this place, as he has made a point of informing the readers, since he is not the type of person who enjoys going into these "dens of iniquity." His reputation among his friends is that of a somewhat taciturn, reserved, and withdrawn character. His friends even prefer him to be quiet, because he has a tendency to moralize when he does speak. In addition, we the readers, who are frequently addressed directly—whether in the modest singular (our hero once says that he requires only *one* reader, other than himself presumably) or the more ambitious plural—are informed that our narrator has a very low threshold of tolerance for alcohol and that on this particular occasion it was necessary for him to do some catching up with his companions. We are also informed that our narrator tends to be rather a spectator of than a participant in life, being somewhat of a voyeur, so that it was perhaps because of his unusual and (for him) immoderate absorption of alcohol, as he was watching the dancing from his table, that he felt powerfully attracted by a beautiful and statuesque young lady whose dancing partner was a short and vulgar-looking man. With great difficulty the narrator succeeds in freeing the woman from her partner; indeed there is almost physical combat between the two men over the woman. Soon, however, he is dancing with her, entranced by her bodily charms and her mysterious and fascinating smile; a little later, after another altercation with the lady's escort, who at her insistence has been relegated to a corner table of the cabaret, they are sitting at a table engaged in tête-à-tête conversation (strangely improbable and unilateral, since the lady, of Spanish origins, seems to know very little French). Our narrator is suddenly seized, almost involuntarily, with the desire to "tell all" to the lady. He was perhaps encouraged by the suspicion that the lady would be unlikely to understand much of what he was saying.

What now comes bubbling out of our "normally taciturn" narrator is an uninterrupted flow, a continuous and interminable confession of his most intimate secrets, fears, desires, and shames. All the while he is talking he is encouraged to ever greater heights of self-revelation and self-deprecation by the mysterious but seemingly encouraging smile of the woman. His "performance" comes to dominate the evening, and soon everyone in the place is listening to him, reacting first with amused disbelief, then with scorn and horror, at his indiscretion and abysmally bad taste.

The narrator—although he remembers very well the circumstances of his long confession, even through the clouds of alcohol, and although he delineates carefully the effect his words have on what is now an audience of considerably more than one—is curiously silent on one obvious point: *that is, what exactly it is he is supposed to have said.*

He claims not to remember a single word. Always anxious to anticipate his ever-present reader's objections and doubts, the narrator uses this seemingly inexplicable gap in his memory as a pretext for a long Tristram Shandy–style apology:

> Qu'on ne m'accuse pas de rester sciemment dans le vague quand il s'agit d'exposer la nature de mes aveux, et d'abord il n'est justement pas question de passer ceux-ci en revue; si vous brûlez d'en prendre connaissance, je vous préviens que vous préparez une fameuse déception, car n'en déplaise aux gens irréfléchis, prompts à croire qu'un autobiographe est doué d'une mémoire sans défaillance et qu'il est légitime qu'on attende de lui un compte exact de ses faits et gestes, si j'ai bien promis d'étudier consciencieusement et sans détours tout le mécanisme complexe de mes crises, je n'ai pas l'ambition de tout rapporter, y compris ce que je n'ai jamais su. Il ne dépend pas de moi que le plus important m'échappe, que dis-je, m'ait échappé quand il semblerait que j'aurais pu si facilement le saisir. J'ai déjà dit que je ne dénaturerais les faits à aucun prix; quand certains d'entre eux me feront défaut pour la compréhension de l'ensemble, je saurai renoncer au bénéfice que me vaudrait une impression plus forte produite par quelques faits inventés de toutes pièces sur l'esprit du lecteur, je ne substituerai pas au vide de l'oubli des mensonges plus vraisemblables. Tant pis si

cela doit désobliger les curieux et les méticuleux. Je préfère m'exposer à l'accusation injustifiée de passer sous silence des confidences qui me compromettraient—et j'ajoute que je veux bien être pendu s'il existe quelqu'un qui ait la naïveté de croire que j'en suis encore à éviter de me compromettre. Peu m'importe qu'une omission ou un véritable oubli jettent une ombre sur ce qui dans son ensemble ne saurait être sujet à caution. Mais j'entends qu'on me demande comment j'ai pu oublier ce qui précisément est le plus significatif ou en tout cas le plus piquant? Je n'ai rien à répondre à cela. Et pourtant il me serait peut-être possible d'en donner une explication propre à satisfaire les personnes de bonne foi. Si fâcheuse et si invraisemblable que puisse être à certains égards cette constatation, j'ai complètement oublié quels furent mes aveux pour la bonne raison que pendant que je les prononçais, *je n'y prêtais aucune attention.* Je m'explique. L'essentiel pour moi, c'était de bavarder.*

---

* "Don't accuse me of staying purposely vague when it's a matter of revealing the nature of my confessions, and first of all it's not exactly a matter of reviewing these; if you're so anxious to find out what they were, I'm warning you you're in for a big disappointment, since with all due respect to thoughtless people, ready to believe that an autobiographer is endowed with a foolproof memory and that it's proper to expect from him an exact account of his deeds and actions, even if it's the case that I've promised conscientiously and without digression to study the whole complex mechanism of my crisis, I have no desire to report everything, including what I've never known. It's not my fault that the most important things escape me, how should I say it, had escaped me when it seemed that I could so easily have remembered them. I've already indicated that I won't falsify the facts in the slightest for any price; when one or another of them necessary to understanding the whole fails me, in order to make a stronger impression on the reader, through the interpolation of some entirely invented facts, I'll know how to renounce the benefit of substituting likely lies for the voids of amnesia. Too bad if this annoys the curious and meticulous. I prefer exposing myself to the unjustified accusation of suppressing confidential facts that would compromise me—and I'll add that I'd rather be hung than to believe that there could be a reader naïve enough to imagine I'd avoid a compromising revelation. It matters very little, besides, that an omission or a gap in memory should throw a

Since, in apologizing to his readers, the narrator frequently generalizes that many people, if not most, suffer from this malady (the reader here, as in Tzara, Beckett, and Sollers, lays claim to the uncomfortable "equality"[1] of Baudelaire's imprecation: "Hypocrite lecteur, mon semblable, mon frère"), Des Forêts seems to be making some type of statement—by the attitude of indifference that he professes above to the *actual* words he has uttered—about the culture we live in and our inevitably curious, ambiguous, and insincere relation to the expressive means at our disposal. Des Forêts here mocks us ("qu'on me demande comment j'ai pu oublier ce que précisément est le plus significatif ou en tout cas le plus piquant?")[†] for the demand we invariably make to know exactly what it is he said, the *story* (such as Blanchot and Sollers refuse to tell). By emphasizing such nugatory, vain, and interchangeable externals, we hide from and blind ourselves to the more germane, if threatening, notion that we speak not so much because we have something to say, since we are forced to speak anyway (as Blanchot says to his imaginary interlocutor of *L'Entretien infini*, we must talk or destroy one another), but because we are by the very structure of our situation obliged to talk: we need to lecture for an hour, fill so many pages, make conversation over dinner or a drink. Here we need to know not how to tell a truth but how to embellish one, that is, to lie. The fact is that we at all

---

shadow of doubt over what cannot on the whole be subject to doubt. But I can understand someone asking me how I could have forgotten what precisely was the most meaningful or, in any case, the most provocative part. I have to admit I have no answer to that question; however, it might be possible for me to give on this matter an explanation capable of satisfying people of good faith. As irritating and unlikely as this claim might seem in certain respects—I'd completely forgotten my confession for the very reason that while I was reciting it, *I was paying absolutely no attention to what I was saying*. Let me explain myself more clearly: the important thing for me was not what I was saying but the fact that I was talking"; *Le Bavard*, 86–89 (1963 ed.: 63–64) (author's italics).

   † "You ask me how I could have forgotten the most meaningful, or, in any case, the most provocative part"; *Le Bavard*, 89 (1963 ed.: 64).

events can give the floor, microphone, printed page only to those who have mastered the arts of dissimulation and deceit. The word, therefore, is automatically compromised, "processed," suspect, and cheapened in a culture where what is said is insignificant in comparison to the position or station in our hierarchies of the speaker. Like a newspaper whose articles we already know before we look at them, a writer's words are already *read* before they are printed—in this world where there is nothing left to say that hasn't been said already by what we know about the speaker and the institutions he is forced to function within and from. We say, in the end, what we are obliged to say, repeating our lines that we know so well we don't even have to commit them to memory.

Des Forêts' idea is that we tend to speak not because we have something to say (that possibility, except for certain stubbornly residual "cries" and/or graffiti,[2] having been effectively foreclosed) but out of a need to be heard. We talk to a listener whom we ask not to respond—

> ... un bavard ne parle jamais dans le vide; il a besoin d'être stimulé par la conviction qu'on l'écoute, fût-ce machinalement; il n'exige pas la repartie, c'est à peine s'il cherche à établir un rapport vital entre son interlocuteur et lui; s'il est vrai que sa loquacité grandit jusqu'à l'exaltation la plus folle devant l'assentiment ou la contradiction, elle se maintient en tout cas très honorablement devant l'indifférence et l'ennui.*

—but to give us the illusion that we are talking and being heard. Language, in this perspective, loses much of its traditional prestige, function, and "aura." It no longer enables prayer, comprises an art or literature, or facilitates communication between men. It is ready now for measurement

---

* "A chatterer, chatterbox never speaks in a vacuum; to be stimulated he needs to be sustained by the conviction that he is heard, even mechanically; he doesn't even ask for an answer, he's scarcely looking also to establish any kind of vital rapport between his interlocutor and himself; if it's true that his loquacity swells into the maddest exaltation before assent or contradiction, it holds its own also very well when faced with indifference or annoyance"; *Le Bavard,* 199 (1963 ed., 148).

and quantification; it becomes instrumental, its purpose sardonically reduced to that of physiological release— anatomical, excretory, sexual, and certainly, as in the ultimate Joyce, very *pressing*.[3]

Like monetary wealth (unjustly divided among men, and in unjustifiable ways), language has as its only purpose the distribution of gratification. Significantly, and of course ironically, our narrator will say in closing the long speech that constitutes this book: "Je me suis soulagé."*

It is not necessary that the words we use mean something, only that we speak; although a referent must be offered, at least temporarily, as a pretext for further discourse, this meaning, if taken too seriously, would interfere even with what we now derive from words. Sexual experience, that signifier that is its own signified, with its natural suppression and deflation of intellectual hierarchies, is as convenient a metaphor in *Le Bavard* as it was in *Finnegans Wake*.[4]

Language takes on a quasi-sexual function. The narrator explicitly refers to his ranting speech-confession as "une érection verbale" ("a verbal erection"; 94 [1963 ed.: 68]). Orgasm is presumably achieved when one has spoken enough, a condition that only the speaker is qualified to judge and after which one is "tired": "Or maintenant, je suis las. Allons, Messieurs, puisque je vous dis que je ne retiens plus personne!"† are the last words of the book. The essential point seems to be to talk until one is all talked out; and the main disaster to avoid, as in sex, is being interrupted. It therefore becomes clear that written expression, being unilateral, possesses clear advantages over living verbal expression.[5] The person (and eventually people) to whom the narrator unburdens himself is free to come and go as she pleases—as she has amply demonstrated by cutting herself loose from her first partner so as

---

* "Now I feel quite relieved."

† "And now I feel tired. Well, people, you know the way out, since I'm telling you very frankly I'm no longer retaining anyone"; *Le Bavard*, 214 (1963 ed., 160).

to "listen to" the narrator. The "fou-rire"* with which she
cuts off the narrator's speech is merely evidence of her
liberty to reject a nonreciprocal relation. The narrator, who
abruptly finds himself stumbling out of the bar with the
lady's laughter echoing in his ears, is at great pains to
disguise to himself and to his reader the true nature of his
embarrassment (which, according to our logic, is that he
has been stopped short of a kind of orgasm). He even pretends momentarily to feelings of *peaceful communion* in
the nighttime city and mentions his relief at being away
from a place where, because of the influence of the alcohol
he had uncustomarily consumed, he had violated what he
had assured the reader is one of his fundamental principles: to avoid talking about himself to others! He de-
spises above all people, he tells us now, those who confess
their inmost secrets to others. The reader, however, has
often been invited to regard the narrator's statements as
less than completely truthful; the narrator often claims
proudly that he is prone to lying and in the end even dismisses the entire story he has told as a pure fabrication,
although coyly qualifying this retraction by wondering
what his future reader will do with the problem of "did he
lie when he said he lied."

The true reason for the narrator's unhappiness and
frustration, then, has to be read "between the lines." He is
sad by no means because he has been "false to himself" or
to his *real* values (the typically romantic pose of Baudelaire, "enfin seul"† at one in the morning)[6] but because he
has been interrupted in the middle of his sexual-verbal act
by someone whom he believed to be a willing partner, if
not an accomplice. The advantages of the printed word become obvious in this light. The reader is not able to demand a reciprocity that would seem a natural right for
almost any listener. The pressure and urgency of the situation are then subtly displaced from the character to the
reader: our narrator is manifestly concerned above all

---

*   "Fou-rire" = wild laughter.
†   "Finally alone."

that the reader stay with him to time and space devoted to pleading with the reader certainly occupies a considerable portion of the text. One could even go so far as to say that, as in Beckett's trilogy and other modern texts we have been discussing,[7] the story is progressively eliminated in favor of the author's address to a reader—so that by the third and concluding chapter all pretense of the story having an independent, objective existence has been abandoned. The story (whether true or not) concludes at the end of the second chapter with our narrator's ostensible suicide; the last chapter takes up the reader's natural objection—"well, what are you doing still alive?"—to which the narrator replies, after having expressed at length his annoyance that his reader has the nerve to bother him with such triviality, that the story wasn't really true: the story has merely been used as a tool so that the reader wouldn't interrupt the narrator (put the book down) while he was talking.

The story disappears like a rainbow in a puddle in the bright sun of the narrator's "confession" that he invented only so as to have something to say; in fact, this secret is only revealed to us as a pretext in order for him to keep on talking a bit longer, for the laughter that our narrator says he fears even more than the woman's who interrupted him is his hypothetical reader's. He then *admits* he had misrepresented his mood in leaving the bar by claiming that his was a peaceful state of mind. The fact is he was as upset after hearing the woman laugh as if someone had spat directly in his face (107). Naturally, he anticipates his precious readers' reaction to this sudden and flagrant contradiction of himself: these readers

> seront bien surpris et qui sait? peut-être flattés si je leur révèle que j'ai cherché à les égarer en m'attribuant des pensées de tout repos moins par crainte de la honte que j'aurais pu éprouver à me remémorer ce rire déchirant comme un coup de couteau que parce que

j'avais des raisons de redouter un autre rire, je veux
dire leur rire précisément, oui, votre rire, messieurs!*

The narrator then goes on to deny that there is anything
comic in this situation; I think here he is as serious as he
ever gets. The literary method thus becomes what just
happens to be the chosen tool of a man who (like all of us)
is obliged to speak, who is driven to speak, for physiological reasons, and for whom the content and, a fortiori, the
style of what he says are secondary if not insignificant
beside his crying need to talk, talk, talk.

The narrator is careful to point out that this method
was not chosen out of love of literature, and he is equally
careful to distance himself from "literary" ambition. The
fact that the work is written in masterful prose and is in
its way a masterpiece, or at least a consummate tour de
force, should not obscure Des Forêts' subtle handling of
"the problem of literature."

We are inevitably referred back to the Hegelian critique
of art so central to the surrealist iconoclasm we have seen
at work in Tzara. We have also shown how this "attack on
the privileges of art" is explicitly and dramatically omnipresent in Blanchot, Leiris, and Sollers as well as implicit
but perdurable in Beckett and the ultimate Joyce. The critique that Hegel made of art is that it no longer represents
an absolute and that science and technology would inevitably take the place of art as man's most intense,
authentic, and representative expression of himself: in
other words, that art was already "chose passée" ("a thing
of the past"). Spengler's well-known pessimistic view that
the engineer[8] is the artist of our day and Rimbaud's scandalous refusal of the world of poetry in favor of the so-
called real world are certainly corollaries to this position.

---

* "[The readers] will be surprised and, who knows, possibly
flattered if I tell them that I've tried to mislead them in attributing calm
thoughts to myself less by fear of the shame I would feel at remembering this laughter, that really tore through me like a dagger, than because I had my reasons for fearing another's laughter, I mean their
laughter precisely, yes, your laughter, my dear sirs!"; *Le Bavard*, 108–9
(1963 ed., 80).

We do not mean to apply these generalities in a simplistic manner to the complex human issues that Des Forêts so uncannily elucidates, even if his narrator loses no opportunity to poke fun at mere "literature" and "literary gifts." We simply wish to suggest that his work constitutes, in its indirect, subtle way, the same kind of subversion of Western culture and art, together with the hierarchies and privileges they protect and express, as we have seen at work in other, more clearly radical, writers. In this sense, although Des Forêts' iconoclasm is certainly less explicit than Tzara's, Blanchot's, or Sollers', it is no less total and in its secret, perhaps insidious, way is equally sobering and provocative.

Des Forêts carries his demystifying approach even further in the subsequent stories that constitute *La Chambre des enfants* (*The Children's Room*). These "récits" invoke the ambience of the institutions (military, scholastic, domestic) of an old world gone rotten and having no hope for change or revival, whose inhabitants have no choice but to follow the paths already laid out for them, paths that by common agreement mean nothing and lead nowhere. Thus, after the "project" of literature has been deprived of all function, whether expressive or representative, the narrator of "Dans le miroir" sadly concludes about his single reader: "N'empêche qu'il me faudra lui soumettre la troisième version ce soir."* Human action is reduced in this "empty" world to obeying the letter of a law whose spirit has ceased to exist, to a survival by momentum. The teacher-student relation, in particular, offers Des Forêts a perfect opportunity to describe, through the words of one of his characters, the melancholy "no-exit" quality of this world, in which seeming choices, like rebellion and disobedience, only reinforce a structure of power that oppresses and shapes every instant of our lives:

—Ne comprends-tu pas que les maîtres ont dramatisé le règlement en donnant à nos rapports avec eux qui se

---

* "I've still got to give her the third draft tonight"; *La Chambre des enfants* (*The Children's Room*), "In the Mirror," 283.

substituent à lui le caractère d'un conflit permanent? C'est aux maîtres qu'il faut obéir, c'est par eux qu'on se fait punir, c'est donc à eux qu'on sera tenté de désobéir pour leur permettre, selon la formule insolente de notre élève, *de faire leur métier*. Résister sournoisement à leurs ordres, tromper leur surveillance afin d'encourir une juste punition, c'est rompre sans cesse avec la docilité satisfaite où nous risquerions de nous endormir, mais c'est aussi reconnaître la puissance invincible du règlement qui ne vit en nous que par la fréquence de nos délits. Et qui donc nous invite insidieusement à commettre ces délits, sinon les maîtres eux-mêmes par le rappel de nos devoirs comme par les sanctions dont ils nous menacent sans cesse?*

The young writer who is the main character of "Une Mémoire démentielle" ("A Crazy Memory") in the same collection has concluded that action, in his case literary action, is sheer futility. His initial idea was to preserve or recall certain significant events of his youth, such as a resentful and proud "silence" (natural pendant to the "noise" of *Le Bavard*) that was supposed to have lasted for an extended time and to have culminated in a dream of killing the principal of his school, after which he became a fugitive; but he judges, in conclusion, that dream and reality are so inextricably intertwined in the nevertheless vivid and convincing expression of these events that what

---

* "Don't you understand that the masters have dramatized the rules in giving to our rapport with them, which replace these rules, the character of a permanent conflict? It's the masters that we need to obey, it's by them that we're obliged to be punished, it's therefore them that we'd be tempted to disobey, to allow them, according to the insolent formula of our student, *to practice their trade*. Slyly resisting their orders, eluding their surveillance for the sake of avoiding a just punishment, is to break ceaselessly with the satisfied docility where we would risk lulling ourselves to sleep, but it's also to recognize the invincible power of the rule that lives in us only through the frequency of our violations. And who else therefore invites us insidiously to commit these crimes but the masters themselves by this appeal to our duty as well as by the sanctions they constantly threaten us with?"; *La Chambre des enfants*, 175.

he is preserving for posterity is precisely and only the *fiction of a memory*. He determines, nonetheless, that he must continue to write, even in the absence of any purpose that can withstand inspection, and with the added anguish that he will never know what it is exactly he is writing about or what his readers are reacting to.

We are playing here with a Proustian equation, but we must be careful to subtract from it any pride or consolation in a redeeming or transforming power of art. Time past is there as an area to explore, recapture, and remember, but it no longer pertains to our present. It is more escape, mockery, and lure than a direction for authentic search. The past is there, waiting for us, for Des Forêts as for Proust; but for the former it is no longer *worth* anything. Des Forêts' writer, like similar self-projections of Beckett and Blanchot, has been sentenced rather than rewarded; although this story has been told entirely in the third person singular, Des Forêts switches shockingly to the first person singular in the last few sentences, thus banishing any pretense to authorial detachment from a condition that resembles more nearly a predicament:

> Il rédigea une dernière version qu'il tint pour définitive, bien qu'elle ne fût pas moins caduque que les ébauches antérieures, mais lâchement, mais douloureusement il renonça cette fois à la détruire et rêva—essaya de rêver—qu'elle perpétuerait sa hantise. Préoccupé de lui assurer un prestige posthume, il connut les tourments comiques du littérateur. Je suis ce littérateur. Je suis ce maniaque. Mais je fus peut-être cet enfant.[*]

Des Forêts is obviously taking responsibility for these last

---

[*] "He composed a final version that he considered definitive, although it was no less obsolete than the previous sketches, but cowardly, sadly he renounced destroying it this time and dreamed— tried to dream—that it would perpetuate his haunting memory. Busy assuring himself a posthumous glory, he knew the comical torments of the literary man. I am this literary man. I am this maniac. But possibly also I was this child"; *La Chambre des enfants*, "A Crazy Memory," 222–23.

lines, whether or not we want to identify him with the precocious and sensitive child of whom he has been speaking. The author thus assures us, and personally, that people will continue talking, writers writing, singers singing[9] long after all content and meaning have been expunged from their lives. Man no longer believes in what he is doing, but the process must go on, even without a subject, purpose, origin, or end.

Des Forêts' texts acquire, obliquely, a peculiarly *political* dimension in the subtle and sudden ways they often "slip" from the existential conditions he depicts to include and embrace, while holding at a dignified distance, himself at the time of composition or, alternatively, his interlocutor, neighbor, other, and/or reader. The narrator of *Le Bavard*, who has invited us into his book by posing as a "special case" (11, where he insists on his singularity), concludes by expanding the *crisis*, that is, a mania to talk without having anything to say, to include all of humanity—of which he is only a particularly frank and self-conscious example:

> C'est entendu, je suis un bavard, un inoffensif et fâcheux bavard, comme vous l'êtes vous-mêmes, et par surcroît un menteur comme le sont tous les bavards, je veux dire les hommes. Mais en quoi cela vous autorise-t-il à me reprocher âprement le mal dont vous êtes vous-mêmes affectés? On ne peut me demander de rester dans mon coin, silencieux et modeste, à écouter se payer de mots des gens dont j'ai bien le droit de penser qu'ils n'ont ni plus d'expérience ni plus de réflexion que moi-même. Lequel d'entre vous me jettera la pierre?
>
> Ce que moins que tout autre vous paraissez disposés à me passer, c'est une certaine mauvaise conscience. Quand on a honte d'être un bavard, dites-vous, on commence par se taire. J'en conviens. Mais ce besoin fâcheux qui nous est commun constitue-t-il une tare sur laquelle ceux qui n'en rougissent pas ont le droit de me juger? J'ai la faiblesse de croire que mieux

vaut ma conscience, fût-elle mauvaise, que votre aveuglement.*

That prestigious and consoling quasi-absolute, the work of art, of literature, worthy of the rapt devotions and ardent labors of a Proust, a Flaubert, or a Henry James, becomes in the irreverent (though careful) hands of our narrator a mere means to an end. The process whereby contingent man has been substituted for the absolute (the Nietzschean event par excellence) has resulted in this extreme abdication of any transcendent meaning or value either for man or for his art. Not having a goal beyond himself to devote himself to, man has been reduced to his bodily existence, and all the traditional absolutes and highest cultural "goods" have become mere grist for his mills. The work of art will liberate, justify, or excuse nothing and no one.

That symbolist retreat, excoriated by Tzara,[10] of the artist into isolation, oneiric contemplation, memory (involuntary or not), no longer exists for our narrator. He flirts at one point with the alleged consolations of these methods, even going so far as to wonder about the stupidity of those who complain they can never be happy, when in fact happiness is available to anyone who wants it: all we have to do is close our eyes and dream, or find a peaceful place to

---

* "It's understood I'm a chatterer, an innocuous and annoying chatterer, just like you are, and, on top of that, a liar like all big talkers are, I mean to say men. But how does that entitle you to reproach me bitterly for the evil that you are infected with yourselves? You surely can't ask me to stay in my corner, silent and modest, listening to the idle chatter of people that I'm in my right in thinking are neither more experienced nor more thoughtful than myself. Who among you has the right to throw the first stone?

"What less than anything else you seem inclined to spare me is a certain bad conscience. When you're ashamed of being such a windbag, you at least can begin by shutting up. I'm entirely in agreement on this. But this exacerbating need that we share in common, does it constitute a weakness that those who are not about to blush over it have the right to judge me on? I'm weak enough to think that my conscience, even if it's bad, is better than your blindness"; *Le Bavard*, 191–92 (1963 ed., 143).

rest our gaze upon and that jogs a pleasant memory or
two. Our narrator shows us how this is done when, shortly
after his flight from the bar, he becomes painfully aware
that he is being followed (as we find out later, by the Spanish lady's disgruntled partner). His fear leaves him when
he enters a public garden, finds his favorite bench, and
reminisces about his past pleasures: one of his favorite oc-
cupations in this park was posing as a prospective cus-
tomer for the prostitutes and then enjoying their discom-
fiture when they realized he wasn't really interested. The
"past recaptured" that give him such solace was thus
merely an indulgence of voyeuristic and sadistic whim! His
feelings of superiority to those not able to attain such calm
regions of peace constitute some of the purest effrontery in
the text:

> ... contrairement à ce que voudraient faire croire cer-
> taines gens qui cherchent le bonheur sans jamais le
> trouver, celui-ci éclate sous leurs yeux et retentit dans
> leurs oreilles à chaque heure du jour, qu'ils le prennent
> donc où il est, ne fût-ce qu'un instant, et qu'ils cessent
> de nous fatiguer de leurs inutiles plaintes, c'est ensuite
> pour montrer l'importance que j'attache au rapport
> entre la brusque disparition de ma peur et les souvenirs
> de calme félicité qu'évoquait irrésistiblement pour moi
> la vue de ce banc sur lequel je venais m'asseoir. Il est
> en effet très frappant que j'aie cessé de croire à la réalité
> du péril à partir du moment où je me suis introduit
> dans ce jardin. Ce phénomène me paraît intéressant
> dans la mesure où il est symptomatique de la répercus-
> sion que de tels souvenirs, pour peu qu'ils conservent
> leur violent parfum, peuvent avoir sur le cours d'une
> pensée même dominée par la peur, comme c'est le cas
> ici.*

This "happiness" turns out to be fleeting and evanescent,

---

* "... contrary to what those who look for happiness without ever
finding it wish to make us believe, happiness explodes under their very
eyes and resounds in their ears every hour of every day, let them take it
where they find it, even if it's transitory, and let them stop annoying us

however; the painkilling power of this "music of memory"
is not limitless—and turns out to be quite weak indeed
compared to the perdurability of his fear and a dormant
masochism that now awakens and demands punishment,
fit preliminary to a spiritual regeneration:

> ... j'étais tout entier possédé par la musique fascinante
> des souvenirs, rien n'aurait pu altérer ma jouissance; à
> peine avais-je encore le souci du présent. Et cependant,
> cette musique elle-même, combien de temps subirais-je
> son pouvoir? N'allait-elle pas se dissiper à la longue et
> alors ne serais-je pas de nouveau exposé à expier par
> un cruel dégoût de moi-même la honte d'avoir parlé
> publiquement? Le fait est que tout se déroula suivant le
> processus que je viens d'indiquer, mais cette fois, si
> lourd était le sentiment de ma déchéance que, tenant la
> peur pour le remède le plus efficace, persuadé qu'elle
> seule me permettrait d'éprouver un certain allégement,
> sinon d'échapper complètement l'emprise du remords,
> j'en arrivais à la regretter ainsi qu'à souhaiter l'épreuve
> d'un châtiment dont je ne doutais pas de sortir
> régénéré.†

Another problem connected with the consolations offered by memory is that they frequently disappoint. The
narrator makes great efforts, for instance, to recall a certain feature of the lady's face that he found especially

---

with their useless complaints, it's therefore to demonstrate the importance I attach to the rapport between the brusque disappearance of my
fear and the memories of calm felicity the view of the bench I'd just sat
on evoked in me. In effect it's remarkable how I'd stopped believing in
the reality of the danger from the very moment I entered the garden.
This seems to me interesting inasmuch as it is symptomatic of the
repercussions such memories can have, if only they retain their violent
flavor, on the course of a mood even dominated by fear, as mine was";
Le Bavard, 132–33 (1963 ed., 98–99).

† "... I was entirely possessed by the fascinating music of memory, nothing could alter my joy. I was scarcely even worried about the
present moment. This music, however, for how long would I be subject
to its power? Would it not be dissipated in the long run—then,
wouldn't I be liable again to expiate with cruel disgust with myself the

pleasant to contemplate, her smile, but try as he might, he cannot resuscitate this feature; instead he is invaded by the memory of her laughter, mocking and rejecting him, inhabiting his present and destroying his peace of mind:

> ... j'essayais désespérément de me rappeler comment cette femme avait souri pendant que nous dansions ensemble ... même en faisant de très grands efforts, je ne trouvais plus la moindre trace de ce sourire dont j'ai dit pourtant quelle attraction il avait exercée sur moi. C'était très irritant: je voulais m'en souvenir, je voulais absolument m'en souvenir, je le voulais plus encore que je n'étais disposé à me l'avouer et j'essayais d'abord de me rappeler sa chevelure, quelle sorte de pierres pendaient à ses oreilles et la façon curieuse qu'elle avait de plisser les yeux en me regardant, et son nez, comment était-il déjà? et ainsi peu à peu et comme négligemment je m'approchais de la région brûlante, mais au moment où je croyais déjà tenir ce sourire, c'était un atroce éclat de rire qui envahissait tout le champ de ma mémoire. J'en étais quitte pour recommencer mes travaux d'approche en redoublant de prudence et de ruse, jusqu'à ce que des échecs répétés m'y fassent définitivement renoncer. En revanche, ce rire, je le voyais parfaitement, je ne le voyais que trop, et je craignais même que le souvenir pût m'en rester par-delà la mort.‡

Here Des Forêts is ransacking the "problem of memory" so prominent in the texts we have been exploring, from

---

shame of having spoken publicly? The fact is that everything happened in the way I've just indicated, but now, so overwhelming was my feeling of failure that, holding fear for the most efficient remedy, persuaded that it alone would allow me a certain relief, if not a complete escape from, the grip of remorse, I wound up even regretting my fear as well as ardently wishing for the ordeal of a chastisement from which I had no doubt I would emerge reborn"; *Le Bavard*, 134–35 (1963 ed., 99).

‡ "... I tried desperately to remember how this woman smiled while we danced together ... even with great effort I couldn't find the slightest trace of this smile whose attraction for me I've already admitted. This was annoying: I wanted to remember, I absolutely wanted to remember, I wanted it even more in that I was not disposed to admit

Tzara's strident denunciations of the faculty of recollection, to Beckett's ironic detachment from past comfort and future hope alike, to the "impossibilities" evoked with such verve and candor in the autobiographies of Leiris, to the "slates" that Blanchot and Sollers seem to be cleaning anew with every unprecedented fragment of consciousness they isolate in words.[11]

What seems to frustrate Des Forêts' narrator most is an inveterately Freudian lack of conscious control over our own minds, a weakness whose implication is to put into question, if not disrepute, our entire Western ideology of "making our own destinies." The problem with memories is that we don't choose them, they choose us; our memories, like our dreams, arise out of a deeper space within us than is subject to decision.

Just as our narrator experiences the time of memory as an inherently deceptive dimension, he directs the same withering critique at many other of our cultural expectations and conventions. His attack on commonly believed notions about the explanatory potential of childhood, background, and environment for adult behavior is particularly effective in this connection. For instance, he describes in depth a certain state of mind or mood, going so far as to think out a coherent, even rigorous philosophy to explain it, ushering in data and evidence from his past life, reaching back into his childhood, telling what his friends always thought of him, what his attitude toward women was—all to explain to or justify himself to or convince the reader of the reality and truth of his representations.

---

it and I tried at first to recall her hair, her earrings and the strange way she had of wrinkling her eyes while looking at me, and her nose, what was it like, really? And so, little by little, as if unintentionally I approached the place of my desire, I felt I was getting closer to it, but at the very moment when I believed I already possessed this smile, it was instead an atrocious burst of laughter that invaded my memory. I had to leave off in order to start again on my efforts to approach, with redoubled prudence and ruse, until repeated failures caused me to abandon the project definitively. On the other hand, that laugh, I saw it perfectly, I saw it only too vividly, and I was terrified that the memory of it would haunt me even beyond death"; *Le Bavard,* 105 –6 (1963 ed., 77).

Thus, when he is trying to talk us into believing in his tranquil state of mind after he has "fled" from the laughter in the bar, he describes himself as having always alternated between society and isolation, implying that when he has had enough of the former he goes to the latter (103–4). Although he has established and solidly reinforced a certain image of himself as being the kind of mature individual who could contemplate the recent disturbing events in a spirit of philosophical detachment and calm, it soon becomes apparent that he has built this picture up only to tear it down, for he has to admit presently that the relief he experienced in the beautiful winter cityscape of nighttime street and garden and in his intellectual rationalizations about "what he has always been like" was only a "represented" relief.[12] He is forced into this admission by the very strength of the thoughts and memories that he has not been able to control and that do not have to be represented because they are there already and clearly in charge:

> En voilà assez! Je mens! Je viens de mentir en épiloguant gravement sur le sentiment de détente que j'aurais éprouvé à contempler ce paysage froid et silencieux; pour dire enfin la vérité, je ne m'en souciais pas plus que d'évoquer cette femme qui avait irrémédiablement perdu à mes yeux tout le charme et le prestige qu'elle tenait pour une grande part de son sourire énigmatique. J'ai menti, je regrette de dire que mes dispositions n'étaient guère à la sérénité et quand on venait de me faire subir dans les conditions que je viens de décrire une offense qui m'avait blessé plus que ne l'eût fait un crachat reçu en pleine face, comment aurais-je pu attacher la moindre importance à la pureté glaciale de cette rue où je pressais le pas en rasant les murs comme un être honteux?*

The effect of this passage is to efface entirely the previous pages. What we are confronted with here is a prose that is

---

* "That's enough! I'm lying! I've just lied in discoursing gravely

written in a kind of "fading ink," for it seems to disappear shortly after pen has set it down on paper. This idea of the self-effacing work, self-erasing and autodestructive, is of course a perfectly modern event, one that our own century, with its technologically facilitated penchant for auto-annihilation, has been particularly fond of. The work doesn't wait until time, history, or even criticism has done its job but indicts, judges, and passes sentence upon itself, refusing to plead innocence or to desire or even accept a verdict of "not guilty."

That the work (*any* work) is inevitably culpable, sly, deceitful, we may now take for granted, while we are also very urgently invited to wonder about the motives of those that are obliged to reveal these things to us. As the events of this text, its postures, roles, settings, have been denied as enunciated, so in conclusion, in a kind of mathematics of nihilistic infinity, as of mirrors[13] reflecting each other, the work denies itself while incriminating this very denial:

> Mais j'espère que vous allez me demander pourquoi je me suis employé avec une ardeur si étrange à mettre au jour mes supercheries et à supposer que vous n'ayez nullement l'intention de me poser une telle question, j'ai quelque raison de penser que vous me la poserez quand je ne serai plus là pour répondre. Je réponds donc séance tenante, ce qui aura du moins pour effet de me mettre à l'abri du soupçon injuste d'éluder ce qui m'embarrasse, tout en me donnant l'occasion de satisfaire le peu d'envie qu'il me reste de bavarder. Je pourrais répondre qu'un remords tardif m'a conduit à

---

about the feeling of calm that was mine in contemplating the cold and silent landscape; to tell the truth, finally, my only thought was to summon up the image of this woman who had irremediably lost in my eyes all the charm and prestige that she had held for me—largely because of her enigmatic smile. I lied, I'm sorry to say that my mood was scarcely serene and since I had been obliged to suffer, in the conditions I've just described, an insult that wounded me more than a gob of spit in the face, how, indeed, could I have attached the slightest importance to the glacial purity of this street where I hurried my step, shadowing the wall like a shameful being?"; *Le Bavard*, 106–7 (1963 ed., 78).

dévoiler ce que j'avais mis tant de soin à voiler, que mon horreur native du mensonge a eu enfin raison de ma honte, qu'il m'a soudain paru inacceptable d'entretenir dans l'erreur ceux de mes lecteurs qui avaient eu la courtoisie de me suivre jusqu'ici; je pourrais répondre aussi, en me prêtant alors des sentiments moins nobles, que je trouvais une sorte de jouissance perverse à détromper moi-même mes propres dupes, que j'ai le goût d'exhiber mes tares ou qu'il me plaisait d'être honni par ceux que j'avais aguichés avec de faux appâts, ou encore je pourrais évoquer le plaisir puéril que nous prenons souvent à détruire ce qu'au prix d'un labeur sans trêve nous avons réussi à bâtir de nos propres mains. Mais naturellement, ce serait encore mentir. La vérité, c'est qu' à court d'imagination et pourtant encore peu désireux de me taire, je n'ai rien trouvé de mieux que de révéler mon escroquerie à ceux qui en étaient les victimes, et vous avez vu que je n'étais guère disposé à vous faire grâce d'aucun détail. Je ne me suis jeté si avidement sur ce nouveau sujet que parce que je n'avais alors rien d'autre qui me permît d'alimenter ma sotte et malheureuse passion. Le risible remplaçait le pathétique. Toujours est-il que je tenais bon, et c'était là l'essentiel: je parlais, je parlais, quelle jouissance! Et je parle encore.*

After once more having introduced the reader into the secrets of his soul and craft, the narrator, under the pre-

---

* "But I guess you're going to ask me why I was so busy and with such stubborn energy in revealing my deceit and even supposing you don't want to ask me this kind of question I have reason to think that you'll want to ask it when I'm no longer there to answer it. I reply then, this very moment, which will at least have the effect of dealing with the unjust suspicions that I've been avoiding embarrassing revelations, as well as affording me the opportunity to satisfy the little remaining need I have to go on chatting a little longer. I could answer that a belated regret caused me to reveal what I was so careful to hide, that my instinctive horror at lying had finally conquered my shame, that it suddenly seemed inacceptable to keep any longer in the dark those of my readers that were kind enough to come this far with me; I could explain also, in assigning less noble motives to myself, that I felt a kind of

tense of anticipating objection, has posed for himself the
further embarrassing question—why has he seen fit to
take down, brick by brick, this carefully constructed
edifice, turned into a facade of a facade? The conditional,
the favored form of other self-refuting, de-realizing authors[14] (Joyce, Blanchot, and Sollers), sets us up for the
subsequent "bursting of the bubble" of his reasoning, "je
pourrais dire," I could say. We are given, in convincing
depth, what could have been the reasons, or what we
could have been told were the reasons, were we dealing
with a less than honest narrator.

Not long before this, in an extended, eloquent, and persuasive figure, our narrator had compared his unveiling
the technique of illusion to the behavior of a bored magician who, tired of always deceiving the audience in the
same way, has decided to reveal to them step-by-step the
method by which they were deceived. One must imagine
Sisyphus happy, but not such an audience:[15]

> Imaginez un prestidigitateur qui, las d'abuser de la cré-
> dulité de la foule qu'il a entretenue jusqu'ici dans une
> illusion monsongère, se propose un beau jour de
> substituer à son plaisir d'enchanter celui de désen-
> chanter, à rebours de tout ce qui fait généralement l'ob-
> jet de la vanité et quitte à perdre à jamais le bénéfice
> qu'il tirait de sa réputation de faiseur de miracles.

---

perverse joy in undeceiving myself my own dupes, that I have a
predilection for exhibiting my own defects, or that I would enjoy being
reviled by those I had hooked with false bait; or else I might attribute
my 'frankness' to the childish pleasure we often take in destroying that
which, often at the cost of extraordinary efforts, we've built with our
own hands. But, naturally, that would still be lying. The truth is that,
short of ideas and nevertheless still with very little desire to stop talking, I found nothing better to do than to reveal my skulduggery to those
that were its victims, and you've seen that I was scarcely inclined to
spare you any detail. I've thrown myself so avidly into this new subject
because I had no other that allowed me to feed my foolish and
unfortunate passion. The ridiculous instead of the pathetic. But still I
was holding out, and that was the important thing. I was talking, I was
talking, what joy! And I'm talking still"; *Le Bavard*, 207–9 (1963 ed.,
154).

Qu'on ne s'y trompe pas, ce n'est pas par un tardif mais louable souci d'honnêteté qu'il lui vient la fantaisie de livrer ses recettes une à une avec la froide minutie d'un horloger qui démonte une horloge, il n'a pas de ces scrupules, c'est tout simplement par volupté de détruire ce qu'il a créé et de flétrir l'enthousiasme qu'il a soulevé, il étale donc ses pièces sur la table, donnant ainsi un air de vulgarité à ses tours les plus subtils, se délectant à décevoir ceux qu'il avait émerveillés, descendant de son propre gré du pinacle où ses dupes l'avaient porté, guettant avidement dans leurs yeux qu'agrandissait hier encore un étonnement d'enfant la première ombre de la désillusion, et pour peu que subsiste sur leur masque triste, pincé par un sourire vide la plus légère lueur de la foi, il se hâte de l'éteindre avec autant de soin qu'il avait pris la veille à l'entretenir. Suis-je cet homme cruel et fou?*

This elegant comparison and explanation must likewise be rejected with all the others. We are going to have to attribute the magician's strange behavior not to these noble or ignoble motives assigned to him by the narrator

---

* "Imagine a magician who, tired of abusing the credulity of the audience that he had maintained till then in a deceptive illusion, proposes one fine day to substitute for the pleasure of enchantment one of disenchantment, just the opposite of what people usually take pride in, and ready to abandon forever the benefit he derived from his reputation as a worker of miracles. Let's not make any mistake about it, it's not through a belated but praiseworthy concern for honesty that he's come upon this fancy of revealing his recipes one by one with all the cold calculation of a clockmaker taking apart a clock; he has no such scruples; it's simply for the joy of destroying what he's created and in order to dash the enthusiasm he's aroused that he lays his cards on the table, making his most subtle moves seem common and vulgar, delighting in baring the deception for those he had most amazed, descending at his own sweet will from the pedestal where his dupes had placed him, looking anxiously in their eyes, that only yesterday were widened in a childlike wonder, for the first hint of disillusion, and lest there remain under their sad faces and pinched empty smiles the slightest ember of faith, he hastens to extinguish it with as much dispatch as he had employed yesterday in maintaining it. Am I this cruel and crazy man?"; *Le Bavard*, 187–88 (1963 ed., 141).

for the reader's benefit (the narrator's fondness for such cold words as "bénéfice" (profit) and "duper," much as in Tzara's *Mouchoir des nuages*,[16] makes literature a matter of exploitation and "getting over," just like any other business) but instead to the crushing fact that the magician had run out of tricks and decided to reveal his act just to have a pretext for staying that much longer on the stage, that is, continuing to talk: "Vous êtes condamné à monter sur les tréteaux, il faut vous résoudre à faire le charlatan."*

The magician who shows his audience how his tricks are performed would be an appropriate symbol of the movement of art toward self-annihilation. That the light of reason is not always benign and altruistic is a commonplace in our time, well recognized by our romantic forerunners—by Shelley, for instance, who said, "We murder to dissect." One thinks also of Nietzsche's uncomfortable antagonism toward Socrates, whose universal application of a questioning attitude toward the totality of existence Nietzsche thought of as setting a noxious precedent for Western culture. Our narrator, as he is quick to admit, is hiding behind reasons and explanations that do not stand up under further investigation (as they never do). It is as if he is caught in a system of infinite logical regress whose bottom he can never touch, a system without any finality, not even the lack of finality.

The apt figure of the magician conveys us as close as we can come to the nature of the narrator. There is certainly something "magic" about this story. Blanchot has suggested it is a "ghost story without a ghost."[17] The text produces compelling illusions of reality that it then disperses in a puff of rhetorical smoke, leaving its reader to wonder whether to believe his eyes *or* his ears. The sensual realism of the descriptions, the "true-to-life" details, as, for instance, the Spanish lady's holding of a cigarette between thumb and index finger (90–91), establish a veracity too

---

* "You've been sentenced to mount the stage, you must be resolved to play the charlatan"; *Le Bavard*, 198 (1963 ed., 148).

indelible and attractive to be affected by any mere denial. Somehow our senses are prone to accept what our intellect is invited to deny. In our secular age we increasingly need this reassurance of the "real world" so we can venture all the more securely on other terrains. Edgar Morin has suggested that it is precisely our hunger for the fantastic that makes us require a foothold in so-called reality: "Realism, this refusal of falsenesss in the name of fiction, is the guarantee furnished to a conscience which is ashamed to engage in magic, *and which can no longer dream freely in the waking state.* A certain likeliness is necessary to the waking state so that it can let itself be captured by the dream . . . a certain guarantee of authenticity."[18]

Another aspect of narrative style that enters into the hypnotizing quality of the work is the predominant use of long sentences. These may run on for as much as a page or two, as, for instance, in the lyrical and evocative descriptions of the garden, parts of which I have cited, or the sinuous, seemingly endless sentences with which the narrator involves us in the bar scene (72–78). As in Faulkner, Proust, Claude Simon, and Michel Leiris, the reader is not given a chance to catch his breath, that is, to think, but because there is no place to stop is swept along irrecoverably into the mood and feeling.

One may remark also the echoes from other writers that permeate the text. Dostoevsky is here, whether we think of the talky drunkard Marmeladov of *Crime and Punishment* or the tortured confiding first-person narrators of *Notes from the Underground* and "Dream of a Ridiculous Man." Elements of the stream-of-consciousness technique are certainly present, as is the strange mixture of fantasy, ambivalent longing, and concrete detail characteristic of Kafka. Blanchot also points out parallels between the "je" of Leiris' overtly self-compromising *L'Age d'homme* and the "je" here, while noticing also that Camus probably borrowed from the concluding chapter of *Le Bavard* in *La Chute* for the themes of regret and guilt.[19]

An abandoned cart pointing toward the heavens has a distinctly symbolist resonance, and the following treatment of it can remind one of Poe, whom Des Forêts resembles not only in stylistic rigor but also in his obvious dedication to bringing off a predetermined effect whose nature has been concealed from the reader:

> Il me serait à peu près impossible d'analyser l'effet lugubre que me produisit cette charette solitaire dont les brancards tendus vers un ciel invisible en une attitude suppliante évoquaient à mes yeux ma propre détresse, sans que j'eusse pourtant sur le moment conscience d'un tel rapport; toujours est-il que ce spectacle me frappa de terreur et m'inspira le désir panique de courir devant moi, de me ruer à travers l'obstacle mouvant des ténèbres. . . .*

In any case these are deceptive comparisons, and they are meant to be. Des Forêts' distance from these techniques is obviously as great as Tzara's from the "literature" he mocks in *Mouchoir des nuages* or Sollers' from the *pastiches* he frequently performs in *Drame*. They are certainly part of his bag of tricks, his "dons littéraires," to which he refers, mockingly, more than once (14, 202); but their use amounts to a "détournement," a turning aside of these borrowed styles into the specially twisted meanings that the context of our author's cynicism gives them. Thus, the confessing "I" of Dostoevsky, Leiris, and Gide, although often an "unreliable narrator," still exists in some fashion, giving us the impression that there is a person behind the mask, whereas the "I" of *Le Bavard* remains thoroughly insubstantial, tending to evaporate as the story unfolds and to disappear behind a voice and mere words, much like the "I" of such experimental prose tracts as Beckett's *Unnamable* or even the nonexistent "I" of Sollers' *Drame*. The special effect of such techniques, therefore, is not to draw the reader into any particular ambience but to create

---

* "It would be very nearly impossible to account for the lugubrious effect produced on me by this solitary cart, whose handles pointing toward an invisible sky in a supplicating posture evoked in me my own distress without my really being at the time conscious of the analogy; still this spectacle struck me dumb with terror and inspired in me the panicky desire to run ahead, racing through the moving horror of darkness"; *Le Bavard*, 122–23 (1963 ed., 90).

little scenes that convince for a while, then vanish and are
erased, like scientific hypotheses that have outlived their
usefulness.

Des Forêts uses the traditional literary styles only to
discredit them—just as Baudelaire, in his mock-devotional
poem "A Une Madonne," creates an image of great sanctity
in order to desecrate it all the better.[20] Thus, in the closing
pages of the second chapter (159–86), our narrator goes to
great lengths to convince the reader of the reality of his
spiritual epiphany. He begins by describing a feeling of
great felicity that was produced by his hearing familiar
music even before he was aware that he was hearing it.
Identifying the sound as coming from a children's choir
turns into blissful musings on the source of his euphoria
(170), which he locates in his vanished childhood when at
school he sang in a chapel choir. A kind of "past recaptured" comes flooding back to the narrator, depicted vividly, eloquently, with great precision in all the richness,
courage, and strength of his youth. Like the young Rimbaud, he loved only the rebel, the outcast, and the
criminal:

> ... celui qui, insoucieux du scandale et faisant fi d'une
> réprobation unanime, lutte crânement à un contre mille
> pour imposer ses vues, fussent-elles erronées; le révolté
> qui, n'entendant pas se conformer à un état de choses
> qu'il réprouve et que tous admettent par veulerie ou par
> intérêt, n'hésite pas à braver les autorités qui le main-
> tiennent dans l'oppression, farouchement résolu à ne
> céder qu'après avoir remporté la victoire, fût-elle illu-
> soire ou trop lointaine; l'accusé, coupable ou non, que
> traque dans son box une société pourrie d'honnêteté et
> de bon sens, bref tous les opprimés auxquels la lutte
> solitaire confère une auréole de pureté.*

There follows an extended rhetorical development in which
the confidence and certainty of his youth are compared to

---

* "[The rebel] ... who, careless of scandal and defying unanimous
reproach, struggles stubbornly one against a thousand to impose his
own views, even if they're wrong; the rebel who, not intending to

the indifference and hopelessness of his recent years. As a standing up to his enemies, he was confident that someday he would be able to, but as an adult, he complains, he has become indifferent to such struggle:

> A mesure que j'avançais dans la vie, mon indifférence allait s'accroissant, rien ne me semblait valoir la peine d'aucun effort, et il en résultait que mon avidité n'était plus dirigée comme autrefois vers des idées de revanche ou de conquête: elle aspirait au contraire à ce qui saurait m'en délivrer. C'est qu'aujourd'hui le fracas des combats me répugne et me lasse, et j'en veux à mort à qui m'arrache de force à mon indifférence. Ne rien entreprendre, veiller, attendre, veiller ...†

We have been treated to an extended descriptive and narrative scene in a definite space and time, wherein our narrator ostensibly attains some fundamental understanding of the course of his life. Time past, present, and future melts into the lyrical simplicity of the conclusion of pardon, self-reconciliation, and the narrator is so carried away that he is ready even to plunge into a nearby river where the choir of children's voices seems to be beckoning, for, he asks himself, how to live past this moment of utter self-surrender? To guarantee the reality of this epiphany, our narrator is careful to specify that there is an *actual*

---

conform to a state of things that he rejects and that everyone resigns himself to out of interest or wickedness, does not hesitate to confront the powers that oppress him, ferociously resolved not to yield till final victory, even if it were illusory or very faint; the accused, guilty or not, whom a society that is rotten in its honesty and common sense hounds before its tribunals, in short, all the oppressed upon whom their solitary struggle confers a halo of purity"; *Le Bavard*, 175 (1963 ed., 130).

† "As I grew older, my indifference grew also; nothing seemed to me worth the effort, and the result was that my enthusiasm was no longer directed as before toward ideas of revenge or conquest; it aspired, on the contrary, to what would deliver me from these. For today the fracas of fighting disgusts me, bores me, and I feel a deadly anger at those who would tear me violently from my indifference. Undertake nothing—just watch, wait, wake ..."; *Le Bavard*,177 (1963 ed., 133).

choir practicing nearby. He has spent the entire night in the garden, much of it obviously unconscious, after having submitted himself gladly to a terrible beating at the hands of the man he had wronged. It is now dawn, and he asks himself exultingly, "j'étais prêt à obéir?"*— a merely rhetorical question whose triumphantly affirmative reply does not even have to be voiced. One is reminded of such classic moments as the "oh earth I will" lines of Rilke's *Duino Elegies*, the "Yes, I will Yes" of Molly Bloom, or the magnificent affirmation that concludes George Herbert's seventeenth-century religious poem, "The Collar":

> But as I raved and grew more fierce and wild
>   At every word
> Methought I heard one calling, *Child*!
>   And I replied, *My Lord*.

All of these "mystical moments," and many others, are relevant, but with one slight modification: when we turn the page, *this sumptuous epiphany has vanished into thin air.*

Chapter 3 then commences with our now crabbed and cantankerous narrator anticipating a certain embarrassing question from the reader: "What are you doing still here?" We are then asked to cancel out in our minds the entire previous scene, as we are told that its only reason for being was to serve as pretext to our narrator's indulging his need to talk some more. The scene has been only a mirage, or an illusion, produced by a master magician who is only too happy now to reveal to the reader "how it was done" as well as a choice of motives from which to select. The reader, certainly convinced that an epiphany took place, having been exposed also to an evocation of a particular person's childhood, with detailed descriptions of identifiable scenes —this same reader is now told that all of the preceding was purest fabrication and that it was meant deliberately to mislead.

---

* "Was I ready to obey?"; *Le Bavard*, 180 (1963 ed., 137).

We are now supposed to recognize, ruefully, the primordiality of the need of the talker to talk over what he is saying, since that *is* what he is saying. It is as if we have been listening to someone who has gone to great lengths to establish that he is a certain person with a specific past, projects, obsessions, and just when we think we've made a new friend, he suddenly informs us that he has totally misrepresented himself and has done so only because he likes to hear himself talk; and what is more, if only we had the honesty to admit it, we are exactly like him: "J'ai la faiblesse de croire que mieux vaut ma conscience, fût-elle mauvaise, que votre aveuglement."* More to the point might be a declaration of love, or some other proposition that demanded participation, or rejection from a listener, suddenly followed by a retraction—cancel all the previous—accompanied by some statement to the effect that the speaker just likes the way his voice sounds when he says "I love you." The listener is thus treated like a passionless machine, a computer, as it were, that can be programmed "clear" and is then ready for a new computation. Such behavior, pathological certainly, would result in the speaker's being treated like a lunatic by the listener. Rare indeed would be the listener who would consent to listen, seriously at least, to a speaker who had undermined the very basis on which human communication can take place. This is in fact what happens to our narrator as an outcome of the crisis in the bar. The Spanish lady refuses to hear him out. The "fou-rire" that accompanies him into his exile and that he will hear for the rest of his life (hypothetically, in view of the subsequent "retraction") is the merited and even just reward for his insane presumption.

We have been describing a situation that might be qualified as belonging to a kind of "bad faith." The endemic "bad faith" of writers in general and literature in particular, according to Sartre and others (certainly Leiris and Blanchot), is that in writing we have a tendency to evoke

---

   * "I've the weakness to believe that my conscience, even a bad one, is worth more than your blindness"; *Le Bavard*, 192 (1963 ed., 143).

dangers and risks that don't really threaten us, to pretend
that our lives and happiness are at stake when they are
not. An answer to this Pla- tonic charge of falsity (for Plato,
the writer is automatically suspect), as preferred by the
surrealists, Bataille, and some tormented others, is to
prefer the kind of writer who "writes with his blood," that
is, the artist who shapes his work out of the very substance of his pain, his risk, and his effort. Creval, Daumal,
Gilbert-Lecomte, Lautréamont, and Artaud have each cut
such a figure in the field of literature—as a writer who is
playing a dangerous game, whether taking mescalin, like
Michaux, in order to bring us some precious evidence back
from the "other side," or getting addicted to opium, like De
Quincey and Cocteau, to narrate their supposed cures, or,
at the other end of a spectrum, becoming politically involved, on the left (Nizan, Eluard, Aragon) or on the right
(Céline, Drieu la Rochelle), so that one's life is at stake or
at least permanently marked by extraliterary scars.

Des Forêts responds to this vulnerability of writing, to
the charge of falsity, escapism, and cowardice—bad
faith,[21] in short—by the subtlety and energy with which he
grapples with these issues, both directly in *La Chambre
des enfants* (where the problem of the relation of writing to
reality is explicitly explored) and by strong implication in
Le Bavard. Not able to achieve satisfaction in the realm of
the spoken, Des Forêts' narrator plays with the resources
of the written word. The unilateral rapport, so necessary to
the compulsive talker, is much more easily attainable in
the written than in the spoken form of the word. No one is
going to interrupt the writer, whereas the live speaker
risks the existential presence of a real interlocutor who at
any moment might avail himself of an option to cut off the
monologue or confession. The only real risk is that the
reader will abandon the work before the writer is done
talking, but his risk can be obviated by a careful and
clever use of traditional (or experimental) prose techniques, the purpose of which is not to express anything in
particular, as is certainly the case with the authors from
which they are borrowed, but only to keep this necessary
reader at his listening post to the end, that is, until the

talker is finished, has had the required satisfaction, orgasm—until he is *done* with the reader.

Once this end is achieved, there is no longer any need for pretense, as after a business deal or professional sexual act has been consummated, signed, sealed, or delivered, the initiator might feel free to reveal to the partner the devious means whereby the act might have been prepared and perpetrated. The writer, having no further motive for keeping his reader in a state of illusion, is free to deliver the secrets of his craft and in fact can get a little extra attention in the process; when he has absolutely no further use for us, when he is tired—as indeed he should be, if the analogy between his need to talk and the sexual act has any bearing—then we are, without any further ceremony, adjourned:

> Je suis arrivé à ce que je voulais obtenir. Je me suis soulagé, et qu'on ne me dise pas que ce n'était pas la peine. Or, maintenant, je suis las. Allons, Messieurs, puisque je vous dis que je ne retiens plus personne!*

It is too late for us to laugh now, or even to close the book. On the contrary, we probably tend to go right back to the beginning to see at least how it is that we, such clever and careful people as we think we are, have been induced to read and even enjoy something that turns out to be nothing—except a product of the need to talk.

---

* "I got what I wanted, I feel relieved now, and don't tell me it wasn't worth the effort. Well now, I'm tired; and, people, you know the way out, since I'm telling you very frankly I'm no longer retaining anyone"; *Le Bavard*, 214 (1963 ed., 160).

9

Madnsss, Theater, Text[1]

J. A. MILLER: So who ultimately, in your view, are the subjects who oppose each other?

FOUCAULT: This is just a hypothesis, but I would say it's all against all. There aren't immediately given subjects of the struggle, one the proletariat, the other the bourgeoisie. Who fights against whom? We all fight each other. And there is always within each of us something that fights something else.

—"The Confession of the Flesh"[2]

I

We have been exploring a literature that suppresses story, plot, action, and event, that refuses to create character, that elides author and reader, and that falls back upon language as a kind of last refuge or generating mechanism, an intolerable but irrefutable and consummately necessary recourse to which some kind of unrecognizable subject has been reduced. This is a fundamentally nomadic literature, which refuses materiality as well as ideality and is at home nowhere, not even in itself, as it declines equally to legitimize or endorse the social hierarchies in which it nevertheless has to admit reluctantly it occurs.

It is, of course, not so easy to be subversive, not simply a matter of deciding which of the discourses, styles, techniques, habits, and institutions are oppressive and then denying or opposing them. The negation becomes a discourse of power in its own right and invites further opposi-

216

tion. The self-eliding author becomes a kind of author, the unreliable character assumes substance in its very lability, while the problematic reader accepts or even enjoys the new status that the very uncertainty may confer. Indeed the refusal to tell the story, as in Blanchot's *Madness of the Day*, becomes the story, or at least enough of one to write. Whether it is a matter of Kierkegaard's antiphilosophy, Tzara's antipoetry, or Sollers' antinovels, anarchic premises must ultimately admit dependence on and continuity with the structures they ostensibly deny.

However iconoclastic, unprecedented, and surprising our subject and language, when we play with literature, we are playing the game of a power that will have the last word as it had the first. What characterizes an antiliterature is not so much its advertised refusal to employ the traditional illusions, deceptions, and seductions—to which, in any case, it must inevitably return, and which it never really left behind—but instead a certain mood of detachment from and aloofness or disdain toward the means it sees itself as being obliged to deploy. The writer is no longer proud, masterful, and controlling but rather ashamed, culpable, and controlled. He acknowledges, perhaps, that he must function within a certain vocabulary and order, say, that of "book" and "work," but he no longer pretends to master these categories that he sees all too clearly that he is mastered by. Instead he sees himself more modestly as living within them for a time, because for now there is no other shelter. Our belief in the things we do and think and in the structures in which we are obliged to perform is now evanescent, transitory, and transitional.

No longer really authors and readers, professors and students, doctors and patients, sellers and buyers, we are now all consummately actors.[3] We throw ourselves, with all the trappings of reality, into whatever role is required, promiscuously simulating involvement or unconcern, gratification or frustration, communication or incomprehensibility—but we are no longer, as in the game of confidence, who we present ourselves to be, as rapidly arriving and equally convincing avatars of our next performance will bear out.

II

It is appropriate, then, that two of the figures for the human condition that modernist literature prefers are those of madness and the stage, for these are consummately temporary stations. Madness is quintessentially the absence (and also plethora) of work, of book, of memory, and of continuity that is so anguishing today; and schizophrenia, restlessly seeking and spiraling ever outward, compelled by its own inner logic and necessity and endemic refusal of accountability, its incessant "and then ... and then,"[4] serves as apt symbol, once it has been demedicalized, of a model for desire, availability, and functional endlessness in some of the most effective and influential texts of our times.[5]

The metaphor of the actor is equally perdurable and ubiquitous, as the direction of advanced theatrical theory and practice in our century has unquestionably been toward the elimination of barriers, frontiers, and limits between public and audience and the increasingly undeniable mutability and contingency of their rapport. There has been correspondingly a devolution of the theatrical from a situation of rarity and exceptionality to its massively therapeutic, corrupting, disorganizing, and/or transmogrifying invasion (through media) of "everyday life."

Modernism in general is permeated by and preoccupied with questions of insanity and theatricality, as we have witnessed, since the romantics, a rehabilitation of both these formerly marginal and intrinsically culpable categories. Madness becomes a crucial focus and center for a "medical gaze," increasingly sliding in a movement from physical to mental in a century-long development from autopsy and diagnosis to analysis and, most recently, conditioning. On another tangent, the romantics, reviving a Platonic connection that a classical "age of reason" had occluded, used madness as inlet into art and as privilege, brand, fate, and message of its perpetrators. The history of literature, from Blake to Baudelaire, Lautréamont, the symbolists and surrealists, to its improbably noncontaining limit and extreme in *Finnegans Wake*, bears witness to the compelling power, flexibility, and relevance of this dimension of experience: madness moves from a position of externality to the text, perhaps inhabiting its author, his characters, or waiting for same, to a position closer to the text and finally inside it. We may follow this evolution from the text's celebration of the author's own irrationality, as with Blake and Whitman, to the corruption of the text through hints as to its inseparability from insanity, outright as with Nerval, or that of the abnormal states chemically induced, as if for the purpose of writing from them, by a Coleridge, a De Quincey, a Rimbaud. Finally we arrive at the modern avatar of the text "gone mad," which may have begun with Mallarmé, through to *Finnegans Wake,* and beyond to Blanchot, Derrida, Sollers, Leiris, and those moderns whose texts convey intentions, structures, and wills of their own—whose connection to authorial agency or even a reading public is problematic. This is the text that Barthes has called "intransitive" and that stands madly and stubbornly aloof from origin as well as destination and utility.

The idea of theater has evolved in an equally remarkable way. Traditionally a barely tolerated and certainly a quarantined activity, its subversive energy and disorganizing potential are well acknowledged in a history of Catholic, then Puritan, containment or rejection. Rousseau's ironic warnings, in a strange letter to the citizens of Geneva, against a theater that he obviously knows all too well, are based on the supposition of the corrupting influence of the art; likewise, Diderot's lucubrations on the paradox of the comedian define a kind of altered state where that actor is best who acts a role that he does not feel. As religious taboos and social proscriptions loosen and church and state become problematic, transitory, and mutable institutions, the sin of acting and actor, as of madness and madman, mutates into a mark of glory and cause for celebration. We also see, in our own century, a merging of madness and theater, as madness becomes the consummate act, in the sense of the Freudian masking symptom, or an effort at communication or expression, as with Georg Groddeck.[6] Theater becomes likewise inextricably intertwined with madness with Artaud and the subsequent "living theater" he inspires.

III

The popularity of these metaphors is probably owing also to the answers they are capable of supplying to the question of the culpability of art that, as we have seen, occupies such a prominent place in the panoply of self-apologizing works we have been looking into. The artist's madness is guarantee of his removal from the ulterior motives of literary endeavor. On another level, the drugged, the compulsively criminal, the author who spends himself in lost causes, are all distanced from their works, consigned to a destiny that glory can very little inflect and where even royalties, when they arrive, may make very little difference.

Just as the mad author, because he is beyond the pale of such benefits, is distanced from the kind of charges that Tzara and the surrealists leveled against art as merely a subtle form of investment, so also is the mad text equally removed from an author who is a mere agent of its production. The *Wake*, for instance, functions as a machine that has been precoded to perform in a certain way, its only rule being a limitless lability shuttling in ever-returning spirals of complexity and simplicity; and we have seen how paradoxically a text so personal and unique as Leiris' nevertheless propels its author all the more surely into a limbo of nonrecognition and nonexistence, where even the avower of most intimate secrets cannot see himself today in the confessions of yesterday. The texts of Beckett are equally mad, denying exit if not entry, theatrical and evanescent, not so much authored as ushered into their public —as an element of a rapport where futility assumes the cosmic dimension of a Kantian a priori, that is, where it is the irremovable basis of perception; likewise, the books of Blanchot and Sollers obey structural imperatives that remove them, as discrete entities, from author and reader alike, while erasing the very words in which they are written. Mad also is the text of Des Forêts, mere discourse that disallows itself and its narrator, while turning the reader into its uneasy, if amused, quasi-sexual accomplice, audience, and dupe.

Above all, these texts make one mad in the reading. Whatever pleasures of novelty, surprise, intellectual stimulation, and colloquy they provide are more than paid for in the disequilibrium and restless insecurity they cannot help but convey. These are, as Kafka and Nietzsche suggest all good writing should be, dangerous books. The reading of a text as threatening sexually, as indigestible morally, socially, or intellectually, as Bataille's little masterpiece, "Madame Edwarda," must be a confused and tormenting experience; for in that tale the mind shows itself no match for the super- or all-too-human powers of a lust that dwarfs all human effort and flattens every pretension to harmony of flesh and world. Mind-altering also is the mood of the *Wake* where thought and language, as we have ever known them, go their separate ways. These texts complicate rather than simplify our lives; we may read them through but can never really put them behind us for the simple reason that when we look back they're not there.

We rather recover from than remember these books. Stories like those of Blanchot and a fortiori Sollers are functionally and structurally incapable of recall, since conspicuously absent from them are the assurances on which memory depends for its associations, or if some coordinates are supplied, they are so utterly refracted, assaulted, denied, and requalified that they serve more as lures than as guides. There is no alternative but to pass through these hells again and endlessly.

These are catalytic, insulting, and arousing texts. Like Tzara's *Seeds and Bran*, with its Sadean visions of universal anarchy, they awaken simultaneously in the reader emotions of fascination, dismay, and incredulity. Or as with the testimony of Beckett's *Unnamable*, Blanchot's pronominal projections, or Leiris' extensive but inconclusive avowals, they will leave us wondering what the author is really talking about or if indeed there is anything (left) really to talk about. They leave us wondering, doubting, questioning, rather than satisfied, informed, and feeling enriched. As in Sollers' strategic fictions that refuse to be (un)real or Des Forêts' canny innuendos that always find their mark, they mock, employ, delude, defy, forbid, seduce, and offend a reader and reading at every turning.

IV

The theatrical metaphor has followed a career in relation to the text that may closely resemble that of madness. The idea of the world as theater is a familiar derealizing device, present, for instance, in the cabalist-alchemical tradition and in the literature of the Renaissance;[7] but theater, like madness, has evolved from a position of externality as subject matter, metaphor, or abstraction finally to invade, occupy, and corrupt the text itself. In a world where reality is dubious because the instances that guarantee it are enfeebled, performance and simulation become the rule rather than the exception. Just as the mad text shatters by refusing to recognize any understanding, communication, or utility between author and reader, so by abolishing the separations on which they are based does the text-as-theater undermine a common ground of connection, ritual, and socially redeeming catharsis between player and public, stage and audience. Theater, like madness, moves from a position of rareness and relegated exception to one that is central, inescapable, necessary, unavoidable, and therefore incapable of being defined as a distinct category or style. In this context the actual stage, just as much as the real asylum, is supererogatory if not superfluous.

For the text-as-theater there is no longer any sheltered domain where the spectacle does not penetrate.[8] In the *Wake* the very language of sleep and the unconscious becomes act, myth, and performance; and for Beckett's subject similarly there is no place apart from the public gaze, since his very poverty, homelessness, helplessness, and abjection make escape from the "panopticon" impossible.[9]

In Leiris also we may witness a kind of culmination of an evolution that, from Rousseau to Freud and Gide, worked in the direction of placing in the public domain all intimacy, secrecy, and reserve; and the confessions of Leiris, however convincing, courageous, and total, assume inevitably the same distance from their narrator that lines do from an actor who is merely voicing the words of another.

A text-as-theater employs words not necessarily as communication, expression, or representation but instead, intransitively, as threshold, simulation, and decor. The words have no meaning and are not meant in any sense that points beyond themselves to some preexistent purpose, design, or message. As in the discourse of Des Forêts' bavard, they say nothing beyond the fact that they are said, recited, performed—and in the end we know nothing except that somehow we have been lured into listening to them. The texts of Blanchot and Sollers bring out even more explicitly and undeniably a disconnection of the word from any substance, identity, or reality, for identical verbal formulations float interchangeably among authors, characters, readers as so many lines that anyone can say but that can belong to no individual. The madness of the text, infinitely available, disposable, floating, insecure, and mutable, is the theatricality of a word that can only echo indefinitely in an auditorium from which there is no exit.

V

A modernist discourse that denies, elides, and abolishes all exclusions, privileges, and separations nevertheless constitutes an interdiction in itself; we have gone beyond the interdicted to come up against the fact of interdiction itself. The judgments, opinions, ideas, and pronouncements of language may all be negated by, for instance, playing them cunningly against each other; but there remains the fact that language, word, verbalization, text are interdictory, prescriptive, and proscriptive in themselves. Our culture limits any significant access to discourse to a very tiny minority by a subtle but pervasive network of exclusions, inhibitions, and prohibitions. No domain of resources is guarded more heavily or parceled out more stingily than the right to speak. We go in terror, as Foucault says,[10] of the prospect of the unleashed, uncontrollable power of a liberated word that would dissolve our society in a flash flood of incoherence and noise. Our "disciplines" function, then, as tyrannical mechanisms whose fundamental purposes are relegatory and defensive.[11] Experimentation, flexibility, and invention, while tolerated or even encouraged in the limited domain of restricted access that constitutes modernist writing, carry heavy penalties and enormous risks where they occur outside of quarantine—as in the "crime" of graffiti.

Modernist discourse does not so much liberate us from the "tyranny of the word" as reveal or unmask this tyranny for what it is, as belonging to the exclusionist, segregated, and segregating function of the word in our society. Rather than freeing us, this discourse reveals our situation as intrinsically unfree, trapped, and hopeless; the society in which such a predicament is inevitable is correspondingly negated, delegitimized, and discredited. The potential for subversion of this discourse, therefore, does not lie in its ability to liberate us from conventions, traditions, and illusions, which it does not do except by replacing them with others that ultimately are equally stifling. What is most iconoclastic about this discourse, instead, is its ability to reveal, by experimenting with its realization, that freedom is a purely formal category in our culture,[12] that in fact it does not even have to be revoked since it is—because of the vested interests that prevail—a pure impossibility, fiction, and lure. What modernism does is call into question by calling the bluff of a power that, in order to command the assent necessary for its hegemony, must promise so much but is able to deliver so little.

VI

La conscience sort des ténèbres, en vit, s'en alimente,
et enfin les régénère, et plus épaisse, par les questions
mêmes qu'elle se pose, en vertu et en raison directe de
sa lucidité.*

—Paul Valéry

A culture for which the unknowable is nonexistent
is incapable of accepting the modernist text on its own
terms or taking seriously its claim to proud uniqueness
and intransitivity.[13] The very anomaly and strangeness of
the work cry out in social terms for commentary, normalization, criticism, and entry into or exclusion from a canon.
The difficult text spawns all the more surely an industry
whose function it is to find some way for it to fit in or some
rationale for shutting it out. Just as madness and other
related nonconformity (crime, drugs, suicide, homelessness) invite the birth of a class of professionals that act to
rationalize, reduce, or, as a last resort, exclude the perpetrators, so the anarchic in art supports a thriving industry
that lives off the attempt to explain it. The problematical
work invites commentary by its very refusal to communicate. Its madness provides investment, games, livings, rep-
utations, activity, careers, excuses, subsidies, educations,
energy. Its disorganization and disorganizing potential
mobilize the resources of a society—to channel, turn back,
correct, and protect itself from its dangerous example and
nerve, just as in other areas where the threat and/or
promise of the unknown call forth the professionals whose
function it is to "understand" such doings.
     This critical, professional, and normalizing function
often occurs, of course, synchronically with the anarchic,
creative, and disruptive—frequently in the same individual

---

* "Consciousness emerges from darkness, lives on it, feeds on it,
and finally regenerates it, and an even deeper one, by the very questions it asks itself, by virtue and reason, directly, of its light"; *Tel Quel*
1:62.

and work. Just as a marginal person may feel called upon
to rationalize his behavior in terms of circumstances,
categories, and courses that may give him entry and some
kind of status in the society that has excluded him, so an
anomalous author of an incomprehensible text, within
and/or without the work, may furnish a critical apology or
justification that creates a framework necessary for artistic
or even biological survival; and so we have the familiar
modern figure of the writer who functions as his own first
and worst critic and judge, in a kind of split of personality,
role, and identity—anticipating and responding to the elements that require interpretation and domestication.
Writers whose works strain the limits of acceptability tend
to provide an ideological superstructure to contain, channel, and explain the anarchic rush of chance encounter
and iconoclastic energy.

For the surrealists—Tzara, Breton, Gilbert-Lecomte,
Daumal, and others—that superstructure is a compound
of Freud, Marx, and alchemy. Such a writer was also the
Joyce of the *Wake* (and to a lesser extent the earlier Joyce),
so frequently apologizing, interpreting, instructing both
within and without the work, organizing, orchestrating,
and, by pseudonym, even participating in a critical chorus
that chants its hosanna of welcome even before the book is
really born.[14]

First and most exhaustive and suspicious critic of himself is also such a writer as Leiris, fanatically, hypersensi-
tively, and neurotically anticipating all conceivable artistic,
social, political, or moral objections. In Leiris the critical
function has become so automatic it is inseparable from
the creative since his text operates systematically as commentary on itself.

For Blanchot these functions, whatever the penetration
of theory and even philosophy into the text, are distinct;
however, he sets up a formidable critical apparatus that,
discretely avoiding self-commentary, nevertheless shelters,
nourishes, and celebrates specifically those fragmentary
and problematic works whose relation to his own is close
and cordial.

Likewise, Sollers' reviews, *Tel Quel* and now *L'Infini*, provide a critical arena where his works can be received, explained, and justified. Self-judging also is the text of Des Forêts, whose book is at once accusation, defense, and commentary on itself and whose public is synchronously present, anticipated, and constantly related to in the very act of narration.

Critical commentary and judgment, however, are not necessarily, at least in their eventual consequences, always normalizing and domesticating instances. Once the unknown seems to become known, the writer may be allowed, or allow himself, to return refreshed and reassured to his arsenal of anarchy and disruption. A movement may be described from the unknown to the known and back to the unknown. In this sense the commentary can be seen not so much as an end but as a phase.[15] The commentary may also work to delegitimize itself: the greater the display of critical acumen, brilliance, and ingenuity, the more clearly its own futility and irrelevance may stand revealed—and correspondingly the necessary failures of our society in its incapability of providing any real place for authentic artistic endeavor in general or individual expression in particular. Works like the *Wake*, Sollers' antinovels, Blanchot's or Des Forêts' forbidding tales may emerge intact at the end of the critical tunnels that have been mined for them to pass, as so many finally indigestible particles—impossible for a social body either to absorb or eliminate and therefore a continuing and permanent threat to the homeostasis of the organism.

Critical commentary may also operate disruptively and radically by a sort of smuggling, ushering the anarchic writer into the innards of a system where his sabotage can be more effective, as may be the case in Sartre's rehabilitation of Genet.[16] An effective critical intervention can deprive the repressive social structure of the interdictory and exclusionary powers it needs to operate, at least insofar as this structure stands by means of consensual validation. Such a criticism may eliminate or render problematic, weak, and porous the quarantined category of the freak,

the mad, the socially useless, the incorrigible, or the irreconcilable—by making of these terms so many indictments
against the institutions that profit and prevail by their formulation and application.

What commentary finally may reveal in relation to the
modernist text are the very limits of knowledge, the inability of thought to cope with, judge, justify, and control its
processes and products; for commentary finds blocking its
progress, hegemony, and path those works that are impossible to fit into any preexisting or conceivable scheme or
category, that reject glory while at the same time refusing
oblivion, that resist definition as well as defy exploitation.
These works point us toward an unattainable freedom, a
nonexistent subject and desire, and away from any accommodation with a ruling ideology or prevailing political theory or practice. They suggest without suggesting anything;
they evoke the sense that something is happening somehow without trapping us into the modalities of definition
and categorization as to what exactly it is. They carry out a
dynamic strategy rather than express anything, pushing
writer and reader into an indeterminate realm where everything is open to further exploration and doubt.

These works contest endlessly all roles, ideas, notions,
and stabilities, including their own sufficiency and reliability. The formulations they make are all profoundly re-
vocable, all exquisitely a matter of situation and condition,
taking away the worlds they summon as fast as they appear. They are models, if anything, of the fact that there is
no model or guide, and not even that.

Indefatigably preferring situations, quandaries, predic-
aments, and problems that are incapable of explanation
and rationalization, these texts reveal the insufficiency
and inadequacy of any conceivable cultural apparatus that
pretends to be capable of dealing with them and so work
toward invalidation of the systems of social control in
which they occur. Denying all substance and any reliable,
stable identity to author, reader, text, story, character, or
critic, they exist, if anywhere, in an intangible *between*
—where all is anticipation, movement, and (dis)connec-
tion.

It is finally necessary to invent a critical discourse and vocabulary that, no longer hoping to account for these texts, can at least approach them in feeling, spirit, and intention. As a Russian formalism attempts to respond to Rabelaisian or Dostoevskian polyphony, or a structuralist poetics to correspond to the aesthetic of Proust and Claudel, so the deconstructive and other allied poststructuralist approaches relate to these opaque and intransitive texts of modernity.

The very words, therefore, that inform deconstructive critical practice are necessarily entities that shy away from solid statement, judgment, and definition. They are terms, as in the Derridean thesaurus[17] of floating signifiers, of relay, hesitation, ambiguity, and delay, that call attention to lines and vectors of energy and thought rather than to points where things arrive. This is a no-man's-land where all is vulnerability, hazard, and waiting-to-be, where all *depends* and nothing can be established except in relation to something else that refers us indefinitely in all directions except home. The signs here are entities like nexus, network, structure, pattern, system, design, process—an array of interchangeable (or overlapping) items whose meanings, directions, goals, and import vary with place, conjuncture, and situation. In this sense deconstruction's role is to elide all meaning and fixity by directing attention toward aspects of the textual apparatus that forbid all security as they deny all knowledge and certainty. Deconstruction points us toward the humbling recognition and reversal that we must admit that we do not (and are not able to) know what we are really talking about, and when in fact we think we do, it is because we have not examined the texts and contexts carefully enough.

Deconstruction pushes us from the stations, decisions, and values where we have taken residence back into the arena of chance, risk, event, and performance. Deconstruction's delight is to bring out the uncertainties, ambiguities, dualities, and irresoluble quandaries in texts that our culture has most securely relied upon, chasing us always from positions that we occupy in relation to them, showing us how we have minimized the anarchic potential of these works and suppressed and channeled their energy into supports for our complexes and vested interests. When deconstruction deals, on the other hand, with works that directly inspired it (Heidegger, Artaud, Bataille, Blanchot, Valéry),[18] therefore manifestly and undeniably projecting a withering critique upon all stability and also their own existence, then its role is rather to prevent any closure, conclusion, or certainty from forming around the work itself. Deconstruction, then, aims to prevent the work from becoming established in any comfortable social or academic setting, rejecting hypostatization as well as codification and hierarchy to maintain freshly provocative its subversive potential,[19] defending it, even, if necessary, against the "author" himself, who, subject to pressures of his own, may sooner or later be inclined to deny it.

The critical function in this deconstructive mode, therefore, is to isolate the work from author and reader alike, to grasp what is at stake in the textual mechanism that has been unleashed, to protect the text against its originator as well as against its reader and the institutions that work to contain it. The fidelity that is deconstruction's is not to any reputation, work, accomplishment, or achievement but to the operation, process, and event, of which the literary text is only a passing, if crucially significant, moment. It is in this sense that we may conceive of deconstruction as being as much an ethics as a critical theory. Deconstruction works, then, to keep the intrinsic "madness of art" from devolving into sanity and code. For deconstruction, the interesting moments and elements in any system, work, and structure are not those connected with its utmost eloquence, pertinence, viability, power, and control but instead those wherein these entities seem to be coming apart—points of futility, ambiguity, contradiction, and doubt.

Those works are profoundly deconstructive and deconstructions for which failure (to make any kind of total sense) is endemic, pointless, and inevitable, works that functionally forbid and dismay understanding and comprehension, as they resist also the capturing and co-opting potential of our memories and desires. With the literature of deconstruction it is a matter, therefore, of the perpetual and paradoxical I between[20]—that necessary gap and absurd hiatus, connection, and distance that is to be neither accepted nor abrogated but always instead *contested.* Ultimately, deconstructive man can claim nothing but an inaptitude for complacency.

Renvoi

Who is this "person" who wrote all the above? If there is someone to answer, "Yes, I am he," does that make it so?
  Or is the mask now saying, the voice behind the mask,
    I am the mask on the mask
Do you wear the mask of who you want to be (loved)?
And what do masks feel in their turn? We know masks *pretend* to feel.

It's only a demon who would say there is nothing behind but another one (devil = inventor of infinity, of never as of ever)
Glas doesn't end but is cut off
    Glas means end
        We never stop ending
Or you could sign it with your tear

Notes

Chapter 1. Introduction

1. Jacques Derrida, *Writing and Difference*, 24.
2. David Carroll, *The Subject in Question: The Languages of Theory and the Strategies of Fiction*, 169–200.
3. *Théorie d'ensemble*, an important collection (1968) of writers connected with Sollers' radical review, *Tel Quel*, where these philosophers and novelists were all "working" together.
4. Christopher Norris, *Deconstruction: Theory and Practice*, 22–24.
5. Nothing, however, *inherently* limits the deconstructive "method" to any specific age (Renaissance, baroque, eighteenth century, even early Christian period), as two far-ranging recent treatments show: Ralph Flores, *The Rhetoric of Doubtful Authority; Deconstructive Readings of Self-Questioning Narratives*, St. Augustine to Faulkner; G. Douglas Atkins, *Reading Deconstruction, Deconstructive Reading*. Derrida, questioned in *Positions* about "the relation of your work to the textual work called 'literary,'" explains the special attention he has given the moderns, for it is they who have taught us how to read those who anticipated them: "Yes, it is incontestable that certain texts classed as 'literary' have seemed to me to operate breaches or infractions at the most advanced points. Artaud, Bataille, Mallarmé, Sollers. Why? At least for the reason that induces us to suspect the denomination 'literature.' ... These texts operate, in their very movement, the demonstration and practical deconstruction of the *representation* of what was done with literature, it being well understood that long before these 'modern' texts a certain literary practice was able to operate ... against this representation. But it is on the basis of these last texts ... that one can best reread ... the law of the previous fissures." Derrida, like Blanchot, who "taught him how to read them" (see n. 9 below), finds most relevant those moderns who make the very existence of their literature problematic, for their works already constitute bold deconstructions of the "literature" of the past.

6. Wallace Martin, in his introduction to *The Yale Critics: Decon-struction in America*, edited by Jonathan Arac et al., cites Paul de Man and J. Hillis Miller in this connection. The latter he sees making the "argument that literature demystifies or de-constructs all attempts to accord it a special status" (xxviii).

7. Donald G. Marshall, "History, Theory, and Influence: Yale Crit-ics as Readers of Maurice Blanchot," in *The Yale Critics*, 146: "Blanchot begins his inquiry with those for whom writing is a question."

8. Atkins, *Reading Deconstruction*, 1: "Inaugurated in America in 1966 by Jacques Derrida's devastating critique of Lévi-Strauss at a Johns Hopkins symposium, deconstruction has become the critical rage." At that meeting, however, Derrida uses the word only once, and not very notably: "It is a question of putting expressly and systematically the problem of the status of a discourse which borrows from a heritage the resources necessary for the deconstruction of that heritage itself" ("Struc-ture, Sign, and Play in the Discourse of the Human Sciences," 252), preferring the more ludic term "free play," which punctu-ates his speech. Thus deconstruction turns out to be a little like conversion, a retrospective science. Derrida's exposition of what he calls "a general strategy of deconstruction" waits for the later *Positions*, 41, where he makes of it simultaneously an extension and overturning of Hegelian dialectic, without, how-ever, the controversial moment of synthesis, which would only constitute a new order to deny. We reread the Hegelian page more than definitively turn it, since by "turning the page," or pretending to, we merely stay in the same logocentric, phonocentric metaphysics and tyranny of presence that we have not escaped by merely changing its vocabulary. Those "certain marks" (42), Derrida's overlapping (but not inter-changeable) indications or signs that are meant to point to no real referent ("hymen," "trace," "supplement," "écart," "dissémi-nation," "pharmakon"), then operate in deconstruction to "re-sist and disorganize" the dialectical oppositions (e.g., "true-false," "real-illusory," "good-bad," "bourgeois-proletariat") that they continue to "inhabit" (43) but wherein they "can no longer be included ... *without ever* constituting a third term, without ever leaving room for a solution in the form of speculative dia-lectics" (43). Georges Bataille probably said as much in the strange motto, cited frequently by Blanchot and Sollers, "Il faut lever l'interdit sans le supprimer" ("We must lift the interdic-tion without eliminating it"). It should be noted also that here Derrida may be hypostatizing a notion of deconstruction that functions more innocently elsewhere. For Paul Ricoeur, for ex-ample, deconstruction works in harmony with other terms like

demystification and demythologization as elements in what he calls our modern "task of consciousness" that we are led to through a "hermeneutics of suspicion." Cf. *The Conflict of Interpretations, Essays in Hermeneutics.* Ricoeur has, of course, been for a generation now an articulate opponent of Derrida and the philosophy of difference he stands for. For instance, for Ricoeur the Derridean (Nietzschean and Freudian) fragmentation of the subject constitutes the challenge that man must accept to reformulate his identity on more enlightened grounds. The subject, for Ricoeur, is like the morality of Kant, open to debate and even modification, but certainly not to refutation, *for we simply cannot live without it.*

9. François Brémondy, "Derrida et Blanchot," in *Les Fins de l'homme, à partir du travail de Jacques Derrida,* Colloque de Cerisy, 214–18; and, cited by Donald G. Marshall (*The Yale Critics,* 136), Derrida's pronouncement on Blanchot, from "Pas," in a special issue of *Gramma,* is unequivocal in its praise: "Never so much as today have I pictured him so far ahead of us. He waits for us, still to come, to be read and re-read even by those who have been doing it since they knew how to read and *thanks* to him" (tr. Marshall); cf. also Derrida's essay on Blanchot (and Jacques Ehrmann), "Living on/Border Lines," 76–176.

10. Marshall, "History, Theory, and Influence," 135–55.

11. Geoffrey Hartman, "Maurice Blanchot: Philosopher-Novelist."

12. Paul de Man, "Maurice Blanchot," 256.

13. "What he saw, the garden, the winter trees, the wall of a house; while he looked, no doubt in the way a child does, at his play area, he got bored and slowly looked higher toward the ordinary sky, with the clouds, the grey light, the day flat and without distance. What happened then: the sky, the *same* sky, suddenly opened, black and absolutely empty, revealing (as if the window had been broken) such an absence that everything is since forever and for forever lost, to the point at which there was affirmed and dispersed there the vertiginous knowledge that nothing is what there is there, and especially nothing beyond" (Maurice Blanchot, from "Une Scène primitive," in *Première Livraison*). Miller makes the connection with Kant (and modernity) on the basis of arguments in the *Critique of Judgment* that refute an empirical approach or ground to aesthetic phenomena or taste. Professor Miller's speech, which was delivered in November 1983 at New York University, appeared as "The Search for Grounds in Literary Study." Blanchot's own early text, "A Primitive Scene," surfaces, in italics, in a recent collection of "fragments," *L'Écriture du désastre,* 117.

14. Derrida, "Les Fins de l'homme," in *Marges de la philosophie,*

136–37: "Sartre's major concept, the theme of last recourse, the horizon and the irreducible origin, is what they called 'human reality.' What they meant thereby was a translation of the *Dasein* of Heidegger, a *monstrous* translation in so many regards ... the history of the concept of man was never interrogated, just as if the sign 'man' had no origin, no historical, cultural, linguistic limit" (translation and second italics mine —PB). In an interesting note at the bottom of these same pages, Derrida remarks that the Sartre of *La Nausée* deconstructs the same 'humanism' that was to constitute his ideology of after-the-war. What excuses Sartre's error (and his generation's) for Derrida is the conjuncture of the aftermath of the war, when the 'human' needed emphasis especially. Heidegger made no such allowances in the brilliant and biting refutation of Sartrean philosophy that constitutes the "Lettre sur l'humanisme." For Heidegger the 'human' in itself represents a step away from primordial Being, in the direction of a manipulative and illusory, if unavoidable, conquest of nature.

15. Jean-Paul Sartre, "Aminadab, ou du fantastique considéré comme un langage," and "Un Nouveau Mystique," in *Situations I*, 148–229.

16. *Les Temps modernes* was particularly cold to the adventures of *Tel Quel*, a matter I document further in my essay on Sollers later in this book.

17. Jean-Pierre Faye, "Sartre, entend-il Sartre?" in *Le Récit hunique*, 286–302.

18. Michel Foucault, "Distance, Aspect, Origines."

19. Rodolphe Gasché, "Joining the Text: From Heidegger to Derrida," 156–73.

20. "Je ne suis pas un lecteur fanatique des commentaires qui concernent 'mes' ouvrages—si peu *miens*" ("I am not a fanatical reader of commentaries on 'my' works—so little *mine*"; from a letter by Blanchot to Philip Beitchman, August 26, 1983; quotation marks Blanchot's, italics and translation mine—PB).

21. Carroll, "Dogmatism of Form: Theory and Fictions as *Bricolage*," in *The Subject in Question*, 161–200. However, Derrida deconstructs Lévi-Strauss's notion of *bricolage* itself in "Structure, Sign, and Play," 253–58.

22. Elmer Peterson, *Tristan Tzara, Dada and Surrational Theorist*, 91–92; and Micheline Tison-Braun, *Tristan Tzara, l'inventeur de l'homme nouveau*, 44.

23. Norris, *Deconstruction*, 56–71; Flores, *The Rhetoric of Doubtful Authority*, 22–24. In *The Structuralist Controversy*, ed. Macksey and Donato, Derrida mentions "the Nietzschean critique of metaphysics, the critique of the concepts of being and truth, for which were substituted the concepts of play, interpretation

and sign" (250).

24. I am referring to a certain eloquent, passionate, but neverthe-less forbidding and foreboding orthodoxy that inhabits the pages of *Tel Quel's* colloquies on Artaud and Bataille. These famous conferences took place in the early 1970s —with many important speakers *about* Artaud and Bataille—who were seen through the ideological (Maoist, radical, anarchist) eyes of the time and of Sollers' review, *Tel Quel,* which was the sponsor. The tone was sometimes a bit hysterical and dogmatic, as in the insistence in finding proto-Maoism in Artaud!

25. Wlad Godzich, "The Domestication of Derrida," in *The Yale Crit-ics,* 20–40; and Jonathan Arac, writing in an "Afterword" in the same volume, 184, about Gasché's article (n. 19 above), hints at an American misinterpretation and distortion of Derrida: "He [Gasché] implies that 'deconstructive criticism' in America rests upon a misinterpretation of Derrida. . . . It treats text as a phenomenal entity—writing on paper—rather than recognizing in Derrida's use of it something closer to a transcendental con-cept. . . . Finally, Gasché finds in Derrida's work a deep critique of Romantic notions of the reflexive totality of a work or image, but he finds in American deconstructive criticism a reinforce-ment of these notions."

26. *Finnegans Wake* was the subject of many articles over the years in *Tel Quel* and its successor *L'Infini,* and it also has been a fre-quent theme in the writing of Sollers, Kristeva, and Derrida. The latter's "involvement" with the book is recounted in Daniel Giovannangeli's *Écriture et répétition, approche de Derrida.*

27. Maurice Blanchot, "Les Paroles doivent cheminer longtemps," in *L'Entretien infini.*

28. Norris, *Deconstruction,* 1: "To present 'deconstruction' as if it were a method, a system or a settled body of ideas would be to falsify its nature and lay oneself open to charges of reductive misunderstandings." Rodolphe Gasché, whose purpose in *The Tain of the Mirror: Derrida and the Philosophy of Reflection* is to translate Derrida into traditional philosophical language, finds that method needs to be introduced in quotation marks: "To the extent that Derrida's work is a genuinely philosophical in-quiry that takes the standard rules of philosophy very seri-ously, its 'method' is certainly not characterized by any ex-teriority to its object . . . deconstruction seems to flirt with the scientific idea of method that is characterized precisely by its exteriority to its object. But . . . this point of exteriority to the totality is not that of the subject. Deconstruction is never the effect of a subjective act of desire or will or wishing. What provokes a deconstruction is rather of an 'objective' nature. It is a 'must,' so to speak. 'The *incision* of deconstruction . . . can

be made only according to lines of force and forces of rupture that are localizable in the discourse to be deconstructed' (Derrida, *Positions*, 82)" (*The Tain of the Mirror*, 122–23).

29. Guy Debord, *La Société du spectacle*.

30. Vincent B. Leitch, *Deconstructive Criticism:* "The Subversion of Foundations" (24); "Extensions of Subversion" (39). It is certainly no coincidence that deconstruction was initiated and so quickly caught on in a politically volatile, if not revolutionary, climate; Derrida's "revolutionary" reinterpretations of the Hegelian themes of the end of history, together with his stirring deconstruction of Sartre's humanist misreading of Heidegger—these signal developments took place in the context of France of May 1968; Derrida's role in America, self-ascribed, was to give some account of changes going on over there ("Les Fins de l'homme," reprinted in *Marges*). Less specifically, but no less surely, a certain context of radical ferment (Germany of the 1920s) must have entered into Heidegger's *Destruktion* of Western ontology and metaphysics, of which deconstruction is both an updating and a bypassing. The idea that a radical change in man's political, social, and economic being was imminently possible made ideas necessary, coherent, and acceptable (if and because scandalous) where radical reversals on other levels were indicated. In both cases, perhaps, as the waves of revolutionary energy and confidence subside, or are dammed, blocked, or obstructed, or, maybe a worse fate, *institutionalized*, we are left with some very militant abstractions that can be neither abandoned nor fulfilled. The great change, in the case of Heidegger, is found to have already occurred, and it becomes a matter of nourishing, shepherding it in its "house" or temple of poetry. With deconstruction, the "subversion" becomes pandemic, epidemic, a "turning upside down" where something is left very much standing, and on more solid footing—as, for instance, as is frequently said, literary studies are all the stronger for having passed through its storms and challenges.

What is it exactly that has been changed, threatened, or modified in the kind of subversion that Gasché deals in in *The Tain of the Mirror*? Does not the repetition of the word (permutations of which we'll italicize for illustration) in the following sentences slide into the mode of ritual mantra or sign of allegiance to a certain chic but very recuperable "school of thought"?: "'Literature' thus acquires a *subversive* function with regard to philosophy and the literature under its dominion, not by restoring its specificity at any cost but precisely by recognizing that it can effect such a *subversion* only by hardly being literature. 'Literature' (is) almost no literature. It appears, then, that the disruptive and *subversive* effects of 'literature' are directed not against logocentric philosophy alone but against literature as well, to the extent that the latter submits to philosophy's demands. Hence what *subverts* philosophy is not in fact literature, for it also solicits the very foundations of literature, depriving it of its external foundation in philosophy, or in other words of its being" (259). Remote from all social relevance, risk, or statement, subversion becomes armchair revolution: one makes one's revolution in the library, where the texts, the disciplines, the works subvert each other endlessly—they *take care* of all of that.

31. Paul de Man, *Blindness and Insight: Essays in the Rhetoric of Contemporary Criticism.* De Man is the major figure in the application of deconstruction to literary criticism. De Man's work on Derrida, as Stephen Melville shows so eloquently in *Philosophy Beside Itself: On Deconstruction and Modernism*, is a very nuanced synthesis of reception-rejection (acknowledgment). Recent unearthing of de Man's prolific early work for a fascist Belgian newspaper throws a retrospectively comic light on a sentence that Melville surely now wishes he had not written: "I suppose the first thing that should be said about de Man is that his career has been much longer and more consistent than has been generally thought" (*Philosophy Beside Itself,* 116).

32. Umberto Eco, *Opera Aperta.*

33. Roland Barthes, *The Pleasure of the Text,* 38: "The bourgeoisie has no relish for language, which it no longer regards even as a luxury, an element of the art of living (death of 'great literature'), but merely as an instrument of decor (phraseology)."

34. Jean Franklin, *Le Discours du pouvoir,* 168–69: "What is this mutism? That of the CONTROL which has spared no sector of the space-time, that where the 'semantic field' of a society extends from the space of the sign-flashing environment to the time of adequate response . . . the message realizes its essence in *order* and control, at the moment when the noumenal yields to the signal . . . a uniformity, that of the information market, whose only transcendence is that of the emitter. . . . The repetition of messages forms the only intelligibility here. . . . Identically, this reign of the instant conveys a control of memory; we are entering into the kingdom of the Great Forgetting, which is also that of mnemonic planification" (my translation).

35. *Poétique* 26, special issue on *Finnegans Wake,* edited by Hélène Cixous, where many of the articles stress this point.

36. Jacques Derrida, "D'Un Ton apocalyptique adopté naguère en philosophie" ("On an Apocalyptic Tone in Recent Philosophy"), in *Les Fins de l'homme* (*The Ends of Man*), Colloque de Cerisy,

478: "La fin approche, or il n'est plus temps de dire la vérité sur l'apocalypse. Mais que fait-on, insisterez-vous encore, à quelles fins veut on en venir quand on vient vous dire, ici, maintenant, allons, viens, l'apocalypse, c'est fini, je te le dis, voilà ce qui arrive?" ("The end approaches, now there is no longer time to speak the truth about apocalypse. But what are we doing, you still ask, what is my end who come here to say: 'well now, let's go, come on, apocalypse is over and done with, I'm telling you now, you can believe me, that's what is happening'?").

37. Tristan Tzara, *Grains et issues*, in *Œuvres complètes*, ed. Henri Béhar (hereafter referred to as *Œ. C.*), 3:12.
38. Geoffrey Hartman, *Criticism in the Wilderness*, 157.
39. Blanchot, *L'Entretien infini*, 510, 594–95: "[modernity], bypassing the conception of the work united and closed in itself, organizing and dominating values transmitted by traditional methods, explores the infinite space of the work, with inexorable rigor, but under a new postulate—not necessarily satisfying concepts of unity, totality, or of continuity . . . the guiding thread through this process is that with literature we are dealing with a statement that is not reducible to any unifying process . . . (but) frees thought itself from always having to be the thought of unity" (translation and parentheses mine—PB).

Chapter 2. Symbolism in the Streets: Tristan Tzara

1. Jürgen Habermas, *Theory and Practice*, 282, 40.
2. Virginia Woolf, *The Waves*, 56.
3. Tristan Tzara, *Œ. C.*, 3:13: "On peut aisément se figurer la nouvelle nature de ce temps si l'on admet qu'à tous les cadrans des montres que l'on continuera à remonter on arrachera les aiguilles à même leurs racines" ("You may easily imagine the nature of this time if you grant that they'll rip entirely the hands from the watches that nevertheless they'll continue to wind").
4. Francis Picabia neatly summed up this mood: "Il est inadmissible qu'un homme laisse une trace de son passage sur la terre" ("For man to leave a trace of his passing on earth is inadmissible"; quoted by Tzara in a radio broadcast on the days of dada: *Œ.C.* 5:539). Tzara has of course left us more than a few marks, too; these, though, as I hope to demonstrate, constitute a kind of *theory* that will stand as isolated and meaningless events for a future that does not inscribe them in a living revolutionary *praxis*. Tzara is by no means the only one the survival of whose work depends on social changes yet to be seen. How much sense will Sartre make for a future (or present) gen-

eration in an unfree, centrally controlled technocracy?

5. This point is made brilliantly and exhaustively in Henry Adams's *Mont St. Michel and Chartres.*

6. Tzara is, of course, as interested in "subliminal methods" of literary creation as his contemporaries; where he often parts company with them (ruptures with Breton, suspicion of *Le Grand Jeu's* mysticism) is in his refusal to relax his intellectual vigilance: "Mais l'homme ne pouvant pas être conçu, en ce sens, comme isolé, les lois de la réalité extérieure étant telles que toutes les coordonnées par rapport à lui doivent toujours, à tout moment, se conjuguer et que même son inconscient est forcé de s'y soumettre afin que rien n'entrave la tyrannique ordination" ("But man is incapable, in this sense, of being conceived as isolated, the laws of external reality being such that all guidelines concerning him must be constantly changed and even his unconscious is forced to submit to them so that nothing may upset the tyrannical ineluctability of this order"; *Œ.C.* 3:239).

7. Though there is room for plenty of irony here: the Khmer Rouge were and still are also led by French-educated intellectuals. What they attempted to realize so suddenly and brutally in Cambodia was that dream of a classless society, which goes back through Nizan, Aragon, then Proudhon ("all property is theft"), Marx, and Lassalle at least as far as to Rousseau and Babeuf, and which they came so firmly to believe should not stay just a dream when they were students in Paris. Pol Pot was educated at the Sorbonne. . . . Humanitarian considerations aside, Phnom Penh was emptied for the best of *reasons.*

8. Tzara's banker may perhaps be seen in relation to the poet as William Burroughs's junkie, in *Naked Lunch,* sees the Buddha: he envies him because he possesses the internal, therefore permanent, "fix."

9. In Elias Canetti's *Crowds and Power,* power is seen as always being exercised at a distance. By reducing that distance, Tzara threatens that power. Those that are near to us can never secure our *obedience;* the best they can hope for is our cooperation, if we agree with what they are doing.

10. Grail Marcus, "Lilliput at the Cabaret Voltaire."

11. Since I believe it will make for less choppy reading, and because of the availability of a good translation (by Mary Ann Caws), I'll be citing Tzara in English.

12. This analogy was made by the Russian symbolist Dmitri Merejkowski in *Atlantis/Europe: The Secret of the West,* citing Bartholomeo Diaz's *Conquest of Mexico:* "Eighty thousand sacrifices fall at the consecration of one great pyramidal temple in the city of Mexico" (average was 50,000 a year); but we mod-

erns match or surpass these figures on our roads alone.

13. Tzara speaks often and eloquently on the theme of the domination of man by the machines that were meant to serve him, as in the following passage from a prose poem in *Résumé of Night* (1934): "It would be difficult to convince me that a given individual (let's take the one who is right now synchronizing as best he can his organic needs with the time he has at his disposal until the bus comes) sees, hears, feels, perceives at the same speed and in the same dimension as I do what is going on around him and that his watches, meters, and adjectives have not been, from the moment of his birth, rigged by the unanimous and constant relationship of things and beings to which he has subjected the norms of his judgements" (*Approximate Man and Other Writings*, 223). The passage quoted in n. 6 above is from further on in this prose poem. For Tzara, subliminal methods (drugs, hypnotism, and what he calls a kind of "waking sleep"), while not to be blindly trusted, may be useful to break the conditioned patterns and routines that our machines and noxious social structures force upon us. These "underground" techniques can only give us a glimpse of what it will take a "new man" to really see.

14. "In time of Dearth bring out Number, Weight and Measure"— Blake, from *The Marriage of Heaven and Hell*.

15. Tzara, *Approximate Man*, where our translator remarks the change in tone: "Unexpectedly the final wait in the desert for the coming of the flame rejects the approximate" (258).

16. Cited by A. K. Coomaraswamy, *The Dance of Shiva*, 122. Coomaraswamy does a comparative study of Indian Vedanta and the eschatological-apocalyptic themes typical of French (Marcel Schwob: *Le Livre de Monelle*) and especially Russian symbolism. His approach is therapeutic, similar to such popular but very erudite treatments as Alan Watts's *Psychotherapy East and West*. Symbolist novels, works like Bely's *St. Petersburg* or Sologub's *Petty Demon* (which, according to Henri Peyre's concluding note in his book on symbolism, represent the summit of the movement in literary achievement), which were written in Russia early in our century, are all haunted by the theme of the end of (our) civilization. As far as Viscount Torio goes, whose statement seems to sum up the symbolist theme of apocalypse in its most extreme form, I've never been able to find out more about him, though I've looked. Perhaps he's a pseudonym for one or another of the strange spirits that haunted Russian culture at the beginning of the century— Rozanov, Solov'ev, or Ivanov—far easier, at all events, to say such a thing than own up to having said it!

17. Another "prophetic" extended prose poem that Tzara wrote in

close proximity to *Grains et issues* was *Personnage d'insomnie*. In the latter text men are envisioned as metamorphosing into trees or other forms of plant life. This is nature's revenge on man for his colossal pride and the negligent way he has handled his world: "car les lois végétales, malgré tout, ne s'exprimaient que dans leur propre matière selon une conscience dont l'essential échappe encore aux hommes qui, depuis longtemps, avaient oublié la leur et confirme les volontés d'autonomie de la nature que l'homme, qui s'en est profondément détaché, considèrera toujours comme une insulte perpétuelle à son désir de tout accaparer" ("For the vegetable laws, in spite of it all, only expressed in their own way a consciousness whose central meaning still escapes man—who long ago has forgotten his own and thereby confirms the will to autonomy in nature, from which man has utterly detached himself and that he will always treat as a perpetual insult to his desire to own everything"; *Œ.C.* 3:207). *Personnage d'insomnie*, a consummate tour de force, lyrical, dense, persuasive, and utterly unique, is a bit of a bibliographical enigma. It was never published in Tzara's lifetime, by conscious decision, according to Henri Béhar (*Œ.C.* 3:561–62), who examines one by one the possible motives Tzara had in withholding it from the public but finds none of them sufficient.

18. This interpenetration of life and poetry is Tzara's fundamental message, refined, repeated, and clarioned all through his career not only in his poetry but also in his persistent critical production, which incessantly turns on the problems and prospects of finding and preserving the poetic quality in everyday life. A few quotes may be detached almost at random from a life's work that says, in the end, *nothing else:* "Toute œuvre poétique elle-même, en tant qu'expérience, n'est pas uniquement un produit de la raison ou de l'imagination, elle n'est valable que si elle a été *vécue*. L'image poétique est un produit de la connaissance; ou, la connaissance ne peut être une leçon qu'il faut avoir *apprise*, elle doit être *prise* au monde extérieur, c'est-à-dire résulter d'une action plus ou moins violente sur la réalité qui nous entoure. Toute création est donc, pour le poète, une *conquête*, une affirmation combative de sa conscience" ("Any poetic work itself, as an experience, is not only a product of reason and imagination, it is worthwhile only if it has been *lived*. The poetic image is a product of knowledge. Now knowledge cannot be a lesson that it's necessary to have *learned*, it must instead be *seized* from the external world, that is to say, it must be the outcome of an action, more or less violent, on the reality that surrounds us. All creation is therefore, for the poet, a *conquest*, a combative affirmation of his

consciousness"; "Les Écluses de la poésie" ["The Dams of Poetry"], *Œ.C.* 5:95).

"Le poète non seulement vit l'histoire, mais en partie il la détermine. Pour lui, l'existence elle-même est un phénomène poétique à l'inverse de ceux pour qui écrire des poèmes constitue une profession" ("The poet not only lives history, but he in part determines it. For him, existence itself is a poetic phenomenon, just the opposite of what it is for those to whom writing poetry is a profession"; ibid., 109).

19. *Grains et issues, Œ.C.* 3. For the last paragraph or so I've been paraphrasing parts of pages 9–25.

20. The Marquis de Sade's astounding pamphlet, "Français encore un effort pour devenir vraiment républicains" ("Frenchmen One More Effort to Become Real Republicans") figures prominently in surrealist political thought. See, for instance, "L'Utopie sociale du Marquis de Sade," by Roger Gilbert-Lecomte, in his *Œuvres complètes* 1:261–65. See nn. 21 and 22 below.

21. Roger Gilbert-Lecomte, along with René Daumal and René de Renéville, edited during the early 1930s an influential review, *Le Grand Jeu*, where this essay first appeared. It has recently resurfaced in the *Fata Morgana* anthology (10/18) and in the *Œuvres complètes* of Gilbert-Lecomte. The group of the Grand Jeu, dissatisfied with what they considered to be the reigning materialism but agreeing in principle with the surrealists about the importance of dreams, the present moment, and spontaneity, attempted to astralize or spiritualize surrealism, especially by importing Eastern religion and philosophy. René Daumal, for instance, made himself into a proficient scholar of Sanskrit, and he is the author of the posthumously published *Mount Analogue: A Novel of Symbolically Authentic Non-Euclidean Adventures in Mountain Climbing*, somewhat of a "hippie classic" in America of the 1960s. From surrealism the road led, although of course not straight, to Woodstock.

22. For Gilbert-Lecomte, we no longer dream because being no longer human we will no longer feel the pang of desire; for Tzara the oneiric faculty will dry up because we won't need to dream, our desires having been satisfied by our activities. In either case the days of dreams are numbered. Tzara, *Œ.C.* 3:16: "Le sommeil tournera vide et sec car les rêves ne viendront plus concasser les pierres de l'existence avec leurs vis d'Archimède, les désirs étant comblés pendant le temps de veille" ("Sleep will turn empty and dry for dreams will no longer come to smash the stones of existence in their Archimedean vice, desires having been fulfilled during the time one is awake").

23. This "love," unlike the "amour fou" Breton evoked so haunt-

ingly (*L'Amour fou*), involves no mystical or seemingly predestined encounter between two people meant to meet at a certain astral and earthly conjuncture; its nature, instead, is to be indistinguishable, like Tzara's ideal of poetry, from the pulse of life itself. For Tzara, we won't so much *find* love and poetry as *breathe* it. Tzara, worthy like a very few others (Eluard, Aragon, Neruda) of the name "communist poet," needs a love and an art that rises above particulars: "Sous une forme bien différente de celle qui nous apparaît comme telle, la poésie deviendra acte *unanimement employé et exercé*, principal moyen de connaissance, quand elle aura transpercé le stade de champ d'observation et de déviation spécialisée, voisine du délire et de la simulation, qu'elle occupe encore, pour suivre son destin révolutionnaire qui se confondra avec celui de l'amour" ("In a very different way than now appears to us as such, poetry will become a unanimously *employed* and *exerted* act, a principal means of knowledge, when it will have pierced through the stage of specialized observation and deviance, classed with delirium and simulation, that it now still occupies, to follow its revolutionary destiny where it will merge with the voice of love"; Tzara, *Œ.C.* 3:103).

24. Tison-Braun, *Tristan Tzara*, 78: "il a du faire hausser bien des épaules de Paris à Moscou" ("He must have caused much shrugging of shoulders in Paris and Moscow"). Tison-Braun, deeply versed in the literature and lore of dada and surrealism, is a splendid student of the specifically *poetic* side of Tzara's project, which she ingeniously *isolates*. She may not be so satisfactory, however, as a commentator on his theory, which she insists on demarcating I think a little too neatly from his practice. She is eloquent and clever, for instance, on the logical paradoxes and contradictions between Tzara's (or any) revolutionary theory and the living practice of poetry. But she fails to see that, for Tzara, theory and practice are inextricably intertwined, like flesh and bone on a living organism, and that cutting one away from the other means only that you are dealing with a corpse. In the prose poetry especially, theoretical pronouncement alternates with lyrical effusion, often within the same paragraph or sentence. Tison-Braun, attached as she is to a concept of the work of art (owing much to Malraux) as expression of a "human essence," is perhaps badly placed to sympathize with the wilder ideas and passions of such visionaries as Tzara, for whom the *real* human is an entity yet to be created.

25. Cf. Jean Baudrillard, *La Société de consommation* (*The Consumer Society*), where a major thesis is that the true function of publicity in our societies is not so much to sell the product as

to ease the guilt, inherited from our Puritan-Christian tradition, that we have at consuming it. Baudrillard's later book, *L'Échange symbolique et la mort* (*Symbolic Exchange and Death*), is largely concerned with what he considers to be the unilateral relations between modern states that give all and their citizenry who can give nothing in return *except their lives.*

26. The metaphor of speed, rapid transformation, and metamorphosis is one of the constants of Tzara's critical and poetic vocabulary. Tzara's play *La Fuite* (*Escape*) is one of his more systematic expositions of this philosophy of "permanent change." Michel Leiris' enthusiastic introduction to Tzara's text could describe his own project as well as the poet's: "Le thème directeur en est ce déchirement, ce divorce constant, cette séparation qui répond au mouvement même de la vie. Fuite de l'enfant qui pour vivre sa vie doit s'arracher à ses parents. Divorce des amants qui ne peuvent rester l'un à l'autre sans aliéner leur liberté et qui doivent nier leur amour s'ils ne veulent pas eux-mêmes se nier. Mort d'une génération dont se détache peu à peu, pour monter à son tour, une génération nouvelle. Fuite de chaque être vivant, qui se sépare des autres, souffre lui-même et fait souffrir, mais ne peut faire autrement parce que pour se réaliser il lui faut une certaine solitude. Fuite des hommes. Fuite des saisons. Fuite du temps. Cours implacable des choses, qui poursuit son mouvement de roue. Fuite historique enfin: exode, déroute, dispersion de tous et de toutes à travers l'anonymat des routes et dans le brouhaha des gares où se coudoient civils et militaires. Faillite, effondrement, confusion, parce qu'il faut ce désarroi total pour que puisse renaître une autre société impliquant d'autres relations entre les hommes, entre les femmes, entre les femmes et les hommes" ("The main theme of the play is this rending, this constant divorce, this separation whose movement is one with life. Escape of the child who must tear himself away from his parents to live his own life. Lovers' separation who cannot continue belonging to one another without alienating their liberty and who must deny their love if they don't want to deny themselves. Death of a generation that another generation separates itself from little by little, to give rise, in its turn, to a new generation. Escape of every living being, who separates himself from others, suffers and causes others to suffer, but cannot do otherwise because to realize himself he needs a certain solitude. Escape of men. Escape of seasons. Escape of time. Implacable course of things on the turning wheel of fortune. Escape in history, finally: exodus, rout, dispersion of men and women into the anonymity of roads and into the clamor of railway stations where civilians and soldiers rub elbows.

Failure, collapse, confusion, because we must have this total disarray for there to be created a new society, implying other rapports between men, women, and between men and women"; "fuite en avant" = escape into the future; extract from Leiris' "présentation," 21 Jan. 1946, Théâtre du Vieux Colombier —Tzara, *Œ.C.* 3:623).

Among contemporaries, J.M.G. LeClézio assumes perhaps most obdurately and masterfully the mantle of this "tradition of the transitory" so intrinsic to dada-surrealism in a series of remarkably provocative but unclassifiable "fictions." See, for instance, as directly pertinent to the "fuite en avant" praised by Leiris above, *Le Livre des fuites*. That speed, and the accelerating tempo at which we are all obliged to live, is not always libertarian in its implications, is one of the telling points made recently by Paul Virilio, for instance in *Vitesse et politique*, where speed is seen as the fundamental strategy of established (military) power for allowing its subject populations time only for conditioned reaction, not calm reflection.

27. Antonin Artaud, *Œuvres complètes* 1:247–51; cf. also the hilariously Swiftian statement of Gilbert-Lecomte (dead at 36 of an overdose) on the issue, "Monsieur Morphée empoisoneur publique," in Gilbert-Lecomte, *Œuvres complètes* 1:118–29.

28. It is most unlikely, however, that Tzara would have followed Reich into the further reaches of his sexual pilgrimage. For the former, sexual desire would change in nature and quality in a better world, whereas for the latter this was an unalterable quantity or energy that could only be repressed or liberated. Among Freud's students Tzara was perhaps most profoundly influenced by Otto Rank and, specifically, his idea of "birth-trauma." The latter concept enabled Tzara to rationalize certain connections between primitive culture and a meaningful direction for modern art, on the basis of what he saw as a shared experience of terror or recoil at the fact of living.

29. Tzara memorably expresses this millennial aspiration of a consciousness that is liberated from debt in the final two lines of a late (posthumously published) poem from *40 Chansons et déchansons* (*40 Songs and Ditties*), *Œ.C.* 4:280: "je dis comme je vis / je vois comme la voix / je prends comme j'offre / ma vie est ainsi / je ne dois rien à personne / je dois tout à tous les hommes" ("I speak as I live / I see as a voice / I take as I give / My life is like this / I owe nothing to anyone / I owe everything to everyone").

30. Tzara distinguishes dada from cubism and futurism on precisely these grounds: "On sait que, aussi bien les Cubistes que les Futuristes, ont employé des éléments de la réclame, phénomène moderne, en tant que composantes plastiques ou

valeurs poétiques. Dada, lui aussi, a usé de la réclame, mais non pas comme d'un alibi, d'une allusion, d'une matière utilisable à des fins suggestives ou esthétiques ... la signification des œuvres dada ... prenait le pas sur toute préoccupation esthétique ou moralisatrice ... Dada ne prêchait pas, car il n'avait pas de théorie à défendre, il montrait des vérités en action et c'est comme *action* que désormais il faudra considérer ce que l'on nomme communément art ou poésie" ("It's well known also that the Futurists as well as the Cubists have used elements from advertising, modern phenomenon, as plastic components or poetic values. Dada itself also used advertising, but not at all as alibi, allusion, or material utilizable for suggestive or esthetic ends ... The significance of Dada works lies not in any esthetic or moralizing preoccupation ... Dada didn't preach, because it had no theory to defend, it showed truth in action and it's as *action* that from now on we'll have to think of what is commonly called art or poetry"; "Dada contre art," *Œ.C.* 5:354–55).

Tzara eventually rejected Breton and surrealism on grounds very similar to these, especially in his intransigent lecture at the Sorbonne, "Le Surréalisme et l'après-guerre" (*Œ.C.* 5:59–105), which is probably one of the most severe (and intelligent) judgments ever pronounced by a major living writer on another.

René Daumal, replying to Breton's criticisms in the *Second Manifesto of Surrealism* of the *Grand Jeu* venture, had also taxed Breton with being overly interested in his place in the history of literature ("Lettre ouverte à André Breton," *L'Évidence absurde,* 153–59). The enormous anger at Breton, on the part of Tzara as well as Daumal, reveals, of course, the equally enormous respect they had for him.

31. See my introduction, pp. 10–12.

32. This argument is equally valid for the lottery and gambling, surely by no mere coincidence increasingly sponsored or sanctioned by the state: wealth is preserved as a theoretical possibility and reduced to a merely financial dimension for the impoverished (in so many ways) masses.

33. The invocation of risk and peril is a passionate and convincing repair in Tzara's many studies of other poets (especially the "poètes damnés" and the Romantics) that comprise *Les Écluses de la poésie* (*Œ.C.* 5:5–223). These "appreciations," obviously written over many years, are remarkable, as Tzara was himself, for their consistency of tone and determination; for Tzara had decided firmly, for himself and others who made the "dangerous choice," that one is not a poet with impunity: "L'exemple de Rimbaud nous convie à considérer la connaissance comme

un objet dont on ne peut s'assurer l'acquisition qu'au péril de sa vie, en s'emparant de haute lutte" ("The example of Rimbaud invites us to consider knowledge like an object that we can acquire only at risk of one's life, taking possession of it only in the throes of combat"; Œ.C. 5:151). These demands that Tzara makes of the poet he doesn't neglect to make also of the revolutionary: "la lutte sera dure et l'échange demandera la décision du sang. Voilà qui fomentera la terre et scellera la plante nouvelle, du sang" ("the struggle will be hard and the exchange will demand the decision of blood. This is what will foment the earth and seal the new plant, blood"; Œ.C. 3:80).

34. Tzara, Œ.C. 3:46–47, 104n, my translation.

Chapter 3. A Question of Culture/Culture in Question: Beckett

1. Samuel Beckett, *Three Novels: Molloy, Malone Dies, and The Unnamable*, 112–13.

2. Quoted by Ruby Cohn in "Philosophical Fragments in the Work of Samuel Beckett," 169.

3. E.M. Cioran, *The Trouble with Being Born*, 212: "Not to be born is undoubtedly the best plan of all. Unfortunately it is in no one's reach."

4. Georges Bataille, *Œuvres complètes* 6:444: "J'aperçois la précarité de l'être en moi, non la précarité classique fondée sur la nécessité de mourir mais une nouvelle, plus profonde, fondée sur le *peu de chances* que j'avais de *naître*" ("I remark the precariousness of my being, not classical precariousness based on the necessity of dying, but a new, more serious one, based on the *very small chance* that I would be *born* in the first place").

   Guido Ceronetti, *Le Silence du corps* (*Silence of the Body*), 37: "L'homme ose se permettre encore des cruautés, alors qu'il commet déjà, tranquillement et de façon répetée, l'acte le plus cruel de tous: engendrer, donner aux horreurs de la vie des êtres qui ne sont pas et n'éprouvent pas de douleur" ("Man dares to allow himself to be cruel, when he's already committed, tranquilly and repeatedly, the cruelest act of all: engendering, condemning beings that do not exist or suffer to the horrors of life").

5. This argument, based on the increased responsibility of the carrier of the child, is made persuasively by Jérome Peignôt, *Les Jeux de l'amour et du langage*. Such nice ethical distinctions will, of course, disappear in a future of laboratory gestation.

6. Beckett, *Molloy*, in *Three Novels*, 84: "I had bent on settling this

matter between my mother and me."
7. Jean Baudrillard, "The Orders of Simulacra," 83–159.
8. Ernst Cassirer, *Substance and Function in Einstein's Theory of Relativity*, 264: "To describe a group of phenomena, then, means not merely to record receptively the sensuous impressions received from it, but it means to transform them."
9. See pp. 14–15.
10. The phantom of repetition has haunted and perhaps helped to derange many an able mind. One thinks of Nietzsche's attempts to deal with it, culminating in his triumphant discovery of the Eternal Return, which constitutes the *enlightenment* at Sils—and also of the problem of redundancy posed, but not satisfactorily solved, by Artaud, so well described by Derrida in *Writing and Difference*.
11. Ludovic Janvier, "Style in the Trilogy," 87.
12. Sixties' graffiti.
13. Rainer Maria Rilke, *Duino Elegies*, 75. See also above, 41–42, for a comparison of Rilke and Tzara.
14. Rilke, *Elegies*, 75–76.
15. Beckett, *The Unnamable*, 551: "There were three things, the inability to speak, the inability to be silent, and solitude."
16. T.S. Eliot, *Ash Wednesday*, section five: "Will the veiled sister pray/For children at the gate/Who will not go away and cannot pray."
17. E.M. Cioran, *The Fall into Time;* Blanchot, *L'Écriture du désastre.*
18. J.D. O'Hara, ed., *Twentieth-Century Interpretations*, 5, quoting an interview with Beckett.
19. Richard Demarcy, *Éléments d'une sociologie du spectacle*, 298. Brecht felt he was successful at this technique if his audience was ready to sit back and "light up their cigars," symbol of their meditative distance from the spectacle! See above, my discussion of Tzara's *Mouchoir*, 30–36.

Henri Béhar has drawn the analogy between Tzara's style and Brecht's in a note discussing "un effet de distanciement par lequel, loin de 'participer,' le public est appelé à garder sa lucidité. Esthétique brechtienne en quelque sorte si un perpétuel humour, un traitement désordonné de l'espace et du temps, une donnée abstraite sans rapport avec l'être social n'empêchaient toute formalisation" ("a distancing effect, through which, far from participating, the public is called upon to keep its lucidity. Brechtian esthetic, kind of—if it weren't that a constant humor, a disorganized handling of space, time, an abstract given unconnected to social being did not prohibit all formalization"), *Œ.C.* 1:690.

A brilliant recent discussion of the influence of Brechtian

"consciousness art" on cinema occurs in the French film critic Youssef Ishagpour's *D'Une Image à l'autre.*

20. For instance, in "Theme of the Traitor and the Hero," in Jorge Luis Borges' *Labyrinths.*

21. Louis-René Des Forêts, *Le Bavard.* Des Forêts' first-person narrator denies any truth to the story he has just told. The reader then is left with the insoluble question, "Did he lie when he said he lied?" This position is similar to the one Beckett leaves us in: we don't know quite how literally to take what his narrators are telling us, and we're not supposed to know. See above, 26, and my chapter on Des Forêts.

22. Maurice Blanchot, *L'Attente l'oubli* (*Wait Forget*). Here is a case of the almost total subtraction of fiction from any normative context of time and space, with purposive inconsistency of style to make sure that the reader can never "get his bearings." By refusing and removing the habitual conventions of fiction, and at the same time tantalizing us with them, Blanchot is making us more aware of what these conventions were and the role they served. See above, 23–24, and my chapter on Blanchot.

23. Henry James, "The Art of Fiction," 544, where he accuses Trollope of "betrayal of sacred office" for having admitted to the reader that he has only been "making believe."

24. Des Forêts, *Le Bavard*, 207–9, actually comes close to this perspective when he has his narrator inform his reader that the secrets were revealed only so that he could talk a little longer.

25. This resembles very closely the French situationists' indictment of urbanism; Guy Debord, *La Société du spectacle*, 116: "The 'new cities' of the technological pseudo-peasantry inscribe clearly into the terrain the rupture with historical time upon which they are built. Their motto could well be: "Here On This Spot Nothing Will Ever Happen, And Nothing Ever Happened Here" (my translation—PB). According to the Marxist critic Lucien Goldmann, in *Structures mentales et création culturelle*, such "neutrality" forms the background for modern art in general and the alienation it responds to: Mathias, for instance, is to discover, in Robbe-Grillet's *Le Voyeur*, the utter apathy and indifference of an environment where no one cares, except himself, about the crime he has committed.

26. Vincent Descombes has very succinctly but adequately described the influence an "end of history," as projected by Nietzsche and Hegel, had on Blanchot, but his remarks apply as well to Beckett: "At the end of history, the human species enters into an irremediable idleness, an aimlessness without end. This was Nietzsche's doctrine. By announcing the 'death of God' and the 'aimlessness of the last man,' he invokes the great modern utopia of a 'close of history.' Kojève [see chap. 4,

n.5] had already said that the end of history was equivalent to the death of man. In all his works, Blanchot described this life-after-death which is the lot of man in the aftermath of history, and to which modern literature is the supreme testimony" (*Modern French Philosophy,* 112–13). The rapprochement of Blanchot to Beckett, especially of the *Unnamable,* is common in modern French criticism, where the connection is made, not especially on the basis of the pathos of the human condition (omnipresent in Beckett but intellectualized in Blanchot), but on the level of the structural robbery committed on the subject by a language that preexists and predetermines identity and action—an identity that paradoxically we are both forced to be and to will. The hero of Blanchot's *L'Idylle* (see above, pages 108–9) was recently described as "Condemned, like the narrator of 'The Unnamable,' to express himself with the words of others, he fails to integrate himself into the community through a common language, or to find his own identity with his own language; and so, in a certain way, we find anticipated what will become the Beckettian laceration of language, based on the suspicion that *The Idyll* and *The Last Word* (by its title alone) both convey: 'Your language only pleases me halfway. Are you sure of what you say?—No, I said, shrugging my shoulders; how could I be sure? It's a risk to run?' And the risk to run is that of the *misunderstanding,* and of the impossible community. Caught between the impossibility of speaking (because he speaks without knowing what he's saying) and the impossibility of keeping quiet (because the temptation is irresistible to add always another to his last word), the narrator is sworn to the ineffable" (Michel Jarrety, "Maurice Blanchot, Figures de la Limite," 69–70; my translation—PB).

27. The blow on Flaubert is of course more telling in Beckett's French text as "le mot juste."

28. Dorrit Cohn, *Transparent Minds: Narrative Modes for Presenting Consciousness,* 177.

29. R.M. Albérès, *Métamorphoses du roman,* 142.

30. Maurice Blanchot, *L'Éspace littéraire,* 10–20.

31. Max Weber, *From Max Weber,* 355: "The intellect, like all cultural values, has created an aristocracy based on the possession of culture (rational) and independent of all personal ethical qualities of man. The aristocracy of intellect is hence an unbrotherly aristocracy. Worldly man has regarded this possession of culture as the highest good. In addition to the burden of ethical guilt, something has adhered to this cultural value which was bound to depreciate it with still greater finality, namely senselessness—if this cultural value is to be judged by its own standards. . . . For the perfectibility of the

man of culture in principle progresses indefinitely, as do the cultural values; and the segment which the individual and passive recipient or active co-builder can comprise in the course of a finite life becomes the more trifling the more differentiated and multiplied the cultural values and the goals for self-perfection become. Hence the harnessing of man into this external and internal cosmos of culture can offer the lesser likelihood that an individual would absorb either culture as a whole or what in any sense is 'essential' in culture. Moreover there exists no definitive criterion for judging the latter. It thus becomes less and less likely that 'culture' and the striving for culture can have an inner-worldly meaning for the individual. . . . For this very reason culture's every step forward seems condemned to lead to an ever more devastating senselessness. The advancement of cultural values, however, seems to become a senseless hustle in the service of worthless, moreover self-contradictory, and mutually antagonistic ends . . . and appears the more meaningless the more it is made a holy task, a 'calling.'

"Culture becomes ever more senseless as a locus of imperfection, of injustice, of suffering, of sin, of futility. For it is necessarily burdened with guilt, and its deployment and differentiation thus necessarily become ever more meaningless." It is certainly in response to such irrefutable arguments as the above that Maurice Blanchot, in probably his most explicitly revolutionary collection, *L'Entretien infini,* announces, "The artist as creative personality, literary figure as exception, poet as genius—the heros have fortunately no place in our myths. . . . Immortality, hope for posterity, glory and the desire to be known by all, have gone the same way" (my translation—PB).

32. See also my introduction, p. 12.
33. Umberto Eco, *L'Œuvre ouverte.*

Chapter 4. The Rules of Michel Leiris' Game

1. "Au fond, je ne peux écrire, je n'arrive à écrire — à peu près! . . .—que sur ce qui me touche personnellement, d'une façon affective. C'est pour cela que j'ai été amené à toute cette littérature autobiographique" ("[B]asically I can only write, I only manage to write, just about, on what touches me personally, affectively. This is what drew me into all this autobiographical literature"; "Entretien avec Madeleine Chapsal," in Pierre Chappuis, *Michel Leiris,* 113).
2. I am not minimizing Michel Leiris' very important and expert

work in other genres (poetry, criticism, a novel, and a surrealist "glossary") and even in another profession (he is a trained ethnologist) but simply pointing out the centrality of autobiographical projects, which are (all editions Paris: Gallimard): *L'Âge d'homme*, 1939; *La Règle du jeu I, Biffures*, 1948; *La Règle du jeu II, Fourbis*, 1955; *La Règle du jeu III, Fibrilles*, 1966; *La Règle du jeu IV, Frêle Bruit*, 1976; *Le Ruban au cou d'Olympe*, 1981 (*A Man's Age*, 1939; *The Rule of the Game I, Bifurcations*, 1948; *The Rule of the Game II, Gadgets*, 1955; *The Rule of the Game III, Filaments*, 1966; *The Rule of the Game IV, Faint Noise*, 1976; *The Ribbon on Olympia's Neck*, 1981).

3. Jeffrey Mehlman describes Leiris' aesthetics as a "poetics of lack" in his Lacanian-structuralist study of Leiris, "Reading with Leiris," *A Structural Study of Autobiography*, 65–150. Rodolphe Gasché's very lucid remarks on the traditional imperative of "accounting" for philosophical statements I think may shed a certain light on the particular anguish of a writer as private *and* public as Leiris, whose text *lacks* in the permanently paradoxical sense that it can neither be excused nor go without excuse: "Since Plato, all reasonable speech has been held to be that which not only asserts but also always accounts for what is asserted, by stating the grounds or reasons for it ... Just as in ancient Greece the individual laid his entire life bare in the public square of the *agora* to receive the civic stamp of approval of the whole community, without which his life as a citizen would have been incomplete, so too the appeal to public approval is a necessary and intrinsic element of philosophical accounting, without which philosophy could not claim universality. . . . The individual also responds to the demand of accounting for himself before the community in order to receive recognition of his status as a self-conscious public being" (*The Tain of the Mirror*, 142–43).

4. See my next chapter, "The Fragmentary Word of Maurice Blanchot," pp. 112–13.

5. This is part of the well-known master-slave dialectic from Hegel's *Phenomenology of Spirit*: the master's superiority to the slave turns on his willingness to risk his own life. Marx turned this dialectic "on its head" by calling for proletarian revolution, that is, a reversal of roles—and Leiris and his generation (Blanchot, Bataille, Tzara, Breton, Sartre, and of course many others) further twist it by applying it to intellectual acts as well. It should be noted that I am not passing on the validity of this reading of Hegel but saying only that this interpretation was very important for French philosophy, writing, and (revolutionary) politics in the period 1930–60. Descombes, in *Modern French Philosophy*, is very informative, if a little cynical, on this

subject: the culprit, for Descombes, was Alexandre Kojève, who gave seminars in the 1930s as influential, apparently, as those Lacan (a student of Kojève's also!) was to preside over later. Kojève's important course took place at the École Pratique des Hautes Études between 1933 and 1939. In frequent attendance were Merleau-Ponty, Sartre, Bataille, Klossowski, Lacan, even André Breton. Descombes more than hints that Kojève's reading of Hegel was some kind of distortion, calling it even a "bloody" one, and citing Kojève on May '68, about which he commented: "Since there was no bloodshed, nothing had happened" (10).

6. Philippe Lejeune, *Lire Leiris, autobiographie et langage*, 155: "Je ne prendrai donc plus l'œuvre de Leiris comme un objet à interpréter, mais comme un exemple à suivre, une pratique de l'écriture, d'où on peut dégager les règles d'une savoir-faire" ("I won't therefore be treating Leiris' work as an object to interpret, but as an example to follow, a practice of writing, from which we may deduce the rules of a *savoir faire*").

7. Leiris, *La Règle du jeu III*, 87–88. Another important "reason" was the "double-bind" of an infidelity: "n'ayant d'autre choix qu'entre la trahir elle en ne lui disant rien ou trahir l'autre en livrant mon secret" ("having no other choice than between betraying her by saying nothing or betraying the other by confessing my secret"); 3:292. Leiris' "concluding" interpretation of his inconclusive act, from which it seems only fitting that death should be "lacking," is very much in the spirit of that Hegelian "risk," as described briefly in n. 5 above, that alone can confer seriousness to his words: "je me reporte à mon suicide manqué comme au grand et aventureux moment qui représente, dans le cours de mon existence à peu près sans cahots, le seul risque majeur que j'aurai osé prendre. Et il me semble aussi que c'est à ce moment-là que, mariant vie et mort, ivresse et acuité de vue, ferveur et négation, j'ai embrassé le plus étroitement cette chose fascinante, et toujours à poursuivre parce que jamais tout à fait saisie, que l'on croirait designée à dessein par un nom féminin: la Poésie" ("I think of my failed suicide as a great and adventurous moment that represents in the course of an existence without shocks the only major risk I ever dared to take. And it seems also that at that very moment, marrying life and death, drunkenness and sobriety, fervor and negation, I embraced most closely this fascinating thing, always ahead of us, because never really seized, that we would almost think is designated purposely by a feminine noun: poetry [la poésie]"); 3:292.

8. By this pejorative I mean an inevitable infidelity, whose "objective correlative" might be the symbolic role that Leiris'

adulteries (blown way out of proportion to their actual importance, or at least frequency, it seems to me) play in the autobiography. On another level, Leiris-the-bourgeois "cheats" on
Leiris-the-revolutionary, and vice versa. Inauthenticity, insin-
cerity, and a concomitantly perpetual anguish and anxiety—
these are the givens of Leiris' world: abandon all hope (of
serenity), ye who enter here!

Chapter 5. The Fragmentary Word of Maurice Blanchot

1. Maurice Blanchot, "Gide et la littérature d'expérience," in *La
   Part du feu*, 209. My translation, as elsewhere, unless otherwise noted.
2. Maurice Blanchot, "Joubert et l'espace," in *Le Livre à venir*.
3. Ibid., 71.
4. A contemporary Argentine-French author, Julio Cortazar, in
   Hopscotch (chap. 133) wryly invents the "NATIONAL CORPOR-
   ATION OF CHURCHGOING GUARDIANS OF COLLECTIONS
   AND THEIR HOUSES OF COLLECTION (all houses of collection, and *idem*, houses—deposits, warehouses, archives, museums, cemeteries, jails, asylums, homes for the blind etc. and
   also all employees of said establishments). (Collections: example: an archive keeps files in a collection; a cemetery keeps
   corpses in a collection; a jail keeps prisoners in a collection.)"
5. Maurice Blanchot, *L'Entretien infini*, 514, paraphrasing
   Adorno's *Theory of the New Music*.
6. Maurice Blanchot, *L'Écriture du désastre*, 154–55: "Le don
   d'écrire est précisément ce que refuse l'écriture. Celui qui ne
   sait plus écrire, qui renonce au don qu'il a reçu, dont le langage ne se laisse pas reconnaître, est plus proche de l'inex-
   périence, inéprouvée, l'absence du 'propre' qui, même sans
   être, donne lieu à l'avènement. Qui loue le style, l'originalité du
   style exalte seulement le moi de l'écrivain qui a refusé de tout
   abandonner et d'être abandonné de tout. Bientôt il sera notable; la notoriété le livre au pouvoir: lui manqueraient l'effacement, la disparition.
       "Ni lire, ni écrire, ni parler, ce n'est pas le mutisme, c'est
   peut-être le murmure inouï: grondement et silence."
       ("The gift of writing is exactly what writing refuses. He who
   no longer knows how to write, who renounces the gift he's
   received, whose language can no longer be recognized, is closer
   to the inexperienced, groundless absence of anything to call
   one's own that, even without being, gives rise to the event. He
   who praises the style, the originality of the author, is only

celebrating the self of the writer who has refused to abandon everything and be abandoned by everything. Soon he will become notable; notoriety will give him over to power: soon he will be devoid of effacement, disappearance.

"Neither to write nor to speak is not to be mute, it's possibly the unheard of murmur, rumbling and silence").

7. Blanchot, *L'Entretien*, 514.

8. Blanchot, "Rousseau," in *Le Livre à venir*.

9. For Blanchot, as for his generation (Bataille and Lévinas), this power has to be read as a nonpower whose efficacy lies precisely in the fact that it confers neither prestige nor privilege: "nul sceptre pour celui qui écrit, fût-il déguisé en baton de mendiant: nul appui et nul cheminement" ("no sceptre for him who writes, even were it disguised as a beggar's staff: no support and no way"; Maurice Blanchot, *Le Pas au delà*, 67).

10. Morse Peckham, "Toward a Theory of Romanticism."

11. Blanchot, "L'Échec de Baudelaire," in *La Part du feu*.

12. Blanchot, *L'Entretien*, 524; or in the terminology of Barthes and Sollers, the signifier with no reliable signified or whose signified is either itself or subject to what Lyotard calls "dérive," a floating, drifting, and mutable rapport between sign and meaning.

13. No one more eloquently than Gilles Deleuze has described the necessary ambivalence of the critical attitude toward these "disturbances": "Chacun risquait quelque chose, est allé le plus loin dans ce risque, et en tire un droit imprescriptible. Que reste-t-il au penseur abstrait quant il donne des conseils de sagesse et de distinction? Alors, toujours parler de la blessure *de* Bousquet, de l'alcoolisme *de* Fitzgerald et *de* Lowry, de la folie *de* Nietzsche et *d'*Artaud en restant sur le rivage? Devenir le professionel de ces causeries? Souhaiter seulement que ceux qui furent frappés ne s'abîment pas trop? Faire des quêtes et des numéros spéciaux? Ou bien aller soi-même y voir un petit peu, être un peu alcoolique, un peu fou, un peu suicidaire, un peu guerillero, juste assez pour alonger la fêlure, mais pas trop pour ne pas l'approfondir irrémédiablement? Où qu'on se tourne, tout semble triste. En vérité, comment rester à la surface, et toute l'organisation de surface, y compris le langage et la vie? Comment atteindre à cette *politique*, à cette *guerilla* complète?" ("Each one risked something, went further into this risk, and derives from it an undeniable right. What remains for the critic when he gives advice on wisdom and distinction? Always to speak of the wound *of* Bousquet, *of* Fitzgerald's and Lowry's alcoholism, *of* Nietzsche's madness and *of* Artaud while staying on the shore? Become the professional of these choruses? To hope that the stricken

were not too decimated? Take surveys and produce special
numbers of reviews? Or else go yourself and see a little bit at
first hand, be slightly alcoholic, mad, suicidal—a bit of a
guerilla, too—just enough to open the wound, but not to
deepen it irremediably? Anywhere you turn all seems sad. In
truth, how to stay on the surface without staying on the shore?
How to save yourself and your facade at the same time—the
whole organization of the masquerade, including language and
life? How to attain to these *politics*, to this absolute *guerilla*?");
Logique du sens, 184. A large order, to which doubtless the
"nomadic intensities" and "schizophrenic fluxes" of the author's (and Guattari's) subsequent work was meant to respond.
See also my chapters above on Tzara and Leiris, the first
deciding for a social resolution (revolution) to the challenge of
risk, the second more for a personal one (suicide, adultery, and
general self-laceration).

14. Blanchot, *L'Entretien*, 524–27.
15. Blanchot, *Le Pas au delà*, 61–62.
16. Blanchot, *L'Entretien*, 220. Gilles Deleuze's point in *Nietzsche
    et la philosophie*, one of the books Blanchot reviews in *L'Entre-
    tien infini*, is highly relevant here. There the will to power is in-
    terpreted as being detached from any tangible object, just as
    Proust's desire in Deleuze's *Proust et les signes* is found to be
    independent of Albertine's physical presence: our modern
    world, impatient for answers, noise, substance, sperm, is in-
    capable of respecting that distance that makes possible the in-
    tegrity, therefore the very existence, of philosophy (Nietzsche)
    and art (Proust) alike.
17. Blanchot's position is of course not to be confused with
    Luddism; we cannot defeat the machines by destroying them.
    As in Heidegger, whom he is paraphrasing, technology is seen
    as a kind of destiny, a necessary avowal of man's constitu-
    tional lack or inadequacy, and one that cannot be avoided
    simply by being denied.
18. Maurice Blanchot, *L'Amitié*, 9–61; here Blanchot, opposing
    both optimistic (Malraux and Teilhard de Chardin) and pessi-
    mistic (Duthuit and situationists) evaluations of the technology
    that makes the museum possible, describes the function of
    that institution as not so much to enable us to experience
    other cultures (an impossibility, at all events) as to uproot (dé-
    racinement) us from any trusting rapport to our own environ-
    ment. The significance of the museum in particular and tech-
    nology in general is that they make us all strangers (in a larger
    sense than meant by Camus), nomads, and wanderers on the
    moving surface of the planet.
19. Blanchot, "Le Refus," in *L'Amitié;* or "La Littérature et le droit à

la mort," in *La Part du feu*. The latter essay, translated by Lydia Davis for a recent anthology of Blanchot's criticism, *The Gaze of Orpheus*, establishes a strict correlation between literature and revolution: "The writer sees himself in the Revolution. It attracts him because it is the time during which literature becomes history. It is his truth. Any writer who is not induced by the very fact of writing to think 'I am the revolution, only freedom allows me to write,' is not really writing. . . . Sade is the writer, *par excellence*" (40). Sade's active participation in the French Revolution, lavishly described by Blanchot in *Lautréamont et Sade* (see also chap. 2, n. 20), parallels Blanchot's far from negligible although very self-effacing participation in May 1968. These iconoclastic "affirmations" need to be balanced also with the very nuanced attitude toward rebellion that Blanchot develops in the novel, *Le Très Haut*, whose burden it is to demonstrate the complicity and isomorphism of a guerrilla opposition with a law that it not so much defies as replicates. What attracts the writer, therefore, is the revolutionary energy; what repels him, and in fact evicts and destroys him, is system in any form, even a "revolutionary" one.

20. See chap. 3, n. 31. The (perfectly reasonable) hostility of the masses toward art is discussed by Baudrillard in "The Beaubourg-Effect: Implosion and Deterrence." The masses throng to Beaubourg to celebrate the destruction of art; they have understood, as they have always known, that art has nothing to do with them and is a supreme mockery of their real condition.

21. The passage continues with a version of what was one of Tzara's perennial slogans: "et que je n'en avais pas dans les mains, ni dans les poches" ("and I had no bomb, either in hand or pocket"). "Nothing in the hand, nothing in the pockets" was how Tzara frequently expressed the surrealist attitude of nakedness and vulnerability before the exigency of a revolutionary conjuncture, as well as an opposition to all "investment," whether aesthetic or financial, that blocks availability for change. See above, pp. 30–36, for my discussion of Tzara's *Mouchoir des nuages*, with its theme of the practical interchangeability of poet and banker.

22. It is important to be reminded that for Blanchot the writer does not relax his rigor, logic, or expertise but replies to a "double exigence" by continuing to speak two languages: one, the discourse of power that ensures he either will be heard or cannot be ignored; two, a language of cry, impulse, and violence that means he is saying something: *L'Écriture du désastre*, 101, Blanchot citing Fr. Schlegel: "Avoir un système, voilà qui est mortel pour l'esprit; n'en avoir pas, voilà aussi qui est mortel. D'où la nécessité de soutenir, en les perdant, à la fois les deux

exigences" ("Having a system—that's what is fatal for the spirit; not having one is also fatal. From which the necessity of maintaining, while subverting, at the same time two exigencies").

23. Blanchot, *L'Espace littéraire*, 314.

24. For the intrication, often even interchangeability of the discourses of Blanchot with Bataille and also Lévinas, around the concepts of proximity and communication as nonreciprocity, see the excellent but abstruse Joseph Libertson, *"Proximity"*: *Lévinas, Blanchot, Bataille, and Communication.* Libertson writes that Blanchot, Bataille, and Lévinas project insistently certain principles of "nonpower" and "nonknowledge," inevitably marginal and iconoclastic, that confute if not abolish traditional class- and power-centered philosophy (Platonic and Cartesian) as well as modern phenomenological offshoots that still rely on the authority of the perceiving subject. The realization is inescapable that very much in Blanchot is a more or less manifest dialogue or conversation with Bataille, Lévinas, or both. Reciprocally the presence of Blanchot in the works of the latter two is equally inescapable. See also my remarks about Blanchot, the catalytic figure who is a network of other writers, in my introduction. The writer in Blanchot's sense, then, is not so much someone identifiable as producer of specified works, to which he lays claim, but instead is a kind of general symptom, malaise, or condition that speaks through him and as often through others through him (Blanchot is always, critically at least, dealing with another writer) or through him through others (Blanchot's frequent presence in *Tel Quel*, deconstruction . . .). One may object that intertextuality has always been the nature of the literary beast. To which it may be replied that we are not dealing here with the practically influential but so frequently with the absolutely *indistinguishable.*

25. What is dropped from the second version is all that traditionally went into making a novel: a circumstance, contingency, social setting, psychology, motivation. The other woman of the habitual romantic triangle (a Louise) is similarly elided. Perhaps we can call what is left *nothing* and call that *nothing* the fact of a man and a woman face to face with death, their own and each other's, or as Blanchot says in a later text, *Le Pas au delà*, 177: "Rien, c'est ce qu'il faut: supporter l'insupportable rien" (*The Step Beyond*: "Nothing, that's what is necessary: to support the insupportable nothing"). See also my discussion of Blanchot's *La Folie du jour*, 110–13. Although the differences between the two versions of *Thomas l'obscur* are fully obvious at a glance, Evelyn Londyn compares them exhaustively, if a

bit tediously, in *Maurice Blanchot, romancier.*

26. Françoise Collin, *Maurice Blanchot et la question de l'écriture*, 124. Relying on the theories of G. Canguilhem, Collin states that we don't go to the doctor so much to cure our maladies as to exchange them for social approbation.

27. Daniel Wilhem, *Maurice Blanchot et la voix narrative*, 249–84. Also Roger Laporte, "Le Oui, le non, le neutre.".

28. Londyn complains in the book mentioned in n. 25 above that Blanchot thereby vitiates the aesthetic impact of the book by having Thomas tell us, and at length, exactly what he means. In my view Blanchot's strategy is intentional—since it subverts the tendency of a reader to "appreciate" the novel as a "work of art" and thereby defuse its explosive capacity. The "work of art" that is this novel thereby commits suicide, and what is born in its place is *the word* (*la parole*), which is listened to (as Lévinas has it) not because of its content, message, style, or form but because someone or something is speaking (*prend la parole*).

29. Derrida, "Living On," 103.

30. In this sense Joyce could get away with the magnificent act of sabotage that is the *Wake* because of the credentials to sanity provided by his earlier work. It was too late for his principal source of support (Harriet Weaver) to cut him off once she found out what he was really up to—*destroying the English language.*

31. "Le dehors" is one of the frequent verbal recourses for Blanchot, an *outside*, it should by now almost go without saying, of no inside, simply the temptation (*attrait*) and impossibility of approach to everyone and anything, especially all unity or certainty (even nihilist denials turn into versions of the discredited theology). A very good book that explores facets and aspects of this "dehors" of Blanchot's is Georges Preli's *La Force du dehors; extériorité, limite, et non-pouvoir à partir de Maurice Blanchot.*

32. Just to make sure that you do not, by dint of repetition, mistake this statement for an affirmation, later in the book Blanchot mischievously turns it into a negation, "Fais en sorte que je ne puisse te parler" ("So act that I cannot talk to you"). Like a coin in an unused currency, it is worth as much when you turn it over.

33. The mystical analogy is tempting but must be resisted. Blanchot's "cabala" is too mutable, labile, shifting, and treacherous for any belief to rest in. The words he uses are in perpetual process of mutation and sliding, and their meanings are retracted as soon as they are assigned; they replace each other without difficulty and hindrance, just the very opposite of the *sacred.* Roger Laporte, in "Une Passion," in *Deux Lectures de*

Maurice Blanchot, calls Blanchot, not very seriously, a "mystique dévoyé" ("a frustrated mystic") but I think the religious metaphor reflects a momentary obstruction or fixation of the reader (Laporte) rather than the text, which, by its nature, is always ready to move on.

34. More specifically, at a certain point in time (about 1948), Blanchot abandoned the novel for the récit (a tale with first-person narrator), ostensibly for the increased nudity and simplicity of the latter form. Within the récit form itself there is an evolution away from contingency and circumstance toward the nearly total anonymity and atopia of *L'Attente l'oubli* of 1962 and the unidentifiable interlocutors of the conversations of *L'Entretien infini*. In the recent collections of "fragments," *Le Pas au delà* of 1973 and *L'Écriture du désastre* of 1980, the récit "goes underground," present only by fits and starts, but characters are not so much unnamed as *nonexistent*, just voices that state, argue, doubt, interrupt, implore, cajole—and that ask only to be *heard;* this mixture of philosophy, memory, dialogue, nonwisdom is more of an incitation than a collection, and is obviously meant that way: "Tous les mots sont adultes. Seule l'espace où ils retentissent, espace infiniment vide comme un jardin où, bien après qu'ils ont disparu, continueraient de s'entendre les cris joyeux des enfants, les reconduit vers la mort perpétuelle où ils semblent naître toujours" ("All the words are adults. Only the space where they resound, space infinitely empty like a garden where, well after they've disappeared, there would continue to be heard the joyous cries of children, leads them toward the perpetual death where they seem to be continually reborn"; *Le Pas au delà*, 31), or is the kind of infinitely provocative statement that breaks apart in the mind (or breaks a certain kind of mind apart) as you read and are read by it.

35. Tzara seems very close to Blanchot, though perhaps because of an excess of proximity. Blanchot never mentions him, preferring to deal with surrealism through the more anodyne (than Tzara) Breton. Tzara's genius, whose hallmark was its ability to alternate between the courage and tenacity of deep obscurity and moments of shattering revolutionary vision *and* statement, resembles Blanchot's, where the sheer inexplicability of a look, a cry, or a laugh coexists with the radically undeniable insistence on confronting blatantly the most urgent questions of our time. The following, from Tzara's *L'Écluse de la poésie*, looks like it could come from *L'Entretien infini:* "L'insupportable sentiment d'étouffement que ces êtres éprouvent est dû à l'ambiance où ils vivent et qu'il s'agit pour eux de nier. . . . Le cri, ultime expression de l'homme traqué par sa propre insuffisance. . . . Toute la différence entre les faiseurs

des vers et les poètes enracinées dans la détermination de leur
être entier est contenue dans ce *danger* auquel les derniers ex-
posent à chaque moment leur conscience" ("The insupportable
feeling of being smothered that these beings experience is due
to the ambience in which they live and that they need to deny
... The cry, ultimate expression of the man tracked by his own
insufficiency ... The entire difference between makers of verse
and poets rooted in the determination of their whole being is
contained in this *danger* to which the latter are exposed in
their every conscious moment"); Tzara, *Œuvres complètes*
5:130. Tzara and Blanchot coincide also, and are opposed to
Breton, on an important, sensitive, and controversial issue in
their mutual distrust of automatic writing, arising out of their
almost constitutional antimysticism and anti-Platonism:
automatic writing implies a belief in an ideal essence or truth,
whether transcendental or unconscious, that manifests itself
when conscious control is eliminated.

Chapter 6. The Endless Question: Finnegans Wake, 1, 6

1. A close-to-random sampling: "shows Early English tracemarks
and a marigold window with manlight lights, a myrioscope, two
remarkable piscines and three wellworthseeing ambries"
(James Joyce, *Finnegans Wake*, 127); "hacked his way through
hickheckhocks but hanged hishelp from ther hereafters"(130);
"tronf of the rep, comf of the priv, prosp of the pub" (136).
2. Joseph Campbell and Henry Morton Robinson, *A Skeleton Key
to Finnegans Wake*, 107–32; William York Tindall, *A Reader's
Guide to Finnegans Wake*, 111–30; E.L. Epstein, "The Turning
Point/Bk. I, Chapter VI," in *A Conceptual Guide to Finnegans
Wake*, 56–70; and for a gnostic-emanationist (Blakean), maybe
eccentric, summary: Frances Metz Boldereff, *Reading Finnegans Wake*, 114–21. This list is selective, not exhaustive.
3. In the case of *Ulysses*, the chapter headings from *The Odyssey*
that accompanied its appearance in serial publication were
omitted from the book.
4. Gotthold Ephraim Lessing, *Laocoön*, 91: "Time is the province
of the poet, just as space is that of the painter."
5. This prejudice in favor of space at the expense of time was
attacked in a controversial book by Wyndham Lewis published
in 1927, *Time and Western Man*. In "Le Langage de l'espace"
(378–79), a review of the then "radical fringe" of contemporary
writing (Ollier, Butor, LeClézio), Michel Foucault describes
what he calls the "literatures of time" (Greek, biblical, Renais-

sance) as literatures of return to authority, father, grammar, and source; and Foucault defines the project of modernism (Joyce, Nietzsche) as a refusal of this domination of the past.

6. See David Hayman's comprehensive study of the influence of Mallarméan aesthetics on Joyce: *Joyce et Mallarmé*. The symbolist influence is apparent in the transition to the indirectness and suggestiveness of *A Portrait of the Artist as a Young Man* from the more realistic style of its earlier draft, *Stephen Hero.*

7. "Utterly impossible as all these events are they are probably as like those which may have taken place as any others" (110); "*Just a Fication of Villumses*" (241–42); "as a matter of ficfact" (532).

8. David A. White, *The Grand Continuum: Reflections on Joyce and Metaphysics*, 8: "Because the narrative of the Wake never stops and never starts, the Wake is also defined by the continuous semantic motion. Rest, the classic antithesis of motion, enters the picture only from an extraliterary source, that is, when the reader decides to halt the perpetual seep of the narrative at some point."

9. Margaret Norris, *The Decentered Universe of Finnegans Wake: A Structuralist Analysis*, 78: "The reader is trapped inside the dream in *Finnegans Wake*. A dream can't be analyzed from the inside, because the dream is precisely the place where self-knowledge breaks down. . . . The confusion of the reader of *Finnegans Wake*, is a fitting response to a kind of terror implicit in the world of the dream, a terror confronted by Alice in *Through the Looking Glass* when Tweedledee suggests that she is merely 'a sort of thing' in the Red Knight's dream."

Michael Beausang, "Vivre en Marge (Living on the Edge)," 228, 231: "Marge marque la limite de ce que nous pouvons savoir. En termes scientifiques, '*she introduces herself upon us at absolute zero or the babbling pumpt of platinism*' (164). En apparaissant au zéro absolu, elle apparaît à ce point hypothétique où les substances ne pourraient conserver aucun mouvement moléculaire ni aucune chaleur. Elle désigne aussi les limites du langage ... *Wake,*—sillage: le mot dénonce l'absurdité de toute position fixe dans un monde constamment fluctuant" ("Marge marks the limit of what we can know. In scientific terms, '*she introduces herself upon us at absolute zero or the babbling pumpt of platinism.*' In appearing at absolute zero, she appears at this hypothetical point where substances would be unable to conserve any molecular movement or heat. She designs also the limits of language ... *Wake,*—trail: the word denounces the absurdity of all fixed position in a constantly fluctuating world").

Claude Condou, "Le Corps à lettre (The Body as Letter),"

175–76: "Il n'y a plus de différence entre chanter, manger, penser, entre la Bible et une expression courante, entre l'histoire et le fromage. Tout est nivelé dans une absence de valeur, de hiérarchie, d'opposition ... Ici tous les éléments, dès que produits, s'annulent les uns les autres, et ne se produisent en fait qu'en fonction et en vue de cette annulation mutuelle" ("There is no longer any difference between singing, eating, thinking, between the Bible and a current slogan, between history and cheese. All is leveled into an absence of value, hierarchy, opposition ... Here all elements, as soon as produced, annul each other, and only in fact are produced in function of this mutual annulment").

Gilles Deleuze, *Différence et répétition* (*Difference and Repetition*), 80, 94, 159: "L'éternel retour se rapporte à un monde compliqué, *sans identité*, proprement chaotique. Joyce présentait le *vicus of recirculation* comme faisant tourner un *chaosmos* ... ce qui compte c'est la divergence des séries, le décentrement des cercles, le 'monstre.' L'ensemble des cercles et des séries est donc un chaos informel, effondré, qui n'a pas d'autre 'lois' que sa propre répétition, sa reproduction dans le développement de ce qui diverge et décentre ... il s'agit toujours de rassembler un maximum de séries de points (à la limite toutes les séries divergentes constitutives du cosmos), en faisant fonctionner des précurseurs sombres linguistiques (ici mots ésotériques, mots-valises), qui ne représentent sur aucune identité préalable, qui ne sont surtout pas 'identifiables' en principe" ("The eternal return relates to a complicated world, *without identity*, properly chaotic. Joyce presented the *vicus of recirculation* as causing a turning of a *chaosmos* ... what counts is the divergence of series, the decentering of circles, the 'monstrous.' The ensemble of circles and series is therefore an informal chaos, collapsed, which has no other law than its own repetition, its reproduction in the development of whatever diverges and decenters ... it's a question always of gathering together a maximum series of points (at the limit, all the divergent series constitutive of the cosmos), in bringing into play the sombre linguistic precursors (here, esoteric words, puns) that are based on no preestablished identity and in principle are not even 'identifiable' ").

Umberto Eco, *Le Poetiche di Joyce* (*Joyce's Poetics*), 116, 119, 126: "Nessumo dei personaggi menzionati rimane se stesso ma diviene continuamente qualcos' altro ... un 'epica notturna dell' ambiguita e della metamorfosi ... *riverrun* introduce alla fluidita dell 'universo del Wake: fluidita delle situazioni spazio-tem-porali" ("None of the characters mentioned remains the same but becomes continuously someone else ... a nocturnal

epic of ambiguity and metamorphosis ... *riverrun* introduces
the fluidity of the Wake's universe: fluidity of spatial-temporal
situations").

Daniel Giovannangeli, *Écriture et répétition, approche de Derrida* (*Writing and Repetition, Approach to Derrida*), 152:
"Jacques Derrida a fortement souligné la relativité que rencon-
trent toutes deux les entreprises de Husserl et de Joyce. Alors
que Husserl est conduit par sa problématique de l'univocité à
une réduction méthodique de la langue empirique, destinée à
en isoler 'la transparence actuelle de ses éléments univoques et
traductibles,' à l'opposé, Joyce s'installe résolument dans l'em-
piricité de la culture-facto-historique, 'dans l'equivoque géné-
ralisée d'une écriture qui ne traduit plus une langue dans
l'autre à partir de noyaux de sens communs, mais circule à
travers toutes les langues à la fois'" ("Jacques Derrida has
strongly emphasized the relative nature of the enterprises both
of Husserl and Joyce. While Husserl is led by his problematic of
the universal toward a methodical reduction of the empirical
language, destined to isolate 'the actual transparency (of language) from its univocal and translatable elements,' on the
contrary, Joyce installs himself resolutely in the empiric of the
factual-historical culture, 'in the generalized ambiguity of a
writing that no longer translates one language into another
starting from the nuclei of common sense, but circulates
through all languages at the same time'").

Hélène Cixous, "La Missexualité" ("Miss Sexuality"), 249: "La
féminité du text de *FW*, le text énigme comme féminité. L'im-
prenable" ("The femininity of the text of *Finnegans Wake*, the
text-origin as femininity. The impregnable").

10. White, *The Grand Continuum*, 8, 52: "The classical divisions of
time—past, present, future—lose their powers of differentiation. The relations of 'before' and 'after' become meaningless, if
what is understood from one possible perspective as 'before'
can also be understood from an equally possible perspective as
'after.' ... If, however, a cause does not precede an effect on
temporal grounds, then apparently any cause can be seen as
an effect and any effect can be seen as a cause"; Joyce, *Finnegans Wake*, 482–83: "Now the doctrine obtains, we have occa-
sioning cause causing effects and affects occasionally
recausing altereffects."

11. David Hayman, "Double Distancing" and "Surface Distur-
bances/Grave Disorders."

12. White, *The Grand Continuum*, 53: "With difference overwhelming identity, it then becomes impossible to conceive of time (as
well as everything else) as anything other than a continually
undifferentiated flow. ... " As noticed by Jean-Michel Rabaté,

in "Lapsus ex machina," 157, Joyce is certainly influenced by
the theories of J.W. Dunne on the reversibility of time. Cf.
Dunne's two books: *An Experiment with Time* (1927) and *The
Serial Universe* (1934). Dunne is referred to by name in the
Wake: "the key of John Dunn's field" (516). Dunne also
influenced a certain current of American scientific humanism,
espoused most notably for many years by Oliver Reiser from
his chair of philosophy at the University of Pittsburgh: *Philosophy and the Concepts of Modern Science* (1935), *Planetary
Democracy* (1944), and *The Integration of Human Knowledge*
(1958).

13. Joyce, *Finnegans Wake*, 221: "Time: the pressant"; 295: "Now,
as will pressantly be felt."
14. The formulation, which sounds so much like Henri Michaux,' is
actually Enrico Castelli's from *L'Enquête quotidienne*.
15. See Philippe Sollers and David Hayman, *Vision à New York*, for
a conversation in which Hayman quotes Sollers back to himself
from a recent contribution to a Joyce colloquium (225):

> You are, whether you realize it or not, completely buried
> in a religious consciousness, of whatever sort it is. Joyce
> was possibly the only one capable of taking leave of it.
> D.H.: Really?
> S.: If not Joyce, then *Finnegans Wake*,
> D.H.: As text?
> S.: As *operation*. (My translation and italics—PB.)

Philippe Sollers, "Joyce & Co.," 107: "Since *Finnegans Wake*
was written, English no longer exists. It no longer exists as self-
sufficient language, no more indeed than does any other language"; and Julia Kristeva has talked of Joyce's in the same
breath as Bataille's "fissuration de l'instance logique," and the
common subversion they operate on the "great semantic uni-
ties of ideology and knowledge," in *Bataille*, Colloque de Cerisy,
282–83. The definitive *literal* statement of the contemporary
lineage of the *Wake* is the issue of *TriQuarterly* 38, *In the Wake
of the Wake*, edited by David Hayman and republished in book
form.

16. Norris, *The Decentered Universe*, 1–22.
17. Rabaté, "Lapsus ex machina," 164: "Dans tous les cas, l'opposition vrai/faux est éliminée" ("In any case the true/false opposition is eliminated").
18. Another close-to-random sampling: "a tesseract maker of
mosaics" (100); "a polyhedron of scripture" (107); "collideor-
scope" (143); "farced epistle to the Hebrews" (228); "scribnery"
(229); "a holy cryptmas" (344); "The lewdningblueboltered al-
lucktruckalltraumconductor!" (378); "map of the soul's

groupography" (479); "our book of kills" (482); "allnights newseryreel" (489).

19. Richard Ellman, *James Joyce*, new and revised edition, 32: "Joyce, as later hints make clear, fancied himself as a Parnell. Ireland's 'uncrowned king' was now on his way to becoming her tragic hero. There were three final acts to the play. The first was the attempt of the London *Times* to discredit Parnell by printing a letter, alleged to be in his handwriting, that condoned the Phoenix Park murders of 1882. The villain here was Richard Pigott, whose two sons were at Clongowes with James Joyce; in February 1889, before the Special Commission, Pigott was unmasked as a forger by his misspelling of the word 'hesitancy.'" See also James Atherton, *The Books in the Wake*, 100–104.

20. James Joyce, *A Portrait of the Artist as a Young Man*, first published in 1916, 27–39.

21. Ibid., 27.

22. Joyce, *Wake*, 533: "How I am amp amp amplify"; compare, for example, the thirteen pages of the final version with the single page reproduced by David Hayman below in *A First Draft Version of Finnegans Wake*, 92–93:

What secondtonone myther *rector* & bridgemaker was the first to rise taller through his beanstale than the bluegum baobabbaum or the *giganteous* Wellingtonia Sequoia, went nudiboots into a liffeyette when she was barely in her tricklies, was *well* known to clout a conciliationcap on the esker of his hooth, *sports* [*a chainganger's*] *albert over his*, [*hullender's*] *epulence*, had several coloured serevanmaids on the same [*big*] *white* drawringroam horthrug, killed his own hungery self as a young man *in anger*, [*bred manyheaded stepsons and* [*a*] *leapyourown daughter*, [& *appeared to the shecook*], found food for five when allmarker was goflooded, pressed the beer of ale age out of the nettles of rashness, put a roof on the lodge for Hymn and a cog in his pot for homo, was waylaid by a parker and beshotten by a buckeley, kicks lintils when he's cuppy and casts Jacob's to his childer on the parish, owns the bulgiest bungbarrel that was ever tiptapped in the *privace of* Mullingar Inn, hears the cricket on the earth but annoys the life out of predicants, made Man with *guts* one jerk and minted money n?ong many, *blows whiskey around the head but thinks stout upon his feet*, [*was dubbed out of joke and limned in raw ochre*,] stutters when he falls and goes mad *entirely* when he's waked, is Timb to the pearly morn and Tomb by the mourning night and though he had all the *baked* bricks

of *bould* Babylon *to his lusting placys* he'd be *lost for the*
want of an ould *wubblin* wall?

Answer—Finn MacCool!

23. One writer, for instance, wonders if there is any real "dépense"
(in the sense of Bataille's potlatch and confusion of sex and
death) in *Finnegans Wake*, where nothing is definitive, not even
defintively *lost:* Daniel Ferrer, "Hissheory," 239; "Le texte limite
ses pertes par une récupération si habile, si minutieuse, exerce
une telle maîtrise sur les forces qu'il met en jeu, qu'on peut se
demander si, en fin de compte, il y a dépense réelle ou dépense
mimée" ("The text limits its losses by a recovery so skilful, so
minute; it exerts such mastery on the forces it puts into play
that we may wonder if—in the final analysis there is real or
simulated loss").

24. Allusions abound throughout the *Wake*, but 338–55 focus on a
dramatization of the incident.

25. Norris, *The Decentered Universe*, 28.

26. Nietzsche, *Twilight of the Idols*, 34: "Did he himself grasp that,
this shrewdest of all self-deceivers? Did he at last say that to
himself in the *wisdom* of his courage for death? ... Socrates
wanted to die—it was not Athens, it was *he* who handed himself the poison cup."

27. Norris, *The Decentered Universe*, 11: "The singularity of individual experience—its uniqueness—is undermined by the replica-
tion of events and instability of characters." Ferrer,
"Hissheory," 236: "Le parleur et le parlé, l'accusateur et
l'accusé, le questionneur et le questionné, tout apparaît donc
difficilement différenciable" ("The speaker and the spoken, the
accuser and the accused, the questioner and the questioned,
all appears hardly distinguishable"). Joyce, *Wake*, 626: "But
you're changing, acoolsha, you're changing from me, I can feel.
Or is it me is? Im getting mixed."

28. Interesting that *she* supplies those hilariously unacademic
footnotes to the "lessons" chapter, 260–308: "Come, smooth of
my slate, to the beat of my blosh! ... when I remembered all
your pupil-teacher's erringnesses in perfection class. You
sh'undn't write you can't if you w'udn't pass for undevel-
opmented. This is the propper way to say that, Sr. If it's me
chews to swallow all you saidn't you can eat my words for it as
sure as there's a key in my kiss. Quick erit faciofacey. When we
will conjugate together ... with love ay loved have I on my back
spine ..." (279); and Juan's later "lecture" to the "students" of
St. Brides is hardly less provocative: "Whalebones and
buskbutts may hurt you (thwacaway thwuck!) but never lay
bare your breast secret (dickette's place!) to joy a jonas in the

Dolphin's Barncar with your meetual fan, Doveyed Covetfilles, compulsing paynattention spasms between the averthisment for Ulikah's wine and a pair of pulldoors of the old cupiosity shape" (434).

29. "Turning up and fingering over the most dantellising peaches in the lingrous longerous book of the dark" (251).

30. Adamov, *Le Professeur Tarane,* and Ionesco, *La Leçon.*

31. Atherton, *The Books in the Wake,* 114–23.

32. Ibid., 102–3.

33. Jean-Paul Sartre, *L'Idiot de la famille.*

34. Ellmann, *James Joyce,* 279–81.

35. Samuel Beckett, W.C. Williams, Vladimir Dixon (Joyce), and others, *Our Exagmination Round His Factification for Incamination of Works in Progress,* 14.

36. Margaret Solomon leans this way in her exhaustive survey and analysis of sexual symbolism in the *Wake, Eternal Geomater: The Sexual Universe of Finnegans Wake,* in the introduction to which (viii) she announces her discovery of "the reasons for the major symbols of the book: namely the male and female sexual organs of the human body." But that leaves unanswered the Nietzschean question: "and what does *sex* mean?"

37. The picture conveyed by Ellmann of Joyce's nearly constitutional nomadism is that of a man who tries to solve his problems by moving on once the situation he has been living in becomes too thorny and/or complicated: "Departure from his country was a strategy of combat" (*James Joyce,* 110). "Joyce did not wait for peace of mind. He never possessed it. Instead he moved from crisis to crisis" (210). "No one was in fact quicker to find life tedious, or more eager to shun equilibrium, whether by drinking or moving" (224).

38. Condou, "Le Corps à lettre," 175–76. See middle of n. 9 above.

39. Stephen Heath, "Ambiviolences, notes pour une lecture de Joyce." His commentary on Joyce and Jousse is in the second article, 68–71; Joyce, *Wake,* 468: "In the beginning was the gest he he jousstly says."

40. Hannah Arendt, *The Origins of Totalitarianism.*

41. This tradition, and the system of education whose purpose is to inculcate it, is subject to extensive ridicule and parody in the *Wake,* especially in the "lessons" chapter (260–308); cf. note 28 above.

42. Bernard Benstock, *Joyce-Again's Wake,* 19n: "At various instances Joyce seems to be interrupting to allow the weary reader to plead for a halt." Joyce, 108: "Now patience; and remember patience is the great thing, and above all things else we must avoid anything like being or becoming out of patience."

43. Levy-Bruhl is not, of course, the only object of Joyce-Jones's ridicule. By process of interchangeability and substitution, others are attacked as well: for instance, Wyndham Lewis (see above, chap. 6, n. 5) had infuriated Joyce by branding his work as decadent—that is, as space-obsessed; and so Joyce is especially virulent on Lewis, even more so since his work was popular. No opportunity is lost to parody, mock, and incriminate Lewis, referred to under permutations and plays on "time and space," usually connected to "fallacy"—as in our final extended excerpt from the *Wake* with the "dime and cash (time and space) diamond fallacy," implying that Lewis was some kind of mere dealer or profiteer in ideas. Here we are certainly reminded of the "man" behind the work, the man who was Joyce and missed no chance of settling a score! Joyce is, of course, in excellent company—Alexander Pope, Louis-Ferdinand Céline, to name just a few of its most illustrious members, were not shy about attacking their enemies in their works. With this level of artist, however, we are dealing not with the "man of resentment" that Nietzsche excoriated, but a creative process that turns negativity in life into the affirmation that is art, even in *spite* of itself.

Chapter 7. The Strategy of Interruption: Philippe Sollers' *Drame*

1. Henri Peyre, *French Novelists of Today*, 443.
2. Stephen Heath, *The Nouveau Roman: A Study in the Practice of Writing*, 236; Katherine C. Kurk, "Consummation of the Text: A Study of Philippe Sollers," 126–27; Philippe Sollers, "L'Écriture et révolution," in *Théorie d'ensemble*, 72. See also Allen Thiher's comprehensive account of the place of games in general and chess in particular in modern fiction and the philosophy that grounds it in *Words in Reflection*, 156–87. Chess, for instance, according to Thiher, is an essential and recurrent figure in the formative texts of Wittgenstein, Saussure, Heidegger, and Derrida: "The writer who, like Wittgenstein, Saussure, and Heidegger, is seduced by the chess metaphor may find in it a model of how at least a provisional order can be introduced by fiction into an otherwise absurd reign of disorder. Within the closed space of the chess game the writer can hope to find the model for how to create, with a finite number of elements combining according to the finite number of rules, the paradigm of what a limited combinatory order is. . . . In the hands of a Derrida, however, this model of limited order loses whatever solace it might have offered the writer in search of order. In Derrida's version of the book as chessboard, it becomes 'a

field of infinite substitutions in the closure of a finite ensemble'
for which there is no center that might arrest the 'freeplay' of
substitutions" (*Words in Reflection*, 158). Sollers' use of the
chessboard is closer in spirit and time, of course, to the
Derridean signs of flux, substitution, and anarchy than to the
"limited order" of the precursors. An interesting contrast to
these modern recourses to games and game theory is provided
by Sartre in *Saint Genet*, where he attacks, in the antimod-
ernist mood so frequent with him, this style as a kind of "bad
faith" whereby the writer *pretends* to a place outside of time,
situation, and history—in other words, outside of the human.
Sartre's position regarding games is consistent with his criticism of "mysticism" in the texts of Bataille and Blanchot,
which he also saw as a kind of game of make-believe: "Absurd
and gratuitous, these conventions have no other effect than to
transform in all domains human activity into a ballet. Let us
recall here that prison and the game have always been the
favorite symbols of thinkers who attempted to describe human
activity in placing themselves outside of the human: I'm thinking especially of Pascal, Nietzsche, and Kafka" (*Saint Genet*,
121; my translation).

Whether the wild imaginations and ludic consciousness of
modernity that Sartre is here opposing represent either an
escape from the human or the pretention to so escape should
seem now, in the light of recent explorations of the omnipres-
ence of structure (so that even the game must obey *human*
rules, and even in space we don't leave the world behind),
questionable to say the least. To be human may be instead to
take a position, which would become a *situation*, outside of the
human. Such was the wisdom of the German romantics, indeed, for whom man was only fully human at play—that is, in
the fiction of unreality; as if he can take himself seriously only
when "it doesn't matter." The other *serious* would be *of* the serious: that "spirit of gravity" responsible for, or which facilitates, witch-hunts, oppression, genocide—that Nietzsche opposed and was opposed by at every turning. Before we get too
serious ourselves we may playfully suppose that Sartre's war
against imagination was fueled by his own possession of it in
such enormous and volatile quantities; Sartre's attachment to
the logics of control (Cartesian-intellectual) made him fear the
dark threat of the unknown imagination has always posed,
whereupon he brings *ethics* in, this modern Plato (who burned
his plays so he could become a philosopher), to chase the poet
(in himself) from *his* republic.

3. Sollers, *Drame*, 75–76, 139–40, 150–52.
4. Ibid., 111: ""Il y a . (Un point dans du blanc, c'est cela.)""

(""there is a . [A period on the blank page, that's it.]"") This is likely also to be some kind of allusion to the philosophy of Emmanuel Lévinas, where the "il y a" (borrowed from "es gibt" of Heidegger) at a certain point represents the fundamental terror and opacity of existence. Possibly Blanchot is present here too, as "il y a" is one of the phrases that the narrator of Le Dernier Mot is bewildered by (see above, pp. 109–10).

5. Quotation marks in indented extracts, here and further, are Sollers', coming after an introductory "il écrit" ("he writes") but representing evidently also some kind of "assault on punctuation," since these quoted passages as the reader will see or has seen are of identical provenance and significance (or lack thereof) as those unaccompanied by marks. What Stephen Melville says about quotation marks in the context of de Man and Derrida applies palpably to Sollers' "quoted" text: "The quotation marks can be said to ironize the words they bracket but also to attribute to them or enforce upon them an appearance of deeper intentionality; they work as well to level out the emphasis given in the usual and casual reading of the phrase. . . . the imposition of quotation marks has the effect of repeating the sentence for us as its own rule, recalling its content, its message, to its particularliy—its meaning to being. 'The sentence becomes autonomous'" (Philosophy Beside Itself, 152–53).

On a more general level, the "strategy of citation" in fiction and theory of our time is part of the general assault on self, author, and source. Works become collections of quotations that undermine the sense and attribution of the whole, which becomes aleatory, indeterminate, and ludic. Such an ideology and practice was announced, in reference to the fictions of Michel Butor, by Françoise Van Rossum-Guyon, in the introductory paper that set the militant tone for the colloquium of 1973, at Cerisy, devoted to Butor: "Each reading of the cited texts enriches the text in new ways, opens up new perspectives, modifies the sense of the containing work. . . . A work made of citations advertises its collective character, is a work of collaboration. . . . the multiplicity of collaborators of different times and styles can have as an effect the suppression of the traditional Man-Work relation in favor of a generalized text. . . . Each of the cited authors, in effect, treats the subject in his own way, points of view change, a gap is installed that forces us to become conscious: of the fact that in the text it is a matter only of a certain representation of reality and not of reality, and, therefore, of the relativity of our own representations of things" (Rossum-Guyon, "Aventures de la citation chez Butor," 19–20; my translation). See also Allen Thiher's abundant and far-ranging exploration of citation in modern literature, in *Words in Reflection*. The learned Germans are especially fond of this kind of "research" in their writing: ". . . the practice of montage and quotation has resulted in texts in which all writing is citation. Writing has thus lost its referential function (*Verweisungscharakter*). Literature has become a kind of mechanical process—a writing machine perhaps—as the author has liquidated himself. He has become a machine for reading other texts (which is seen as) . . . a sign of the writer's ideological rejection of the traditional novel as a form of individual accomplishment. The abolition of the writer as the determination of the writing's meaning is, for these German writers, a means of demystifying literature and the bourgeois ideology that goes along with it" (*Words in Reflection*, 184). Citation introduces aporias, problems, paradoxes very difficult to handle by a linear totalizing logic, because of the tendency in this style toward infinite proliferation and *mise en abyme* (for instance, the one I construct here with my string of citations on citation-ality). Sollers' practice is, of course, to use *citation* in all the above senses, then to normalize them by using quotation marks structurally, as we have seen. In addition, Sollers undermines the already very limited reliability of the quotation by frequent use in his text of the three ellipsis dots already familiar to readers of the unmentionable Céline. The readers of Sollers' readers won't know who's left what out. . . .

6. Deleuze, *Différence et répétition*, 94, 252; Eco, *L'Œuvre ouverte*, chaps. 1, 4.
7. Maurice Blanchot, *De Kafka à Kafka*.
8. Deleuze, *Différence et répétition*, 375.
9. Jacques Derrida, *La Dissémination*, 351.
10. Henri Peyre, quoted above, is one of many. Sartre's *Les Temps modernes* has been particularly hostile to *Tel Quel* in general and Sollers in particular; for example, Annie Leclerc, "Sollers, poète d'un certain drame."
11. For instance, "If you met on the binge a poor acheseyeld from Ailing, when the tune of his tremble shook shimmy on shin, while his countrary raged in the weak of his wailing" (148). The "bubble" that is the *Wake*, may be seen perhaps, like the dream some say it is, as an extended contrary-to-fact condition, a survival of the subjunctive in our modern age of indicative "certainty."
12. Barthes, *The Pleasure of the Text*, 38; see also above, pp. 11, 15.
13. See bibliography. Sollers' *L'Intermédiare*, for instance, a collection of earlier essays and stories, is a charming, accomplished,

and even, in places, a wonderfully funny book. "Introduction aux Lieux d'Aisance" ("Introduction to Toilets"; 31–44), it seems to me, has no equal in any language for slyly scatological hilarity.

14. Philippe Sollers, *Logiques*, 237.

15. Barthes, *The Pleasure of the Text*, 52.

16. "". . . what I could do would become readable, translatable . . . which is to say empty, incomplete, no good . . . "" (Sollers, *Drame*, 112; *Event*, 57)

17. Ibid., 86: ""Ce que je choisis ou ne choisis pas de t'écrire me paraîtra bientôt inutile. . . . Comme si écrire, c'était rendre faux . . . ."" ""What I choose or do not choose to write you will soon seem a waste of time to me . . . As though writing were lying . . ."" (Sollers, *Drame*, 86; *Event*, 43).

18. A little Zen or Tao may enter into the conjuncture here too. Sollers at this point is fascinated by the Orient; *Tel Quel* is soon going to take its notorious turn toward Maoism, and Sollers' *Nombres* (1968), the text that attracted such passionate allegiance from Derrida and Kristeva, is going to go so far as to incorporate Chinese letters. In *Drame*, Sollers exploits the ambiguity of the French "est" ("is" as well as "east") to demonstrate the direction of his interest: "Mais l'est? je vous demande comment aller lentement vers l'est? . . . " ("But east? . . . How to head gradually east?"; *Drame*, 31; *Event*, 12).

19. Sollers, *Drame*, 41: "Le plan tourne, se présente sous l'une ou l'autre face" ("The map turns, offering another surface for us to regard").

20. Søren Kierkegaard, *Concluding Unscientific Postscript*, 105: "Reflection can be halted only by a leap."

Chapter 8. A Deconstructed Epiphany: Des Forêts' Le Bavard

1. See above, my comments on "equality" in Tzara (44–45), Beckett (66–69), and Sollers (162–64). Blanchot further characterizes the author-reader relation that Des Forêts creates as that of "étranglement" ("La Parole vaine" [*The Word in Vain*]), in *L'Amitié*, 143: each has the other "by the throat."

2. See above, pp. 101–2.

3. See above, p. 131.

4. See above, pp. 138–45.

5. Blanchot, "La Parole vaine," 142: "Le lecteur de tout livre est pour l'auteur le compagnon malheureux à qui il n'est demandé que de ne pas parler, mais d'être là" ("The reader for any book is for the author the unfortunate companion of whom it is demanded not to talk but simply to be there").

6. Baudelaire, "A Une Heure du matin," 16: "Enfin! seul! On n'entend plus que le roulement de quelques fiacres attardés et éreintés. Pendant quelques heures, nous posséderons le silence, sinon le repos. Enfin! la tyrannie de la face humaine a disparu, et je ne souffrirai plus que par moi-même" ("Finally alone! I can hear only a few late and worn-down carriages. For a few hours we'll have quiet, if not repose. Finally the tyranny of the human face has disappeared, and I'll suffer only alone").

7. See above, pp. 64–69.

8. Oswald Spengler, *The Decline of the West*, 2:505: "One figure is even more important than all the energy of enterprising master-men ... the *engineer*, the priest of the machine, the man who knows it. Not merely the importance, but the very existence of industry depends upon the existence of the hundred thousand talented, rigorously schooled brains that command the technique and develop it onward and onward."

9. Louis-René Des Forêts, "Les Grands Moments d'un chanteur," in *La Chambre des enfants*, 101–54. In this Kafkaesque tale (owing perhaps to "Josephine the Singer ...") it is a matter of an individual who is able to manufacture, seemingly out of nowhere, a musical talent that wins him the adulation of the public. His subsequent sabotage of this talent reveals, or deconstructs, the basically exploitative, shallow, and hollow nature of the rapport between audience and performer.

10. See above, pp. 27–30.

11. To this résumé we may add the onslaught on the faculty of memory that constitutes *Finnegans Wake*, which has dissolved that cage of language; language can therefore no longer even contain, much less "recapture."

12. E.M. Cioran, *Précis de décomposition* (*A Short History of Decay*), 114: "Que la vie ne signifie rien, tout le monde le sait ou le pressent: qu'elle soit au moins sauvée par un tour verbal! Une phrase aux tournants de leur vie,—voilà à peu près tout ce qu'on demande aux grands et aux petits. Manquent-ils à cette exigence, à cette obligation, ils sont à jamais perdus; car, on pardonne tout, jusqu'aux crimes, à condition qu'ils soient exquisément commentés" ("That life is meaningless everyone knows or suspects—may it be at least redeemed by some verbal play. A phrase at the turning points of their lives—that's about all we ask of great and small alike. If they fail this test, this obligation, they're forever damned; for we can forgive everything, even crimes, on condition they're exquisitely commented").

13. Des Forêts' fascination with mirrors is undeniable, as is also our epoch's (Lacan's *mirror* phase). *Le Bavard* opens with "Je me regarde souvent dans la glace" ("I often look at myself in the

mirror"), and the story "Dans le Miroir," in *La Chambre des enfants*, uses the mirror as a figure for the inevitably deceptive rapport between writer and reader: the writer, who must pretend he is holding the mirror up to the reader, is actually holding it up to himself. In another register, Cash, the character who goes mad in Faulkner's *As I Lay Dying*, is also fond of looking into mirrors, as if to verify that he's still *all* there. Mirrors are probably so habitual in fiction because they convey the deep attachment in our culture to truth as reflection and representation. For a comprehensive, insightful, and very systematic exploration of this philosophical tradition, in the light of Derrida's handling-deconstruction of it, see Gasché, *The Tain of the Mirror*.

14. See above, pp. 168–69.
15. The reader of modern text is Sisyphus, like the modern proletarian in Camus' famous rendition of the myth, because the labors, unlike those of Hercules, are incapable of termination. In contradistinction to Camus' hero, however, the modern reader cannot be imagined as particularly happy (though we can't rule out the chance of a certain strange pleasure in sharing the *text* of his travail).
16. See above, pp. 33–35.
17. Maurice Blanchot, "La Parole vaine," 138.
18. Edgar Morin, *Le Cinéma, ou l'homme imaginaire*, 139; italics Morin's, translation mine—PB.
19. Blanchot, "La Parole vaine," 139, 142.
20. See above, pp. 76–77.
21. This (Platonic, Hegelian, Sartrean) idea of the "bad faith of writing," a point I raise with Tzara, Leiris, and in my conclusion, comes down to a search for a risk to take (revolution, surrealism, futurism—or, more personally, addiction and adultery) so that the slave (scribe) would then equal the master (sublimely above literacy). This conflict, bloodbath, struggle, is perhaps our inevitably Western way—to which the magical, cabalistic, alchemical tradition has been all along offering an antidote (although perhaps an increasingly indigestible one). The Eastern traditions, at all events, seem kinder, less aggressive, more humane; and a thinker like Michel Serres may represent a rejection of the master-slave dialectic. Enough blood has been spilled, he says in a recent memoir with the appropriately Eastern title of *Détachement*. Like Thoreau, he pretends to be quitting the game, or like the late John Lennon, "just watching the wheels go round." Some type of (absurd?) *leap* is required in all such postures of surrender to keep them from falling back into passive although passably effective strategies for coming out ahead in the game.

Chapter 9. Madness, Theater, Text

1. By madness and theater I don't mean empirical entities but more what Foucault calls "discursive formations," that is, concepts that are used as tools to deal with our circumstances. Generally I am trying to bypass and eschew what I see as the attendant dangers of reformism. Marx, for instance, in a renowned passage from the "Introduction to the Critique of Hegel's *Philosophy of Right*," locates the injustice that the proletariat must deal with not in any condition or error that it is possible to change or rectify (by shorter hours and better pay, for example) but in the appalling inhumanity and sheer unacceptability of the proletariat's existence as a class whose only reason for being is to be exploited. For this (early) Marx, the proletariat is "a class which is the dissolution of all classes, a sphere of society which has a universal character because its sufferings are universal, and which does not claim a *particular redress* because the wrong which is done to it is not a *particular wrong but wrong in general*" (*Early Writings*, 58). A fascinating and unfinished chapter in intellectual history leads directly from this statement through Trotsky, Luxemburg, and Liebknecht to the provocative conclusions drawn from it, inspired by the French May 1968, in Debord's influential *La Société du spectacle*, 77: "No qualitative amelioration of its poverty, no illusion of integration into the hierarchy can be a lasting remedy for its dissatisfaction; for the proletariat cannot recognize itself truly in a particular wrong which has been inflicted upon it or, therefore, in the *reparation of a particular wrong*, nor in a great number of these wrongs, but only in *the absolute wrong* of having been rejected into marginality by the masters of this world" (my translation). The proletariat, therefore, is that class that is called into being in order to abolish itself as a class at the same time as all other classes. This is known popularly as the *generic* theory of revolution, and, I believe it goes a long way toward accounting for the otherwise incomprehensible "irrationalities" of such episodes as the Paris Commune of 1870, and May 1968, and in another, crueler sense, the irrationalities of the Khmer Rouge of Cambodia.

My point of view is, then, by analogy, that the modernist writer who "knows nothing" is the functional equivalent of the proletarian who "has nothing." The natural affinity of the modern writer for revolution is based on the attempt by the revolutionary proletariat to realize an ontological vacancy, that is, to accomplish in actuality what the former tries to do in words —to sweep away all preexisting prejudices, hierarchies, vested interests, and constraints. Blanchot and Tzara, for instance, are particularly articulate and insistent on this idea and in drawing the appropriate conclusions in the practice of their art and the way they see the art of others (see chap. 5, nn. 19, 21). The direction, then, of the "limit-text" is not toward any expansion or reform of the cultural apparatus (such indeed may be the attitude of Sarraute, Robbe-Grillet, or even, recently, Sollers,—proud of the "freedoms" that writers now enjoy because of their pioneering efforts), which, in tune with Deleuze and Guattari's analyses in *Capitalism and Schizophrenia*, is always ready to develop another corollary to include another "exception." These texts rather refuse permanently any accommodation with the social structures in which they are obliged to operate, like that proletariat of Marx, Trotsky, Luxemburg and Debord that generically must aim not toward amelioration but toward abolition of the social order.

I have selected, therefore, the ideas of madness and theatre, and parenthetically that of text, to demonstrate the fundamental derealizing antagonism toward and distance from our world that these works inevitably assume, for the statement they make is radical, uncompromising, unacceptable. Like a proletariat, "with nothing to lose but its chains," they seek not to make us over and better but to destroy what or the way we are.

2. Colin Gordon, ed. and trans., *Power/Knowledge. Interviews and Other Writings of Michel Foucault, 1972-1977*, 208.

3. Blanchot remarks in a recent essay that, in view of the changes he has been through, he rather thinks of himself as an *actor* who has had many roles to play rather than as an *author* who is responsible for maintaining consistency of identity or purpose: "Ainsi, avant l'œuvre, l'écrivain n'existe pas encore; après l'œuvre, il ne subsiste plus: autant dire que son existence est sujette à caution, et on l'appelle 'auteur'! Plus justement, il serait 'acteur,' ce personnage éphémère qui naît et meurt chaque soir pour s'être donné, exagérément à voir, tué par le spectacle qui le rend ostensible, c'est-à dire sans rien qui lui soit propre ou caché dans quelque intimité" ("And so, before the work, the writer doesn't exist yet; after the work he doesn't subsist; as much as to say that his existence is conditional, and yet you call him 'author.' More exactly he would be the 'actor,' this ephemeral personage that is born and dies each evening, in treating himself as an exaggeration to be seen, killed by the very spectacle that makes him ostensible, that is with nothing that is his own or hidden in any intimacy"; *Après Coup* [*After the Fact*], p. 87). This essay serves as afterword to the reissue of an older work, *Le Ressassement éternel* (*The Eternal Recapitulation*), from which Blanchot wishes to take his distance while all the same accepting a kind of responsibility

for it.

Also relevant is the figure of the theatrical that Sollers projects in his most recent novel, where the interplay between pseudonym and civil status takes on a rococo, bizarre, possibly paranoid complexity, as Sollers, whose *real* name is Joyaux ("Gems"), represents himself as Diamant ("Diamond").

Finally, the actor, on such a stage, would have the last word, if there was one: "Qui sommes-nous à ce moment-là ? Des acteurs? De simples acteurs? Ou bien plutôt, sous nos masques de fantasmes grimaçants, des fantômes enfin réels, enfin chacun soi-même en plain coeur de la comédie? Au cœur, oui, car il n'y a pas plus loin. Ni sa vie, ni la mienne, ni celle d'un des millions de figurants en train d'accomplir les mêmes gestes, plus 'normalement' si l'on veut. Comme si la vieille machine avait sauté, celle de l'ancienne fascination ou terreur. Plus rien. Des fonctions. Des positions provisoires sur un échiquier fou" ("What are we at such moments? Actors? Simple actors? Or rather, under our masks of grimacing fantasies, phantoms that are finally real, finally each one himself at the heart of the comedy? At the heart, yes, for there is no farther. Neither her life, nor mine, nor that of millions of performers in process of performing the same motions, more 'normally,' if you wish. As if the ancient machine had exploded, that of old fascination and terror. Nothing more. Functions. Provisory positions on a mad chessboard"; *Portrait du Joueur* [*Portrait of the Gambler*], 151–52).

4. Gilles Deleuze and Félix Guattari, *Capitalisme et schizophrenie, l'anti-œdipe*, 11.

5. R. D. Laing, *The Politics of Experience*, and Gilles Deleuze and Felix Guattari, *Anti-Œdipus: Capitalism and Schizophrenia*.

6. Georg Groddeck, *The Book of the It*.

7. The theater of the Renaissance and the alchemical-cabalist tradition cancel reality in favor of another (Platonic) world. The modern avatar dissolves the world in favor of no other.

8. Philippe Sollers, *Logiques* (*Logics*), 115: IL NOUS FAUT DONC RÉALISER LA POSSIBILITÉ DU TEXTE COMME THÉÂTRE EN MÊME TEMPS QUE DU THÉÂTRE ET DE LA VIE COMME TEXTE" ("WE MUST THEREFORE REALIZE THE POSSIBILITY OF THE TEXT AS THEATER AS WELL AS OF THEATER AND LIFE AS TEXT"). Sollers is commenting on Mallarmé, capitals his own.

9. A central figure in Michel Foucault's *Surveiller et punir* (*Discipline and Punish*), this is Bentham's eighteenth-century invention of a centrally located watchtower from which just a few guards could watch and control the doings of a vast number of prisoners in the encircling, tiered, and uncurtained

cells. This was a metaphor, of course, for the kind of control that was then planned and is now fully operative for a modern population-at-large "under surveillance" (panoptically through computer) in that other cage they are still calling freedom!

10. Michel Foucault, *L'Ordre du discours*, 10.

11. Ibid., 31–38.

12. Thus an improbable if not statistically *impossible* freedom for the few (in art, stimulating professional activity, winning the lottery, etc.) legitimizes the stifling oppression and manipulation of the vast majority, who are led to acquiesce to a system that makes success a theoretical, if farfetched, possibility. Our societies must claim the ability to deliver a freedom that they cannot extend without undermining the deeper, mostly hidden, structures of hierarchy and privilege that constitute them. The real risks of freedom, impossible to grant, live, or apply except *formally*, that is, *rhetorically*, become spectacle, circus, exception, and diversion; this is a central theme of Debord's insurrectionary text, *La Société du spectacle*, an indispensable theoretical resource for May 1968 and its aftermath—and this strategy or remedy is one that power has been applying to the body politic at least since Ancient Rome. As the uncanny and insightful Poe commented in a random note more than a century ago, the pain that security (bread) won't heal, distraction (circus) will dull: "It is by no means clear, as regards the present revolutionary spirit of Europe (1848), that it is a spirit which 'moveth altogether if it move at all.' In Great Britain it may be kept quiet for half a century yet, by placing at the head of affairs an experienced medical man. He should keep his forefinger constantly on the pulse of the patient and exhibit *panem* in gentle doses, with as much *circenses* as the stomach can be made to retain"; in *The Works of Poe*, 7:216, suggestion no. 25.

13. Even Blanchot, as much an "intransitive writer" as any, stresses emphatically in *Après Coup* (*After the Fact*, referred to in chap. 9, n. 3), this same inevitability of explanation: "Même Mallarmé, le plus secret et le plus discret des poètes, donne des indications sur la manière dont il faut lire le *Coup de Dés*" ("Even Mallarmé, the most secret and discreet of poets, gives instructions on how to read *A Throw of the Dice*"; 89). There is, of course, the familiar figure of the writer who refuses explanation, in a take-me-or-leave-me attitude, as in the sovereignty of Bataille: "Se conduire en maître signifie ne jamais rendre de comptes; je repugne à l'explication de ma conduite. La souveraineté est silencieuse ou déchue" ("Conducting yourself as sovereign means never offering explanations. I loathe all explanation of my conduct. Sovereignty is either silent or

fallen"; Georges Bataille, *Le Coupable* [*The Guilty One*], 51).
Bataille, however, is explaining, and *well*, his very failure to explain. This same paradox inhabits his theories of sex as transgression: in the afterword to the provocative *L'Erotisme*, Bataille mentions that Jean Wahl had objected that the moment
of awareness of the transgression (which Bataille's project
cannot elude without ceasing to be in the public domain as
text) constitutes a recuperation and normalization of its
violence and disruption. To this Bataille had no other answer
than to admit both the cogency of the objection and the contradiction inherent in his own position (a weakness that Sartre
also exploited by calling Bataille a "nouveau mystique"—see
above, p. 5; chap. 1, n. 15. Stephen Melville is very lucid on
this aspect of the "expressed transgression" in Bataille: "But if
the very affirmation of an experience of this sort tends already
to be a betrayal of that experience, Bataille's own writing is
subject to the same threat to which he claims Hegel has
succumbed; it may itself become the annulment of what it
intends to communicate" (*Philosophy Beside Itself*, 76).
14. Beckett, Williams, Dixon, and others, *Our Exagmination Round
His Factification For Incamination of Work in Progress.*
15. Ricoeur, for instance, sees Freud's (and also Hegel's, Husserl's,
and Nietzsche's) unsettling and irrefutable (what Derrida calls
'incontournable' ['unsurpassable']) assaults on the subject as
being no cause to end in pessimism, despair, fatalism, and res-
ignation but instead as a catalyst, stimulation, and challenge
to attain a more comprehensive, reliable, and relevant human
theory and practice: "Freudian realism is the necessary stage
to bring the failure of reflective consciousness to its completion. . . . this failure is neither fruitless nor utterly negative.
For aside from its pedagogical or didactic value and its
potentiality for preparing us to understand the lessons of
Freudianism, this failure begins a process of converting consciousness in such a way as to understand the necessity of
letting go all avarice with regard to itself, including that subtle
self-concupiscence which may be what is narcissistic in the
immediate consciousness of life. Through this failure, consciousness discovers that its immediate self-certainty was mere
presumption and thus gains access to *thought*, which is no
longer the attention that consciousness pays to itself so much
as to *saying, or rather to what is said in the saying*"; *The
Conflict of Interpretations*, 103. For Ricoeur's comparable reaction to Derrida, see chap.1, end of note 8. Remarkably similar
is the way in which another major religious (it should be admitted!) phenomenologist (whose intrication with Blanchot we
have commented on, chap. 5, n. 24) insists on the primordial-

ity and irrefutability of the ethical rapport with the other. The explosions that modernity has detonated, the doubts, insecurities, vagaries, existential quandaries, do not, for Emmanuel Lévinas, abolish responsibility and associated moral action but, on the contrary, make the ethical all the more urgent, "naked" (disinterested, since unsupported now by any earthly or heavenly system of rewards and punishments) and undeniable: "The suspicions engendered by psychoanalysis, sociology, and politics weigh on human identity such that we never know to whom we are speaking and what we are dealing with when we build our ideas on the basis of human facts. But we do not need this knowledge in the relationship in which the other is a neighbor, and in which before being an individuation of the genus *man*, a *rational animal*, a *free will*, or any essence whatever, he is the persecuted one for whom I am responsible to the point of being a hostage for him, and in which my responsibility, instead of disclosing me in my 'essence' as a transcendental ego, divests me without stop of all that can be common to me and another man. I am then called upon in my uniqueness as someone for whom no one else can substitute himself. . . . Thus it is not as a freedom, impossible in a will that is inflated and altered, sold or mad, that subjectivity is imposed as an absolute. It is sacred in its alterity with respect to which, in an unexceptionable responsibility, I posit myself deposed of my sovereignty. Paradoxically, it is *qua alienus*—foreigner and other—that man is not alienated" (Emmanuel Lévinas, *Otherwise than Being or Beyond Essence*, 59). We don't mean to conflate, of course, two thinkers as different as Ricoeur and Lévinas—except in the fact that both attempt to transcend or bypass modernity by accepting what they see as its challenge. Even in the passages cited above we may notice, however, that the two diverge clearly. Ricoeur's recourse to "consciousness" is social objective–Platonic–Hegelian, whereas Lévinas' appeal to "uniqueness" is Kierkegaardian, existential, and subjective. Lévinas obviously also is much closer to Derrida and Blanchot (having written about both and been written about by both—all in very approving terms) and to the mad, theatrical, (un)apologetic literature it is a question of here.

16. "Apotheosis" is probably a more accurate word than "rehabilitation" (even so radical a writer as Bataille has been suspicious of Genet) for what Sartre does so appallingly well in *Saint Genet*.

17. See chap. 1, n. 8. It is relevant also that Foucault's very influential structuralist vocabulary is composed of terms of passage, liaison, and momentary connection rather than of finality, firm ties, or substance: "L'écart, la distance, l'inter-

médiaire [a Sollers' title], la dispersion, la différence ne sont
pas les thèmes de la littérature d'aujourd'hui, mais ce en quoi
le langage maintenant nous est donné" ("separation, distance,
intermediacy, dispersion, difference are not merely themes of
today's literature but the ways in which we now experience the
reality of language"; "Le Langage de l'Espace" ["The Language
of Space"], 378–79). These terms of connection, movement,
fluidity are very much in evidence also in Gasché's recent interpretation of Derrida's "non-Marxist notion of infrastruc-
ture. . . . The infrastructures . . . represent the *relation—connection, ratio, rapport . . . between* concepts, levels, argumentative
and textual arrangements . . ." (*The Tain of the Mirror*, 147, first
two and final emphases mine).

18. See chap. 1, n. 5. .

19. In the very thought-provoking conclusion of *Philosophy Beside
Itself*, Stephen Melville owns up to being inspired partly by a
"desire to assure something very much like the purity and integrity of the Derridean position. . . . Given the overarching
subversive force of Derrida's writings, it seems that such an
assurance ought to take the form of a guarantee of that force."
The passage continues with the protesting disclaimer of nihilism and license, and even a (re)affirmation of *tradition* that
is now a frequent protective recourse (in Hillis Miller, for example) for deconstruction-on-the-defensive: "The desire to
guarantee something that would be pure subversion, pure
play, and so on is simply incoherent. Deconstruction does indeed invite and encourage us to talk nonsense; this is a major
and genuinely risky philosophical move, but it would be a
mistake to think that it offers a general license to nonsense.
That maneuver has no claim on us at all. So the risks deconstruction runs include the making of sense and the recovery of
sense, the chance that part of what we come to will not be so
terribly different from what we have left behind" (*Philosophy
Beside Itself*, 155).

20. The paradox lies in the fact that there is nothing between us
(connection, tie) unless there is something between us (barrier,
obstacle). It is interesting to note the importance that Heidegger attributes (in a lecture given in the mid-twenties that was
part of the program that *Being and Time* would later articulate
with such pervasive effect) to this idea of the "between," that he
says very slyly would be the very place of Dasein, if indeed
there were such a thing as a subject and a world for it to be between! Heidegger's strictures against hypostasis of this useful
notion are most salutary in the sense that they are a caution
that in these times we are at home nowhere, not even in no-
man's-land: "The being of Dasein is not the mode of being of

the world, it is neither the being-handy nor the being-in-hand of something. It is just as little the being of a 'subject,' whose being would repeatedly, in a formally unexpressed way, have to be taken as being on hand. Should we be permitted to maintain the orientation to a world and a 'subject,' however, we could then say that the being Dasein is precisely the being of 'between'; which of course does not first arise by having a subject meet with the world, is the Dasein itself, but once again not as a property of a subject. This is the very reason why, strictly speaking, Dasein cannot be taken as a 'between' since the talk of a 'between' subject and world already presupposes that two entities are given between which there is supposed to be relation" (Martin Heidegger, *History of the Concept of Time, Prologemena*, 251–52).

Bibliography

Adams, Henry. *Mont St. Michel and Chartres.* Boston: Houghton Mifflin Co., 1913.

Albérès, R. M. *Métamorphoses du roman.* Paris: Albin-Michel, 1966.

Arac, Jonathan; Godzick, Wlad; and Martin, Wallace, eds. *The Yale Critics: Deconstruction in America.* Minneapolis: University of Minnesota Press, 1983.

Arendt, Hannah. *The Origins of Totalitarianism.* New York: Harcourt, Brace, 1950.

Artaud, Antonin. *Œuvres complètes.* Vol. 1. Paris: Gallimard, 1956.

Atherton, James. *The Books in the Wake.* New York: Viking, 1960.

Atkins, G. Douglas. *Reading Deconstruction, Deconstructive Reading.* Lexington: University Press of Kentucky, 1983.

Ball, Hugo. *Flight Out of Time, a Dada Diary.* New York: Viking, 1974.

Barthes, Roland. *Leçon.* Paris: Éditions du Seuil, 1978.

———. *The Pleasure of the Text.* Translated by Richard Miller. New York: Hill and Wang, 1975.

———. *Sollers écrivain.* Paris: Éditions du Seuil, 1979.

Bataille, Georges. *Le Coupable.* Paris: Gallimard, 1944.

———. *L'Érotisme.* Paris: Éditions de Minuit, 1957.

———. "Madame Edwarda." Translated by Austryn Wainhouse. In *Evergreen Review Reader* 2 (1962–67): 221–26. New York: Grove Press, 1980.

———. "Le Monde ou nous mourrons." *Critique* 13 (1957): 675–84.

———. *Œuvres complètes.* Vol. 6. Paris: Gallimard, 1974.

Baudelaire, Charles. *Les Fleurs du Mal.* Edited by Ernst Raynaud. Paris: Garnier, n.d.

———. "A Une Heure du matin." In *Spleen de Paris.* Paris: Armand Colin, 1958.

Baudrillard, Jean. "The Beaubourg-Effect: Implosion and Deterrence." *October* 20 (Spring 1982): 3–13.

_____. *L'Échange symbolique et la mort*. Paris: Gallimard, 1976.

_____. "The Orders of Simulacra." Translated by Philip Beitchman. In *Simulations*, 83–159. New York: *Semiotexte*'s 'Foreign Agents' series, 1983, 1986.

_____. *La Société de consommation*. Paris: Gallimard, 1970.

Baudry, Jean-Louis. *La "Création" premier état: l'année*. Paris: Éditions du Seuil, 1970.

_____. "Linguistique et production textuelles." In *Théorie d'ensemble*, 351–64. Paris: Éditions du Seuil, 1968.

Beausang, Michael. "Vivre en marge." *Poétique* 26 (1976): 221–31.

Beckett, Samuel. *Three Novels: Molloy, Malone Dies, and The Unnamable*. Translated from the French by Samuel Beckett. New York: Grove Press, 1955.

Beckett, Samuel; Williams, W. C.; Dixon, Vladimir (Joyce); and others. *Our Exagmination Round His Factification for Incamination of Works in Progress*. New York: New Directions, 1929, 1952.

Begnal, Michael H. "The Dreamers at the Wake." In *Narrator and Character in Finnegans Wake*, edited by Michael H. Begnal and Grace Eckley. London: Associated University Press, 1975.

Begnal, Michael H., and Senn, Fritz, eds. *A Conceptual Guide to Finnegans Wake*. University Park: Pennsylvania State University Press, 1974.

Beitchman, Philip. "The Fragmentary Word." *Sub-Stance* 39 (1983): 59–72.

Benstock, Bernard. *Joyce-Again's Wake*. Seattle: University of Washington Press, 1965.

Berman, Morris. *The Reenchantment of the World*. Ithaca, N.Y.: Cornell University Press, 1981.

Bernal, Olga. *Langage et fiction dans le roman de Beckett*. Paris: Gallimard, 1969.

Bigsby, C. W. E. *Dada and Surrealism*. London: Methuen, 1972.

Blanchot, Maurice. *L'Amitié*. Paris: Gallimard, 1971.

_____. *Après Coup*, précédé par *Le Ressassement éternel*. Paris: Gallimard, 1983.

_____. *L'Attente l'oubli*. Paris: Gallimard, 1951, 1962.

_____. *L'Écriture du désastre*. Paris: Gallimard, 1980.

_____. *L'Entretien infini*. Paris: Gallimard, 1969.

_____. *L'Espace littéraire*. Paris: Gallimard, 1955.

_____. *La Folie du jour*. Paris: Fata Morgana, 1973.

_____. *The Gaze of Orpheus*. Translated by Lydia Davis. Edited by P. Adams Sitney. Barrytown, N.Y.: Station Hill Press,

1981.

————. *De Kafka à Kafka*. Paris: Gallimard/Idées, 1981.

————. *Lautréamont et Sade*. Paris: Éditions de Minuit, 1949.

————. *Le Livre à venir*. Paris: Gallimard, 1959.

————. "La Parole vaine." In *L'Amitié*, q.v.

————. *La Part du feu*. Paris: Gallimard, 1949.

————. *Le Pas au delà*. Paris: Gallimard, 1973.

————. "Réflexions sur le Surréalisme." In *La Part du feu*, q.v.

————. *Le Ressassement éternel*. Paris: Éditions de Minuit, 1951.

————. *Thomas l'obscur*. 2d ed. Paris: Gallimard, 1941, 1950.

Bloom, Harold, et al. *Deconstruction and Criticism*. New York: Seabury Press, 1979.

Boldereff, Frances Metz. *Reading Finnegans Wake*. Woodward, Pa.: Classic Nonfiction Library, 1956.

Bonnefoy, Yves. "Une Écriture de Notre Temps: Louis-René des Forêts." *Nouvelle Revue Française* (July 1986–January 1987): 402–3 (July-August 1986): 1–43; 404 (September 1986): 61–77; 405 (October 1986): 30–50; 406 (November 1986): 29–50; 407 (December 1986): 61–77; 408 (January 1987): 38–55.

Borges, Jorge Luis. *Labyrinths*. New York: New Directions, 1962.

Breton, André. *L'Amour fou*. Paris: Gallimard, 1937.

————. *Manifestes du Surréalisme*. Paris: Gallimard/Idées, 1963.

Brown, Norman. *Closing Time*. New York: Random House, 1973.

Butor, Michel. "L'Usage des pronoms personnels dans le roman." In *Répertoire 2*. Paris: Éditions de Minuit, 1964.

Cain, William E. *The Crisis in Criticism*. Baltimore: Johns Hopkins University Press, 1984.

Campbell, Joseph, and Robinson, Henry Morton. *A Skeleton Key to Finnegans Wake*. New York: Viking, 1966.

Canetti, Elias. *Crowds and Power*. Translated by Joachim Neugroschel. New York: Seabury Press, 1979.

Carroll, David. *The Subject in Question: The Languages of Theory and the Strategies of Fiction*. Chicago: University of Chicago Press, 1982.

Cassirer, Ernst. *Substance and Function in Einstein's Theory of Relativity*. Translated by William Curtis Swabey and Marie Collins Swabey. London: Open Court Publishing Co., 1923.

Caws, Mary Ann. *The Inner Theatre of Recent French Poetry*. Princeton: Princeton University Press, 1970.

————. *The Poetry of Dada and Surrealism*. Princeton: Princeton University Press, 1970.

———. "Text and Revolution." *Diacritics* 3 (1) (Spring 1976): 208.

Ceronetti, Guido. *Le Silence du corps* (*Silence of the Body*). Translated from Italian by André Maugré. Paris: Albin Michel, 1984.

Champagne, Roland A. "The Texts and the Readers of Philippe Sollers' Creative Works from 1957 to 1973." Ph.D. diss., Ohio State University, 1974.

———. "Un Déclenchement: The Revolutionary Implications of Philippe Sollers' *Nombres* for a Logocentric Western Culture." *Sub-Stance* 7 (Fall 1973): 101–11.

Chappuis, Pierre. *Michel Leiris.* Paris: Seghers Poètes d'Aujour-d'hui, 1973.

Cioran, E. M. *The Fall into Time.* Translated by Richard Howard. New York: Quadrangle Books, 1970.

———. *Précis de décomposition.* Paris: Gallimard, 1949.

———. *A Short History of Decay.* Translated by Richard Howard. New York: Viking, 1975.

———. *The Trouble with Being Born.* Translated by Richard Howard. New York: Viking, 1976.

Cixous, Hélène. *The Exile of James Joyce.* Translated by S. A. Purcell. New York: David Lewis, 1972.

———. "La Missexualité." *Poétique* 26 (1976): 240–49.

Cohn, Dorrit. *Transparent Minds: Narrative Modes for Presenting Consciousness.* Princeton: Princeton University Press, 1978.

Cohn, Ruby. "Philosophical Fragments in the Works of Samuel Beckett." In *Samuel Beckett: A Collection of Critical Essays,* 169–77. Englewood Cliffs, N.J.: Prentice-Hall, 1965.

Collin, Françoise. *Maurice Blanchot et la question de l'écriture.* Paris: Gallimard, 1971.

Condou, Claude. "Le Corps à lettre." *Poétique* 26 (1976): 173–79.

Coomaraswamy, A. K. *The Dance of Shiva.* New York: Noonday, 1957.

Cortazar, Jules. *Hopscotch.* Translated by Gregory Rabassa. New York: Pantheon, 1965.

Cross, Richard. *Flaubert and Joyce.* Princeton: Princeton University Press, 1971.

Culler, Jonathan. *On Deconstruction.* Ithaca, N.Y.: Cornell University Press, 1982.

———. *The Pursuit of Signs.* Ithaca, N.Y.: Cornell University Press, 1981.

Daumal, René. *L'Évidence absurde.* Essais et notes 1 (1926–34). Paris: Gallimard, 1972.

————. *Les Pouvoirs de la parole*. Essais et notes 2 (1935–43). Paris: Gallimard, 1972.

————. *Mount Analogue: A Novel of Symbolically Authentic Non-Euclidean Adventures in Mountain Climbing*. Translated by Roger Shattuck. New York: Penguin, 1974.

Day, Tarsis. "Portrait du jouer." *Nouvelle Revue Française* 387 (April 1985): 84–88.

Debord, Guy. *La Société du spectacle*. Paris: Champs Libres, 1969.

De Certeau, Michel. *The Practice of Everyday Life*. Translated by Steven F. Rendall. Berkeley: University of California Press, 1984. Originally published as *Arts de Faire*.

Deleuze, Gilles. *Différence et répétition*. Paris:. Presses Universitaires de France, 1968.

————. *Logique du sens*. Paris: Éditions de Minuit, 1969.

————. *Nietzsche et la philosophie*. Paris: Presses Universitaires de France, 1962.

————. *Proust et les signes*. 2d. ed., enl. Paris: Presses Universitaires de France, 1970.

Deleuze, Gilles, and Guattari, Félix. *Anti-Oedipus: Capitalism and Schizophrenia*. Translated by Robert Hurley, Mark Seem, and Helen Lane. New York: Viking, 1977.

————. *Capitalisme et schizophrenie: L'Anti-Œdipe*. Paris: Éditions de Minuit, 1975.

De Man, Paul. *Allegories of Reading: Figural Language in Rousseau, Nietzsche, Rilke, and Proust*. New Haven: Yale University Press, 1979.

————. *Blindness and Insight: Essays in the Rhetoric of Contemporary Criticism*. Oxford and New York: Oxford University Press, 1971.

————. "La Circularité de l'interprétation dans l'œuvre critique de Maurice Blanchot." *Critique* 229 (1966): 547–68.

————. "Maurice Blanchot." In *Modern French Criticism*, edited by John K. Simon. Chicago: University of Chicago Press, 1972.

Demarcy, Richard. *Éléments d'une sociologie du spectacle*. Paris: UGE, 1973.

Derrida, Jacques. *La Carte postale, de Socrate à Freud et Au-Dela*. Paris: Flammarion, 1980.

————. *De la Grammatologie*. Paris: Éditions de Minuit, 1967.

————. *La Dissémination*. Paris: Éditions du Seuil, 1972.

————. *Dissemination*. Translated by Barbara Johnson. Chicago: University of Chicago Press, 1981.

_____. *Glas.* 2 vols. Paris: Denoël, 1981.

_____. "Living On: Border Lines." In *Deconstruction and Criticism,* by Harold Bloom et al., q.v.

_____. *Marges de la philosophie.* Paris: Éditions de Minuit, 1972.

_____. *L'Oreille de l'autre: otobiographies, transferts, traductions, textes et débats avec Jacques Derrida.* Sous la direction de Claude Lévesque et Christie V. McDonald. Montreal: VLB Éditeur, 1982.

_____. *Positions.* Paris: Éditions de Minuit, 1972.

_____. *Positions.* Translated by Alan Bass. Chicago: University of Chicago Press, 1981.

_____. *Speech and Phenomenon.* Translated by David B. Allison. Evanston, Ill.: Northwestern University Press, 1973.

_____. "Structure, Sign and Play in the Discourse of the Human Sciences." In *The Structuralist Controversy,* edited by Richard Macksey and Eugenio Donato, q.v.

_____. *La Vérité en peinture.* Paris: Flammarion, 1978.

_____. *Writing and Difference.* Translated by Alan Bass. Chicago: University of Chicago Press, 1979. Originally published as *L'Écriture et la différence.* Paris: Éditions du Seuil, 1967.

Descombes, Vincent. *Modern French Philosophy.* Translated by L. Scott Fox and J. M. Harding. London: Cambridge University Press, 1980.

Des Forêts, Louis-René. *Le Bavard.* Paris: Gallimard, 1946.

_____. *Le Bavard,* followed by "La Parole vaine," by Maurice Blanchot. Paris: UGE, 18 October 1963.

_____. *La Chambre des enfants.* Paris: Gallimard, 1960.

_____. *The Children's Room.* Translated by Jean Stewart. London: John Calder Ltd.; New York: Riverrun Press, Inc., 1963.

Douglas, Kenneth. "Blanchot and Sartre." *Yale French Studies* 2(1) (Spring-Summer 1949): 85–95.

Eco, Umberto. *L'Œuvre ouverte.* Translated from Italian by Roux de Bézieux. Paris: Éditions du Seuil, 1965.

_____. *Opera Aperta.* Milan: Bompiano, 1962.

_____. *Le Poetiche di Joyce.* Milan: Bompiano, 1966.

Ellmann, Richard. *James Joyce.* 1959. Reprint. New York: Oxford University Press, 1982.

Epstein, E. L. "The Turning Point/Book 1, Chapter 6." In *A Conceptual Guide to Finnegans Wake,* edited by Michael H. Begnal and Fritz Senn, q.v.

Esslin, Martin, ed. *Samuel Beckett: A Collection of Critical Essays.* Englewood Cliffs, N.J.: Prentice Hall, 1965.

Faye, Jean-Pierre. *Battement*. Paris: Éditions du Seuil, 1962.

_____. *L'Ovale*. Paris: Laffont, 1975.

_____. *Les Portes des villes du monde*. Paris: Belfond, 1977.

_____. *Le Récit hunique*. Paris: Éditions du Seuil, 1967.

Ferrer, Daniel. "Hissheory." *Poétique* 26 (1976): 232–39.

Les Fins de l'homme, à partir du travail de J. Derrida. Directed Ph. Lacoue-Labarthe and J. L. Nancy. Colloque de Cerisy. Paris: Galilée, 1981.

Fitch, B. T. *Dimensions, structure et textualité dans la trilogie romanesque de Beckett*. Paris: Minard, 1977.

Flores, Ralph. *The Rhetoric of Doubtful Authority: Deconstructive Readings of Self-Questioning Narratives, St. Augustine to Faulkner*. Ithaca, N.Y.: Cornell University Press, 1984.

Foucault, Michel. "Distance, Aspect, Origines." In *Théorie d'ensemble*, 11–24. Paris: Éditions du Seuil, 1968.

_____. "Le Langage de l'espace." *Critique* 203 (1964): 378–85.

_____. *Language, Counter-Memory and Practice: Selected Essays and Interviews*. Edited by D. F. Bouchard. Ithaca, N.Y.: Cornell University Press, 1977.

_____. *L'Ordre du discours*. Paris: Gallimard, 1971.

_____. "La Pensée du dehors." *Critique* 229 (1966): 523–46.

_____. *Power/Knowledge: Interviews and Other Writings, 1972–1977*. Edited by Colin Gordon. New York: Pantheon, 1980.

_____. *Surveiller et punir*. Paris: Gallimard, 1975.

Franklin, Jean. *Le Discours du pouvoir*. Paris: UGE, 1976.

Gasché, Rodolphe. "Joining the Text: From Heidegger to Derrida." In *The Yale Critics: Deconstruction in America*, edited by Jonathan Arac et al., q.v.

_____. *The Tain of the Mirror. Derrida and the Philosophy of Reflection*. Cambridge, Mass.: Harvard University Press, 1986.

Gilbert-Lecomte, Roger. *Œuvres complètes*. 2 vols. Paris: Gallimard, 1974.

Giovannangeli, Daniel. *Écriture et répétition, approche de Derrida*. Paris: UGE, 1979.

Godzich, Wlad. "The Domestication of Derrida." In *The Yale Critics: Deconstruction in America*, edited by Jonathan Arac et al., q.v.

Goldmann, Lucien. *Structures mentales et création culturelle*. Paris: UGE, 1970.

Groddeck, Georg. *The Book of the It*. New York: International University Press, 1976.

Habermas, Jürgen. *Theory and Practice*. Boston: Beacon, 1973.

Hartman, Geoffrey. *Criticism in the Wilderness*. New Haven: Yale University Press, 1980.

————. "Maurice Blanchot: Philosopher-Novelist." *Chicago Review* 15 (1961): 1–18.

————. *Saving the Text*. Baltimore: Johns Hopkins University Press, 1981.

Hassan, Ihab. "*Finnegans Wake* et l'imagination postmoderne." *Europe* 657–58 (January–February 1984): 127–233.

Hawthorn, Jeremy. "Ulysses in History." In *James Joyce and Modern Literature*, edited by W.J. McCormack and Alistair Stead. London: Routledge & Kegan Paul, 1982.

Hayman, David. "Double Distancing." *Novel* 12 (Fall 1978): 33–47.

————. *Joyce et Mallarmé*. 2 vols. Paris: Lettres Modernes, 1956.

————. "Nodality or Plot Displaced: The Dynamics of Sollers' *H*." *Sub-Stance* 43 (1984): 54–65.

————. "Reseaux Infrastructurels dans *Finnegans Wake*. " *Poétique* 26 (1976): 207–20.

————. "Surface Disturbances / Grave Disorder." *TriQuarterly* 52 (Fall 1981):182–96.

————, ed. *A First Draft Version of Finnegans Wake*. Edited and annotated with draft catalogue by David Hayman. Austin: University of Texas Press, 1963.

Hayman, David, and Sollers, Philippe. "Some Writers in the Wake of the Wake." *TriQuarterly* 38 (1977): 122–41.

————. *Vision à New York*. Paris: Grasset, 1981.

Heath, Stephen. "Ambiviolences, Notes pour une lecture de Joyce." *Tel Quel* 50, 51 (1972): 22–43; 64–76.

————. "La Déversée." *Tel Quel* 57 (1974): 117–26.

————. *The Nouveau Roman: A Study in the Practice of Writing*. Philadelphia: Temple University Press, 1972.

Heidegger, Martin. *Being and Time*. Translated by John Macquarrie and Edward Robinson. Oxford: Basil Blackwell, 1978.

————. *History of the Concept of Time*, Prologemena. Translated by Theodore Kisiel. Bloomington: Indiana University Press, 1985.

————. "Lettre sur l'humanisme." *Cahiers du Sud* 319 (1953): 385–406.

Hollier, Denis. "Le Déséquilibriste." *Critique* 418 (March, 1982): 189–99.

Houdebine, Jean-Louis. "Joyce: Littérature et Religion." *Tel Quel* 89 (1981): 41–73.

_____. "La Signature de Joyce." "Joyce et Jung." In *Tel Quel* 81 (1979): 52–62; 63–65.

Houdebine, Jean-Louis, and Sollers, Philippe. "La Trinité de Joyce." *Tel Quel* 83 (1980): 36–88.

Husserl, Edmund. *L'Origine de la géométrie*. Translation and introduction by Jacques Derrida. Paris: Presses Universitaires de France, 1962.

Ishagpour, Youssef. *D'Une Image à l'autre*. Paris: Denoël, 1980.

James, Henry. "The Art of Fiction." In *Literary Criticism from Pope to Croce*, edited by Gay Wilson Allen and Harry Hayden Clark. New York: American Book Company, 1941.

Janvier, Ludovic. "Style in the Trilogy." In *Twentieth-Century Interpretations of Beckett's Trilogy, Malloy, Malone Dies, The Unnamable*, edited by J. D. O'Hara, q.v.

Jarrety, Michel. "Maurice Blanchot, Figures de la Limite." *Nouvelle Revue Française* 397 (February 1986): 60–72.

Joyce, James. *Critical Writings*. Edited by Ellsworth Mason and Richard Ellman. New York: Viking, 1968.

_____. *Exiles*. New York: Viking, 1961.

_____. *Finnegans Wake*. New York: Viking, 1958.

_____. *Finnegans Wake*. Translated into French by Philippe Lavergne. Paris: Gallimard, 1982.

_____. *A Portrait of the Artist as a Young Man*. New York: Viking, 1958.

_____. *A Shorter Finnegans Wake*. Edited by Anthony Burgess. New York: Viking, 1966.

_____. *Stephen Hero*. Edited by Theodore Spencer. New York: New Directions, 1963.

_____. *Ulysses*. London: The Bodley Head, 1937.

Kierkegaard, Søren. *Concluding Unscientific Postscript*. Translated by Walter Lowrie. Princeton: Princeton University Press, 1941.

Klossowski, Pierre. "Sur Maurice Blanchot." *Les Temps Modernes* 4 (1949): 298–314.

Kofman, Sarah. *Lectures de Derrida*. Paris: Galilée, 1984.

Kristeva, Julia. "Bataille, expérience et pratique." In *Bataille, colloque de Cerisy*. Paris: UGE, 1973.

_____. "Novel as Polylogue." In *Desire in Language: A Semiotic Approach to Literature and Art*, edited by Leon S. Roudiez, translated by Alice Jardine and Thomas Gora. New York: Columbia University Press, 1980.

_____. "Une Poétique ruinée." In the introduction to *La Poétique de Dostoevski*, by Mikhail Bakhtin. Translated by Isabelle Kolitcheff. Paris: Éditions du Seuil, 1970.

———. *La Révolution dans la langue poétique du dix-neuvième siècle.* Paris: Éditions du Seuil, 1974.

———. *Semiotiké.* Paris: Éditions du Seuil, 1969.

Kurk, Katherine Chenault. "Consummation of the Text: A Study of Philippe Sollers." Ph.D. diss., University of Kentucky, 1979.

Lacote, René, and Haldas, Georges. *Tristan Tzara.* Paris: Seghers Poètes d'Aujourd'hui, 1952.

Laing, R. D. *The Politics of Experience.* New York: Random House, 1967.

Laporte, Roger. *Deux Lectures de Maurice Blanchot.* Paris: Fata Morgana, 1973.

———. "Le Oui, le non, le neutre." *Critique* 229 (1966): 588–90.

Lawall, Sarah N. "The Negative Consciousness: Maurice Blanchot." In *Critics of Consciousness: The Existential Structure of Literature,* 221–65. Cambridge, Mass.: Harvard University Press, 1968.

Leclerc, Annie. "Sollers, poète d'un certain drame." *Les Temps modernes* (June 1965): 282–85.

LeClézio, J. M. G. *The Book of Flights.* Translated by S. W. Taylor. New York: Atheneum, 1972. Originally published as *Le Livre des fuites.* Paris: Gallimard, 1969.

Leiris, Michel. *L'Âge d'homme.* Paris: Gallimard, 1946.

———. *La Règle du jeu I, Biffures.* Paris: Gallimard, 1948.

———. *La Règle du jeu III, Fibrilles.* Paris: Gallimard, 1966.

———. *La Règle du jeu II, Fourbis.* Paris: Gallimard, 1955.

———. *La Règle du jeu IV, Frêle Bruit.* Paris: Gallimard, 1976.

———. *Le Ruban au cou d'Olympe.* Paris: Gallimard, 1981.

Leitch, Vincent B. *Deconstructive Criticism.* New York: Columbia University Press, 1983.

Lejeune, Philippe. *Lire Leiris, autobiographie et langage.* Paris: Klincksieck, 1975.

Lemert, Charles G., and Gillen, Garth. *Michel Foucault, Social Theory as Transgression.* New York: Columbia University Press, 1982.

Lentricchia, Frank. *After the New Criticism.* Chicago: University of Chicago Press, 1980.

Lessing, Gotthold Ephraim. *Laocoön.* Translated by E. A. McCormick. Indianapolis: Bobbs-Merrill, 1962.

Levin, Harry. *James Joyce.* New York: New Directions, 1960.

Lévinas, Emmanuel. *Sur Maurice Blanchot.* Paris: Fata Morgana, 1975.

———. *Otherwise than Being or Beyond Essence.* Translated by Alphonso Lingis. The Hague: Martinus Nijhoff, 1981.

Lewis, Wyndham. *Time and Western Man*. London: Chatto and Windus, 1927.

Libertson, Joseph. *"Proximity": Lévinas, Blanchot, Bataille, and Communication*. The Hague: Martinus Nijhoff, 1982.

Londyn, Evelyn. *Maurice Blanchot, romancier*. Paris: A. G. Nizet, 1976.

Lotringer, Sylvère. "Artaud/Bataille et le matérialisme dialectique." *Sub-Stance* 5–6 (1974): 207–25.

Lynes, Carlos. "Production et théorie romanesque chez Philippe Sollers: Lecture du *Parc*. " *Kentucky Romance Quarterly* 19 (1972): 99–121.

Macksey, Richard, and Donato, Eugenio, eds. *The Structuralist Controversy: The Languages of Criticism and the Sciences of Man*. Baltimore: Johns Hopkins University Press, 1972.

Magliola, Robert. *Derrida on the Mend*. West Lafayette, Ind.: Purdue University Press, 1984.

————. *Phenomenology and Literature*. West Lafayette, Ind.: Purdue University Press, 1977.

Marcus, Grail. "Lilliput at the Cabaret Voltaire." *TriQuarterly* 52 (1981): 265–76.

Marshall, Donald G. "History, Theory, and Influence: Yale Critics as Readers of Maurice Blanchot." In *The Yale Critics: Deconstruction in America*, edited by Jonathan Arac et al., q.v.

Martin, Jean-Paul. "La Condensation." *Poétique* 26 (1976): 180–206.

Marx, Karl. *Early Writings*. Translated by T. B. Bottomore. New York: McGraw-Hill, 1963.

Mehlman, Jeffrey. *A Structural Study of Autobiography*. Ithaca, N.Y.: Cornell University Press, 1974.

Melville, Stephen W. *Philosophy Beside Itself: On Deconstruction and Modernism*. Minneapolis: University of Minnesota Press, 1986.

Merejkowski, Dmitri. *Atlantis/Europe: The Secret of the West*. Blauvelt, N.Y.: Steinerbooks, 1971.

Miguet, Marie. "Sentiments filiaux d'un prétendu parricide: Perec." *Poétique* 54 (1983): 135–47.

Miller, J. Hillis. *The Ethics of Reading*. New York: Columbia University Press, 1987.

————. "The Search for Grounds in Literary Study." *Genre* 17 (Spring-Summer 1984): 19–36 (originally: speech, New York University, November 1983; reprinted in *Rhetoric and Form: Deconstruction at Yale*, edited by Robert Con Davis and Ronald Schleifer. [Norman: University of Oklahoma Press, 1985].

Minière, Claude. "La Musique des îles." *Europe* 657–58 (January–February 1984): 140–49.

Morin, Edgar. *Le Cinéma, ou l'homme imaginaire.* Paris: Denoël, 1958.

Nadeau, Maurice. *The French Novel since the War.* Translated by A. M. Sheridan-Smith. New York: Grove Press, 1969.

Nietzsche, Friedrich. *Twilight of the Idols.* Translated by R. J. Hollindale. London: Penguin Books, 1968. Originally published as *Götzendämmerung* by the author, 1889.

Norris, Christopher. *Deconstruction: Theory and Practice.* London: Methuen, 1982.

Norris, Margaret. *The Decentered Universe of Finnegans Wake: A Structuralist Analysis.* Baltimore: Johns Hopkins University Press, 1976.

O'Hara, J. D., ed. *Twentieth-Century Interpretations of Beckett's Trilogy, Malloy, Malone Dies, The Unnamable.* Englewood Cliffs, N.J.: Prentice Hall, 1970.

Oxenhandler, Neal. "Paradox and Negation in the Criticism of Maurice Blanchot." *Symposium* 16 (1962): 36–44.

Paris, Jean. "Du Monologue et ses précurseurs." *Europe* 657–58 (January–February 1984): 52–64.

Peckham, Morse. "Toward a Theory of Romanticism." *PMLA* 61 (1951): 5–23.

Peignôt, Jérome. *Les Jeux de l'amour et du langage.* Paris: UGE, 1974.

Peterson, Elmer. *Tristan Tzara, Dada, and Surrational Theorist.* New Brunswick, N.J.: Rutgers University Press, 1971.

Peyre, Henri. *French Novelists of Today.* New York: Oxford University Press, 1967.

————. *Qu'est-ce que le symbolisme?* Paris: Presses Universitaires de France, 1974.

Pfeiffer, Jean. "La Passion de l'imaginaire." *Critique* 229 (June 1966): 571–78.

Pierssens, Michel. *La Tour du Babel: la fiction du signe.* Paris: Éditions de Minuit, 1976.

Pleynet, Marcelin. "La Poésie doit avoir pour but." In *Théorie d'ensemble.* Paris: Éditions du Seuil, 1968, 94–115.

Poe, Edgar Allan. *The Works of Poe.* New York: Harper, n.d.

Poétique 26 (1976). Special issue on book 1, chapter 6 of *Finnegans Wake*, ed. Hélène Cixous.

Pollman, Leo. *Der Französischer Roman im 20. Jahrhundert.* Stuttgart: Kohlmann, 1970.

Preli, Georges. *La Force du dehors; extériorité, limite, et non-pouvoir à partir de Maurice Blanchot.* Paris: Encres-Recherches, 1977.

Rabaté, Jean-Michel. "Lapsus ex machina." *Poétique* 26 (1976): 152–72.

―――. "Qu'il faut la chute." *Europe* 657–58 (January–February 1984): 133–39.

Ribettes, Jean-Michel. "Real-Lacan." *Infini* 3 (1983): 87–106.

Ricardou, Jean. *Le Théâtre des métamorphoses.* Paris: Éditions du Seuil, 1982.

Ricoeur, Paul. *The Conflict of Interpretations, Essays in Hermeneutics.* Edited by Don Ihde. Evanston, Ill.: Northwestern University Press, 1974.

Rifaterre, Michael. "Le Formalisme français." In *Essais de stylistique structurale.* Paris: Flammarion, 1971.

Rilke, Rainer Maria. *Duino Elegies.* Translated by J. B. Leishman and Stephen Spender. New York: W. W. Norton, 1939.

Rossum-Guyon, Françoise Van. "Aventures de la citation chez Butor." In *Butor: Colloque de Cerisy,* 17–39. Paris: UGE, 1974.

Rousset, Jean. *Forme et signification.* Paris: Corti, 1963.

Sartre, Jean-Paul. *L'Idiot de la famille.* 3 vols. Paris: Gallimard, 1971–72.

―――. *Saint Genet, comédien et martyr.* Paris: Gallimard, 1952.

―――. *Situations I.* Paris: Gallimard, 1947.

Schlossman, Beryl. "Joyce et le don des langues." *Tel Quel* 92 (1982): 9–30.

Serres, Michel. *Détachement.* Paris: Flammarion, 1983.

Shushi, Kao. "Paradise Lost, an Interview with Philippe Sollers." *Sub-Stance* 30 (1979): 31–51.

Sollers, Philippe. *Drame.* Paris: Éditions du Seuil, 1965.

―――. *Event.* Translated by Bruce Benderson and Ursule Molinaro. New York: Red Dust Press, 1987.

―――. *Femmes.* Paris: Gallimard, 1982.

―――. *H.* Paris: Éditions du Seuil, 1973.

―――. *L'Intermédiare.* Paris: Éditions du Seuil, 1963.

―――. "Joyce and Co." *TriQuarterly* 38 (1977): 107–21.

―――. *Logiques.* Paris: Éditions du Seuil, 1965.

―――. *Lois.* Paris: Éditions du Seuil, 1972.

―――. *Nombres.* Paris: Éditions du Seuil, 1968.

―――. *Paradis.* Paris: Éditions du Seuil, 1981.

―――. *Le Parc.* Paris: Éditions du Seuil, 1963.

―――. *Portrait du joueur.* Paris: Gallimard, 1984.

―――. *Sur le Matérialisme.* Paris: Éditions du Seuil, 1974.

_____. *Théorie des exceptions*. Paris: Gallimard, 1986.

_____. *Writing and the Experience of Limits*. Edited by David Hayman, translated by Philip Barnard with David Hayman. New York: Columbia University Press, 1983.

_____, ed. *Colloques de Cerisy*. 2 vols., *Artaud* and *Bataille*. Paris: UGE, 1973.

_____, ed. *Théorie d'ensemble*. Paris: Seuil, 1968.

Sollers, Philippe, and Hayman, David. *Vision à New York*. Paris: Grasset, 1981.

Solomon, Margaret C. *Eternal Geomater: The Sexual Universe of Finnegans Wake*. Carbondale: Southern Illinois University Press, 1969.

Spengler, Oswald. *The Decline of the West*. Translated by Charles F. Atkinson. 2 vols. New York: Knopf, 1928.

Stephane, Nelly. "L'Homme fiction." *Europe* 657–58 (January–February 1984): 5–12.

Thibaudeau, Jean. *Ouverture*. Paris: Éditions du Seuil, 1966.

Thiher, Allen. *Words in Reflection*. Chicago: University of Chicago Press, 1984.

Tindall, William York. *A Reader's Guide to Finnegans Wake*. New York: Farrar, Straus and Giroux, 1969.

Tison-Braun, Micheline. *Tristan Tzara, l'inventeur de l'homme nouveau*. Paris: Nizet, 1977.

Topin, André. "La Cassure et le flux." *Poétique* 26 (1976): 132–51.

Tzara, Tristan. *Approximate Man and Other Writings*. Translated by Mary Ann Caws. Detroit: Wayne State University Press, 1973.

_____. *La Fuite*. Paris: Gallimard, 1947.

_____. *Œuvres complètes*. 5 vols. Edited by Henri Béhar. Paris: Flammarion, 1975–82.

Valéry, Paul. *Tel Quel*. Vol. 1. Paris: Gallimard, 1941.

Virilio, Paul. *Vitesse et politique*. Paris: Galilée, 1977.

Weber, Max. *From Max Weber*. Translated by C. Wright Mills and H. H. Gerth. Oxford: Oxford University Press, 1958.

White, David A. *The Grand Continuum: Reflections on Joyce and Metaphysics*. Pittsburgh: University of Pittsburgh Press, 1983.

Wilhem, Daniel. *Maurice Blanchot et la voix narrative*. Paris: UGE, 1974.

Woolf, Virginia. *The Waves*. New York: Harcourt Brace, 1931.

Index